D0331214

CHINA'S
JUST
WORLD

CHINA'S JUST WORLD

—— · ——

The Morality of Chinese Foreign Policy

CHIH-YU SHIH

LYNNE RIENNER PUBLISHERS · BOULDER & LONDON

Published in the United States of America in 1993 by
Lynne Rienner Publishers, Inc.
1800 30th Street, Boulder, Colorado 80301

and in the United Kingdom by
Lynne Rienner Publishers, Inc.
3 Henrietta Street, Covent Garden, London WC2E 8LU

Library of Congress Cataloging-in-Publication Data
Shih, Chih-yu, 1958–
    China's just world: the morality of Chinese foreign policy/by
Chih-yu Shih.
    p.   cm.
Includes bibliographical references and index.
    ISBN 1-55587-350-2
    1. China—Foreign relations—Moral and ethical aspects. 2. China—
Foreign relations—Philosophy. 3. China—Foreign relations—1949–
I. Title
JX1570.Z5   1992
327.51—dc20   92-1774
                                                                  CIP

British Cataloguing in Publication Data
A Cataloguing in Publication record for this book
is available from the British Library.

Printed and bound in the United States of America

The paper used in this publication meets the requirements
of the American National Standard for Permanence of
Paper for Printed Library Materials Z39.48-1984.

To Eva and Alison

CONTENTS

PREFACE

Morality is generally seen as irrelevant in literature on foreign-policymaking, and the influence of morality cannot always be determined by empirical tests. However, relying upon counterfactual logic, this book seeks to demonstrate that scholarship on Chinese foreign policymaking and policy motivation has been inadequate and sometimes inconsistent. In addition, it introduces an alternative way of reading Chinese diplomatic behavior.

Many have discussed and critiqued the whole or a section of this manuscript. Some disagreed with its approach; some were excited about it. They all made valuable contributions. These scholars include Jonathan Adelman, John Cassidy, Martha Cottam, Lowell Dittmer, Samuel Kim, Yih-chun Liu, Emerson Niou, Elizabeth Perry, Lucian Pye, David See, Xi Wang, Yue Wei, Rhoda Weidenbaum, Samuel Wu, and Jialing Zhang. Judith Fletcher and Michael Smith provided the patient editing service critical to a non-native writer. The research and writing of this book were primarily done while I was teaching at Ramapo College in New Jersey; the college's dedication to international education was especially encouraging. Finally, it would have been impossible for me to have written this book without access to the East Asian Library at Columbia University. Their generous policy must be acknowledged.

Chih-yu Shih

1

INTRODUCTION

The conventional approach to international organization treats it as a concrete entity, though it fact most organizing efforts in international politics have occurred outside that entity. Many political movements, including détente, Islamic fundamentalism, antihegemonism, and glasnost have significantly affected the normative aspect of international politics, yet none of them is the focus of international organization literature.

One Asian scholar has described international relations as intercultural relations, arguing that international conflicts originate as intercultural conflicts.[1] This keen observation is extremely pertinent to international organizational processes. Since an international organization is always, at least to some extent, utopian, its success depends in large measure on whether those nations involved can share a common understanding of an emphasized vision. Unfortunately, the ideals and norms of international behavior are necessarily culturally bound. This being the case, how can one expect various national leaders to work together for an idealistic world order?

Trends in world politics since the mid-1980s suggest that the illusion of a world community seems once again to be on the ascendancy. Ideology has visibly ceased to be a significant factor in most international conferences, and this has raised widespread expectations that realism will pave the way to improved international organization. Hence, one would assume that in this era of peace and ideological decline economic concerns would dominate all national policymaking processes and scholarly attention would focus on the building of international regimes that reflect underlying political economic structures. If global détente and ideological breakdown in the communist states are only signs of moral chaos and a search for new national identities, however, then academic research should endeavor to uncover those cultural constraints which may seriously obstruct a truly open-minded dialogue among national leaders interested in reorganizing international politics. We need to go back to history in search of the morally sensible alternatives within each major nation that can lead to new attempts at organization.

It is such a turn toward historical precedent that is the rationale behind this book. A normative-cognitive approach is timely in that it acknowledges that the moral search for international justice can start from *within* each nation; this national emphasis has been missing in classic international organization literature. International organization (or, more accurately, the effort to bring it about) is very much a result of the cognitive necessity for national leaders to behave in a morally sensible way in front of their domestic constituency. Accordingly, each move by national leaders on the world stage has not only political ramifications in terms of impact on world power redistribution but also moral connotations of national behavior.

Chapter 2 briefly and selectively reviews sociological literature on organization and asks how it can prove useful in the study of international organization. The concept of organization as a process of seeking common cause maps is adopted in this book, and the notion of role is emphasized. National leaders' role conceptions (self- as well as mutual-role conceptions) particularize for citizens and leaders alike the national identity that bounds the evaluation of world affairs. The chapter emphasizes the national sources of intended international norms and the enacted international context that justifies the national argument. Behavior according to the national self-image has an impact on a people's sense of meaningful existence. Moves toward organizing international politics according to national moral worldviews thus generate theatrical (or self-deceiving) role-playing by each nation according to leadership self-identity and associated role expectations. The process of international organization is one of matching these role plays.

China, with its unique culture, is of particular interest for three reasons. Historically, Chinese culture is primarily rooted in a Confucianism whose concept of power—strongly associated with morality—stands in marked contrast to that of the West. Correct role-playing in China involves moral leadership that helps win respect and attract followers. Openly seeking power indicates a moral decay likely to cost a leader his political legitimacy. The result is thus a need to deemphasize politics in public, reducing Chinese politics to a rhetorical masquerade of ulterior power manipulation; oral power becomes as critical as military and financial power. The ability to cause moral chaos through rhetorical confrontation has been an effective instrument for the Chinese subordinate to shame and therefore to threaten the moral integrity of authority.

Confucian norms and the Chinese style of power struggle certainly affect China's performance in international politics. The Chinese seem obliged to envision international politics as fashioned of some sort of moral hierarchy. Because Chinese state power is relatively weak and constrained within its own borders, it is quite a task for Chinese leaders just to demonstrate that their belief in moral hierarchy is enforceable. They can pretend integrity only through strong rhetorical expression; scholars have noted for years the gap between what the Chinese say and what they do.[2] What makes the Chinese role in international organizational processes dramatic, however, is precisely this oral confrontation resulting from disparity in mutual role expectations between China and other national actors. No nation can afford to comfort itself by assuming the irrelevance of Chinese polemics. As long as the Chinese notion of world order is dramatically different from the status quo, even though Chinese leaders might not intend to use force to change the situation, the world must still be prepared for such a possibility. And yet this kind of preparation would only seem to question China's sincerity and hence compel its leaders to demonstrate their determination through radical policy.

Since 1949 the Chinese search for international justice has been rhetorically conflictive because it has consistently entailed reorganization of the current international order. At certain times the Chinese may seem to accept the status quo while at other times they challenge it. Furthermore, they deliberately ignore any inconsistency between policies of different periods and insist that China has never changed its principled positions.[3] This way, China maintains the appearance of integrity in its moral exemplification. One may contend that this search for justice is de facto fickle and sometimes unrealistic, and indeed it seems all the more unrealistic when the outside challenges China's inconsistency. Within China, there is a genuine interest in protecting the country's image of moral superiority—the key to possessing legitimacy and influence in Chinese society. The implication is that only when the rest of the world ignores their inconsistency are the Chinese willing to be pragmatic and flexible. China's role in international organization hence looks confusing when judged by the sporadic irrational searches for a moral hierarchy that tend to follow on the heels of periods of modestly complying performance. A China expert has described this phenomenon as a union of subconscious rationality and conscious irrationality.[4]

In addition to the Confucian search for moral hierarchy, what makes the Chinese case of great interest is the simultaneous existence of many other normative systems besides Confucianism. Taoism, Buddhism, and legalism have each enjoyed short periods of predominance. One should not deny either the possibility that norms such as socialism might develop, as new norms can always be accommodated in the Confucian search for justice. The existence of multiple norms may help ease moral strain for the Chinese when policy that aims at utilizing the current international organization clashes head-on with rhetoric that purports to denounce it. The interplay of these old and new norms illustrates the role-playing nature of Chinese international organizing behavior. Since a morally sensible re-organization of international politics and benefit in terms of aiding domestic development from such a reorganization are self-contradictory, leaders face the colossal task of maintaining consistency in outlook and justifying pragmatic pursuit of modernization. The coexistence of various norms and principles allows a reinforcement of oratorical power and consolidation of the moral regime in times of distress. The Chinese are thus able to live comfortably with a degree of ambiguity that makes irrelevant Western attempts to elucidate the ranking order of principles applied.

Chapter 3 discusses the coexistence of several guiding principles in China's search for international justice: socialism, peace, revolution and their historical roots in Confucianism, Taoism, and legalism. The diplomatic slogans derived from these principles include anticapitalism, peaceful coexistence, the Four Modernizations, independent foreign policy, anticolonialism, antihegemonism, open door, and so on. Faced with a changing world situation, the Chinese have made sense of the world as well as their role expectations for other national actors in various ways. At times, the search for justice based upon these principles is at best pretension. It is ironic that, in light of the nation's limited capability, China's attempts at reorganizing international politics often appear courageous, though such efforts have never created a more organized world for the Chinese. This multiprincipled diplomacy allows China to maintain a consistent self-perception in spite of inconsistent policy positions over time.

China's dramatic role in international organization can therefore be understood by reviewing how China, on the basis of its own cultural premises, has tried to define proper roles for other nations, how its leaders have endeavored to persuade others to comply with the Chinese notion of justice and play their roles appropriately, and how the Chinese have adapted in the face of adversity. In a sense, studies of China's participation in international organizational processes can thus focus on bilateral relations with superpowers, neighbors, and important international actors: those whose relations with China are presumably being watched by the world and China as well. Because of their high visibility and symbolic importance, policies toward these actors reveal China's notions of international justice, national capabilities, and the possibility of a contradiction between the two. More importantly, bilateral relations can indicate whether China really intends to make world politics more organized in the Chinese sense—what efforts Chinese leaders have made to discipline these other actors. For this reason, my exploration of China's role in international organizational processes is limited to China's bilateral relationships with the (former) Soviet Union, the United States, Japan, and the Third World (especially at the United Nations). Patterns of interaction with these conceptually significant actors best reveal China's foreign policy motivation and testify to China's pledge of moral leadership in international organizational processes.

Since there has always been some degree of superpower confrontation within the past forty-five years, it is important to see how China has balanced its relations with the United States and the (former) Soviet Union. In this regard, it is interesting to see how China's role expectations of the two superpowers have shifted along with the changing notion of world order in China. China's relations with its neighbors since 1949 are complicated. Japan is highlighted in this book because of the historical intimacy and obsession with fraternity between the two peoples. Any change in China's role expectations for Japan has conceptual as well as political significance. Other major neighbors like India, Korea, Pakistan, and Vietnam, or similarly interesting examples such as Burma and Nepal will not be singled out for discussion. Some of these cases involve largely localized interaction; some are discussed under the heading of superpower relations, and most come into play in relation to China's self-declared championship of Third World causes, examined in Chapter 7.

Chapter 4 reviews the role of the Soviet Union in China's search for international justice and Chapter 5, that of the United States. Feelings toward the two have been ambivalent; China's adherence to socialism, antihegemonism, and anticolonialism preclude a smooth relationship with either superpower. Whichever cause Chinese leaders have striven to dramatize since 1949, they have invariably encountered one superpower in their way and the other reluctant to lend a hand; China has certainly proved a difficult partner for either. Save for the period during and right after the Korean War, no superpower has maintained normalized relations with China without simultaneously being the rhetorical target of political struggle emanating from Beijing—at one time or another, Chinese leaders have declared one or both of the superpowers to be corrupt. International organizational movements launched by either superpower have failed to satisfy or include China, while China's own organizing efforts have never granted positive roles to both superpowers at the same time.

Chapter 4 argues that China's USSR policy was designed to shame the Soviet leaders. Contrary to the popular impression that China was driven by security concerns, this chapter contends that the Chinese rarely attached serious weight to the possibility of a Soviet invasion and had not adequately prepared for such a threat. China's policy regarding the Soviet Union centered on the integrity of world communism, which it hoped to maintain by shaming the Soviet Union—a moral pretension that dictated Chinese foreign policy after the mid-1950s. To moralize their position in world communism, the Chinese became obsessed with the notion of revisionism—so obsessed that issues of nation were either avoided, ignored, or belittled. The effect of China's policy on world communism was questionable, but the psychological satisfaction the Chinese achieved by challenging Soviet "social imperialism" can be understood only within the hypothetical context in which China is the only true model of world communism. This moral pretension enabled the Chinese to shame the Soviets; shaming allowed the Chinese to pretend to justice.

Chapter 5 examines China's struggle against U.S. imperialism. World communism is a sensible goal only if China can prove that this struggle can be successfully carried out, and the conceptual need to treat the United States as an enemy in turn makes sense only within China's socialist worldview. China's enlistment of the United States into its antihegemonic united front, then, is ambivalent at best. Antihegemonism as an international organizational principle looks absolutely credible because China behaves as if hegemonism were worse than imperialism (which is bad enough itself). To refute the implication that China has turned pro-U.S., China has struggled on minor issues, dramatizing their significance to irrational levels. Through the rhetorical manipulation of principles, the Chinese pretend that there is no contradiction between antihegemonism and anti-imperialism.

Chapter 6 deals with Japan. In contrast to the superpowers, Japan was traditionally allowed a positive role in the Chinese worldview. Before World War II, the Chinese widely believed that Japan's economic power could benefit China's development. A common Asian origin presumably leads the Chinese to assume Japanese assistance, and they are understandably frustrated when the Japanese reveal their unique version of the East Asian order. But though both China and Japan see a reorganized East Asian sphere as the key to international justice, they have twice ended up at war with each other; a key reason is mutual role expectations that have never coincided. This irony seems to make optimism regarding the emergence of a China-Japan axis a qualified hope at best.[5]

China's ambivalence toward Japan reflects a policy that aims at accommodating the notion of cooperative neighborly relations into China's socialist view. On the one hand, China has been seeking to establish cooperation with Japan with an eye toward development aid. On the other hand, China constantly reminds the Japanese that it is ready to sacrifice their neighborly relations at any time to make a statement about Japan's failure to fulfill role assignments in China's worldview. Neighborship from the Chinese perspective becomes such a drama: China proves its sincerity as a good neighbor by putting aside historical enmity, ideological differences, and competition for leadership in East Asia, but it demonstrates unswerving commitment to socialism and moral leadership in East Asia by periodically and deliberately sacrificing that neighborship. On the surface, there appears to be a new organizational movement in East Asia combining China's political power with Japan's economic power. Further analysis in Chapter 6 reveals that the new alliance is destined to be unstable because neither side has proved successful in satisfying the other's role expectations.

Chapter 7 examines China's united front with the Third World and performance at the United Nations. The primary question is whether China's interaction with Third World countries in the UN contributes to antihegemonism. The nature of role expectation here differs from the previous three cases: China essentially sees the Third World as being on its side, but instead of the Third World's aiding China, China often acts as if Third World countries eagerly expect China to aid them. Again, China's performance here is dramatic in the sense that rhetorical support is always strong whereas material aid is limited and selective. Although mutual role expectations between China and the Third World are compatible, it is not clear that they can satisfy each other in carrying out those roles.

China's major concern is therefore to demonstrate that it is a true friend of Third World countries. Even though China describes itself as a Third World country, it still fails to participate in contemporary Third World movements; China's limited capability compels it to depend on symbolic gestures to demonstrate its friendship and its Third World status. While refusing to describe itself as a Third World leader, China gives zero-interest loans to Third World nations without attaching political strings. Since there is no hope of competing with the two superpowers in terms of resources, China resorts to moral appeals with the conviction that the Third World will eventually realize who its real ally is. Hoping to win countries over this way falls far short of realism but does, according to the Chinese perception, serve to demonstrate the moral superiority of the Chinese state and indirectly shame the superpowers for being self-centered, chauvinist, and immoral.

To study China's role in international organization from this normative-cognitive perspective is critical in evaluating the possibility of a more organized world and assessing China's role within it. Even an optimistic overview of postwar history clearly illustrates that partnership with the PRC is far from being an uncomplicated affair. The Chinese notion of international justice often requires some sort of fundamental change, whereas those powers who enjoy greater control of the international situation generally opt for the status quo. The Chinese role in international organization is negative also because its style is highly theatrical, requiring periodic symbolic moves to demonstrate correctness. These gestures are meant to shame the dominant actors and thus discredit their leadership. The dramatic show of determination to keep moral integrity at its face value only leads to distrust and pollutes the atmosphere of international coordination. International organization, from this perspective, has not evolved far from its primitive beginnings.

The final chapter discusses the changing nature of Chinese foreign policy and the Chinese worldview. Toward the end of the 1980s and into the 1990s, certain "neorealist" ideas seem to have attracted adherents in China. Notions of interdependence, multipolarity, peace, and development have achieved a considerable degree of prominence in official Chinese statements, while leaders of all political stripes have committed themselves to a more open policy. The relative weight of ideology, morality, and justice seem lessened; polemical volume has been lowered several decibels.

Concomitant with the downplaying of morality is the continuing stress on independence, its associated notion of a "new international political order," and the perception of rising hegemonism in the United States. There are therefore two trends working against each other: the neorealist recognition of both the interdependent nature of the world political economy and of the need to participate in and take advantage of the current international economic network, and the statist trend that falls back on the state-to-state metaphor and resists full accommodation with the world market. Only time will tell if classic moral concern will rise again under the counterpressure of lingering cultural tradition.

A final note on the notion of drama. The drama metaphor has been widely used by social scientists to describe interaction. For example, Erving Goffman argues that an individual as an actor normally strives to put on a show and impress the watching social audience.[6] Murray Edleman suggests one of the political functions of using symbols is to maintain political legitimacy.[7] More recently, Raymond Cohen discovered that the critical use of symbols in the "theatre of power" has been furthered in the age of television, which has transformed the metaphor of drama into reality.[8] Cohen argues that diplomats deliberately design signals that have cross-cultural meanings. He avoids the question of motivation or the psychological necessity that leaders play their own dramas, not others'—and therefore manipulate the dramas. As a result of this conceptualization, the notion of drama becomes no more than an extension of realism.

This book uses the metaphor of drama to depict China's foreign policy behavior, focusing on foreign policy motivation. Once the curtain goes up on a drama, leaders are obliged to play their roles, whether they want to or not. Their control of the drama is incomplete at best. This notion of drama has both a conceptual and a behavioral aspect. Drama is a conceptual mechanism that helps make sense of reality,[9] and this may or may not be accurately perceived. Political actors, however, react not to reality but to drama, which is a set of role expectations, a conceptual context, and a structure of logical reasoning. Rationality is a meaningful concept only within a dramaturgic structure. Foreign policy is a drama because it does not automatically respond to reality but to stimuli that meet or fail the role expectation. Recognizing reality is not a source of foreign policy motivation; instead, that motivation comes from a meaningful script.

The notion of drama is different from the notion of culture. Within a specific culture, people are able to communicate in the same language and appreciate one another's points of view. While people who share a culture do not have to agree with one another, people playing the same drama have to develop congruent mutual role expectations in order to continue with the play. Although culture is the source of drama, politicians with a similar cultural background can conceptualize the same reality through different scripts and thus impede one another from establishing legitimacy.

The notion of drama brings a dynamic force to role theory. Every drama has a behavioral aspect: roles must be taken and enacted before they become meaningful. Reality and the environment must both be enacted before the former can exert its influence. The notion of drama therefore directs scholars' attention to the dynamic process of enactment and self-enactment. Leaders hold certain role expectations and must collect information to confirm these beliefs. The best way to enact reality, then, is to behave as if everyone else understands and complies with expectations. Drama can therefore be defined as a collective mechanism for interpretation that leads political actors to fulfill certain role obligations.

International organizational processes accordingly involve attempts to resolve differences among contending dramas staged by different national and subnational actors. The study of China's role is heuristic because the traditional Chinese obsession with being morally correct dictates that its leaders have clear dramatic scripts. Contending dramas within the Chinese context compel the country's leaders to resort to drastic role-playing, both to demonstrate their moral commitment and to shame their political opponents. Consequently, China's quest for a just world always appears to be dramatic, inconsistent, and often irrelevant to the rest of the world; its drastic policy and style of polemics create a threatening countenance. This psychocultural tendency to depend on an uncompromising dramatic script has constrained China's participation in international organizational processes.

NOTES

1. Kenichiro Hirano, "International Cultural Conflicts: Causes and Remedies," *Japan Review of International Affairs* 2, 2 (Fall-Winter 1988): 143–164.

2. Kenneth T. Young, "Adversary Negotiation Style," in U.S. Congress, Senate, Subcommittee on National Security and International Operations of the Committee on Government Operations, *Peking's Approach to Negotiation* (Washington, D.C.: Government Printing Office, 1969); Samuel Kim, "Behavioral Dimensions of Chinese Multilateral Diplomacy," *China Quarterly* 72 (1977): 713–742.

3. The Chinese call this the principle of rigidity and flexibility. See Zhao Quansheng, "Achieving Maximum Advantage: Rigidity and Flexibility in Chinese

Foreign Policy," presented at the American Political Science Association annual meeting, San Francisco, September 1, 1990.

4. Shaoguang Wang, "Deconstructing the Relationship Between Mao and His Followers: A New Approach to the Cultural Revolution," *Chinese Political Science Review* 1 (January 1988): 22–23.

5. See the discussion in Robert Taylor, *The Sino-Japanese Axis* (New York: St. Martin's, 1983); Peter G. Mueller and Douglas A. Ross, *China and Japan— Emerging Global Powers* (New York: Praeger: 1975), pp. 193–199.

6. For a detailed discussion, see Erving Goffman, *The Presentation of Self in Every Day Life* (New York: Penguin, 1969).

7. For a detailed discussion, see Murray Edleman, *The Symbolic Use of Politics* (Urbana: University of Illinois Press, 1964).

8. Raymond Cohen, *Theatre of Power: The Art of Diplomatic Signaling* (New York: Longman, 1987), p. 6.

9. For an operationalized notion of drama, see A. Paul Hare, *Social Interaction as Drama* (Beverly Hills: Sage, 1985).

2

A NORMATIVE-COGNITIVE APPROACH

Many realists might consider anarchy acceptable in the world political arena, but few would extend such acceptance to domestic politics. It is hardly surprising, then, that many national leaders are idealists to the extent that, based upon their domestic experiences, they try to bring some sort of justice to world politics, control uncertainty in the world, and find a meaningful place for their state; organizing international politics is an especially important task for the major powers. Because of differences in cultural background, however, it remains unclear whether world politics can become more organized, despite the efforts of certain national leaders. To assess international organization, one has to consider the psychocultural function of national leaders' organizing efforts in order to appreciate the possibility that such efforts often contain elements of drama and moral pretension in addition to power play. The following sections discuss a normative-cognitive approach that takes into consideration the dramatic aspect of international organization.

SEEKING COMMON CAUSE MAPS

A Social-Psychological Perspective on Organization

The classic notion of organization refers to a body of procedures by which participating members together pursue a set of agreed-upon goals through control of uncertainty.[1] A good example of this conception is the Central Military Commission (CMC) of the Chinese Communist Party (CCP) as an organizational design to control the military. Another way of looking at organization is as a process, a view shared by some social psychologists interested in cognitive processes. Karl Weick, for example, contends that processes involved in organizing must continually be reaccomplished.[2] Organization thus exists in time rather than in space, in continuous enactment of the environment; the process of organization would stop otherwise. To go back to our example, seen from this perspective, the CMC only provides opportunities for dialogue; there is no guarantee of consensual action by the CMC as a unitary actor. Weick further notes that to enact an environment is to create the appearance of an environment;[3] individual CMC members act as if they have common environments so as to get on with their business. Along this line of reasoning, David Hayes and Peter Frost argue that there are coexisting and frequently competing images of what the substance of organization is at any point in time.[4] They deny that there is such a thing as organization in the sense of a concrete social entity.

Realizing the limitations of the classic notion, Hayes contends that a proper definition of organization should make the term an expression of process in which common cause maps, or causal linkages, are sought and established.[5] The process of organization urges people to make sense of the world together. It is probably this idea of organization that leads George Graen and Teni Scandura to claim that organizations are by their very nature negotiated systems.[6] They argue that organization involves a series of role-taking, role-making, and role-routinization activities. Indeed, personal backgrounds and intentions often determine the style and the environment in which the Chinese CMC operates. Beliefs of individual participants as well as the interaction among these beliefs therefore become the focus of research. As Weick contends, the act of organizing is built upon individual behaviors that interlock two or more people.[7] Sometimes a leader such as Mao Zedong is particularly important; at other times Deng Xiaoping, Ye Jianying, and Nie Rongzhen could be equally competitive. This emphasis on individuals is particularly germane to the study of international organization since national actors like China, the United States, and the former Soviet Union have consistently been major sources of contention in world politics.

This stress on individual participants may seem to contradict the notion of organization as a collective process. In reality, compliance of individual participants is essential to the establishment of common cause maps and mutually agreeable role obligations. Actually, it is the contention here that without some sort of common moral pretension, dialogues among actors will not lead to a better-coordinated world in the long run. There has to be a guiding moral view that allows the role of each actor to be specified and evaluated. When national moral pretensions converge, the opportunity to improve organization increases to the extent that dialogues are mutually appreciated and role expectations are mutually congruent.

Individual actors convey information concerning role expectation and imagination defined by cultural premises and worldviews. Accordingly, interaction among individual cognitive structures is the precondition of organizing. Chinese leaders somehow have to be motivated to study, for example, the U.S. leadership's perspectives. The intuitive sources of motivation are self-interests (or national interests in the case of international organization).[8] However, there will be only moderate organization if the Chinese and others merely agree on how to act while the rationales behind doing so are in outright contradiction. The notion of organization as processes of seeking common cause maps thus looks beyond the interest-driven apparent coordination and examines the degree of congruence among various worldviews. It is argued here that when organizing occurs, the Chinese not only promote their interests but also embody a worldview that explains why those interests are worth pursuing.

On the one hand, the Chinese leaders have to know the world before they can judge how to act properly within it. Such an understanding presupposes a worldview that depicts the believed correct order, normal relationships among people and things, and the moral role of the self. On the other hand, they are compelled to act appropriately in order to claim that they indeed know the world. The process of enactment brings about the worldview. The ultimate motivation of human behavior is to secure a sense of meaningful life, to be a part of a just whole. This is self-fulfillment or self-actualization, which some relate to self-worth, self-esteem, self-concept, self-identity, or self-efficacy.[9] While these concepts have somewhat different connotations, they all revolve around the establishment of a stable relationship between the self and its environment. Therefore, the Chinese behave according to what they believe to be true about themselves.[10] The Chinese must behave as if their view correctly depicts the world for them and as if other people surrounding them understand and accept it. That view determines what information is to be attended to, remembered, and utilized.[11] The world becomes more organized in reality when participants in the processes build consensus on, say, what factors caused the Cultural Revolution, what must have gone wrong with Mao, and what must be done to restore the correct order.

The processes of organization at higher levels involve collective actors. How, then, can the concept of motivation at the individual level be applied to the collective level? In fact, just as we all have images of ourselves, we also have images, though perhaps vague, of our groups (families, schools, nations, etc.).[12] Group images are particularly significant in societies like China where group value is constantly being emphasized. This self-group concept tells the correct order within which groups ought to operate, the shares to which groups are entitled, and the behavioral norms that groups should follow. The self-group concept is as important as the self-concept, especially for the Chinese, because the self is conceived of as a part of the group, the existence of which has to be seen as meaningful before the existence of the part can be. The value of the nation-state must therefore be confirmed before the life of individuals can be said to have value.

The concept of motivation can also be applied to the collective level through certain make-believe mechanisms. The normative-cognitive perspective emphasizes leaders of the collective actor who, in the name of the group, seek confirmation of the value of the group and create the sense of self-worth for the concerned group members in general and for themselves in particular. (This can be done either by generating a positive feeling toward the collective identity or by avoiding a negative feeling.) Needless to say, within each group there are competing notions of world justice and role conceptions.[13] Different leaders like Zhou Enlai and Lin Biao therefore may see the same organizing process (for example, Sino-U.S. normalization) in very different moral lights. We have to find out which view dominates in a particular process, during a particular period, and on a particular issue.[14]

Whether a common cause map or an institutional entity can be effectively established between nations depends on how committed national leaders in each nation are to establishing a particular image. A weaker commitment would allow more flexiblity. If such differences of commitment among nations are revealed in international interaction and fed back to each nation, the adjustment can be made accordingly and, in the next-round negotiation, one can expect a higher level of organization to occur. Sino-U.S. normalization was possible in the 1970s, for example, only after the Chinese revolutionary image had failed to convert the world and after the Vietnam War significantly undermined U.S. containment policy. The Chinese revolutionary and the U.S. Cold War models were challenged because policy based upon them failed to achieve anything close to their anticipated result; commitments were weakened.

Features of Organizational Processes

The notion of organization as processes in which common interpretations of events are achieved has the following four characteristics. First, participants and nonparticipants of an organizational process are not differentiated by legal membership. So when China joined the United Nations in 1971, the world was not necessarily more organized. Members are differentiated by the roles they play in a particular interactive process in which a causal interpretation becomes more widely shared among various national leaders. For instance, Sino-U.S. normalization occurred outside any entity but still managed to bring the two sides to the point of agreement on the status of Taiwan. Legal membership in an organizational entity does not guarantee the development of an organizing process.

Second, the process of achieving common cause maps starts by specifying the differences among various cause maps held by the leaders of participating states. Necessarily a process of information and perspective exchange, organization is therefore a process of negotiation in which participants look for mutual understanding. At the beginning of the Sino-U.S. normalization process, for example, the two sides agreed to disagree for the time being. Only by understanding another's point of view can one decide if and how common cause maps may be achieved.

Third, a common cause map necessarily highlights the compatibility of different moral standards, so organization is a process of mutual adjustment to create that compatibility. It involves not only adjustments of cognitive structures but also of subsequent behavior. On the one hand, certain moral codes are more extensively applied in order to encourage previously morally irrelevant behavior. On the other hand, some moral codes become nebulous to allow behavior formerly regarded as deviant; that neither capitalism nor socialism continued to be morally reprehensible in the 1980s played a part in furthering Sino-U.S. normalization.

Fourth and most importantly, organization is a process of self-actualization. Since organization is defined as a process whereby leaders of different nations begin to share common cause maps, successful organizing processes logically clarify the notion of justice and make the world more understandable and psychologically more stable. Chinese leaders, for example, not only found their national self-concept as the sovereignty-holder of Taiwan confirmed in the processes of Sino-U.S. normalization, but they also developed a sense of self-worth because the existence of the Chinese state could be meaningfully attached to a more just world. By being involved in an organizing process, China is accepted by others in the same process. By giving assent to others' worldviews, the leaders and their citizens confirm China's value to other states. Involvement in an organizational process is psychologically rewarding for those Chinese interested in the meaning of the nation-state of China.

The Uniqueness of the Perspective

The moral significance of organizational processes consists in the cognitive necessity of leaders' finding a meaningful role for the state in advancing world justice. This perspective is unique in four senses. Traditionally, organization is assumed to be a concrete body with a set of common goals. The first part of the assumption (that organization is an entity) no longer guides today's research. Most scholars, including neo-realists, however, continue to assume some sort of common goals in the processes of organization, though a nation such as China may enter an interactive process with wholly dissimilar goals. Scholars who study security regimes, for example, usually assume that the goals of a security regime include regulation of armed conflicts. Robert Jervis therefore argues that war's emergence must be seen as costly for a security regime;[15] Roger Smith contends that a nonproliferation regime presumes that the spread of nuclear weapons into many hands jeopardizes prospects for peace.[16] An international trade regime, as another example, would have the goal of facilitating comparative advantages.[17] In contrast, this book does not presuppose goals for an organizing process because of the lack of consensus on what justice is. Instead, it assumes many incongruent goals at the beginning. The function of organization is exactly to sort out the possibility that the incongruence can be reconciled rather than to direct specific state behavior according to previously agreed-upon moral standards (that do not exist).

Second, since nations are believed to start with different moral premises, the focus of research shifts from interactions between the organizational entity and its members to interactions among nations participating in a particular organizing process. So research on Sino-U.S. normalization would examine how each party has adjusted to the other's notion of justice rather than to the recommendation of a bilateral negotiation team. The task of international organization is to create a common cause map, not to assume its existence.

Third, political scientists are traditionally interested in how participating countries affect the performance of an organizational entity and organizational processes. The effectiveness of the United Nations under the constraints of state power, for instance, is a topic that has attracted many scholars.[18] (In fact, many expected China to abuse its veto power after becoming a UN member, but this has yet to happen.) The degree of integration of the European Community as a function of the domestic policies of the member countries is another popular research subject.[19] In contrast, this book is more concerned with how organization as a process affects the norms and behavior of participating countries. For those who accept this perspective, the focus is on change and continuity in state behavior, not in the institutional behavior of the international organizational entity.

Finally, consistent with the argument that organization exists in time and not in space, organization is seen as a consequence of interactions rather than an inception of a set of behavioral norms. Organization is not a constraint but a result. The normalization of Sino-U.S. diplomatic relations in 1979 came about because of bilateral interaction, not because of the norms set when the process began in 1971. In other words, organizational norms are seen neither as a given constraint on state behavior nor a starting point for research.

Two Reminders

Accordingly, there are two major blind spots to the traditional approach. First, participation in an interactive process alone—what one does rather than why one does it—breeds psychological satisfaction.[20] China's radical antihegemonic rhetoric did not keep it from fighting for UN membership, and the polemics continued after China entered the body, regardless of the detrimental effect on the credibility of the UN Charter. Participation may presuppose some goal calculation, even though such calculation is incongruent with organizational goals.[21] But if we agree that organization is a process of self-actualization, then we can appreciate the possibility that nations may interact with other nations for the sole purpose of interaction. China, which joined the United Nations during its antihegemony campaign, may have done so not simply to achieve its revolutionary goal but because its leaders were unable to resist the pleasure of seeing China accepted as a legitimate state. It is a psychological imperative to maintain the appearance of being involved in an international organizing process. While international relations may not be more organized, leaders behave as if there can be better organization, hence the sense of mission and the sense of self-worth.

It is therefore ironic that unilateral efforts to organize international relations may, in effect damage organization because of the futility of forcing a moral consensus in the short run. More nations' participating in an interactive process does not guarantee mutual understanding or mutual adjustment. On the contrary, organizing efforts may reveal just how hopelessly wide is the gap between leaders' interpretations of world events, as Sino-U.S. dialogue in the 1950s and Mao's meeting with Nikita Khrushchev in 1958 illustrated. The traditional approach recognizes that organizing efforts may fail, but it does not seriously entertain the likely debilitating effect of those efforts.

Research Questions

The study of national roles in international organizational processes from the above perspective is divided into five steps. First, we try to determine the notions of justice held by each participating country in an interactive process, each country's mission, and the assumed "fair shares." Second, we must ascertain alternative role conceptions and worldviews within each country. This way, when there is a leadership change within a specific country, we can understand how adoption of a different notion of justice may affect the international organizing process.

The third step is concerned with mutual role expectations derived from various worldviews. We want to know how national leaders expect one another to behave and how they judge one another morally. The fourth question is concerned with the degree of incongruence among mutual role expectations. How is the incongruence perceived and how is it acted upon? Is it regarded as a moral threat? Is it seen as temporary or permanent? The final question is how interactive processes are evaluated within each nation, how they reinforce or revise respective worldviews, and how they change foreign policy behavior in the preceding round of the organizing process.

NATIONAL ROLES IN ORGANIZATIONAL PROCESSES

In light of the anarchical tendency in world politics (meaning the tendency of states to rely on self-help) and the inability of states to survive without emphasizing their own national interests, different leaders often have different conceptions of national interest. It is therefore necessary to find out, for example, whether Chinese foreign policy served Zhou Enlai's or Lin Biao's China, whether it was Deng Xiaoping's assessment of the world or Hua Guofeng's that constrained China's flexibility. A worldview that defines national roles is essential in guiding leaders to clarify national interests. Foreign policy is made accordingly as if international relations were structured as thought. The world is hence interpreted through policymaking based on those expectations.

Political psychologists have for some time recognized the importance of national role conception in foreign policy behavior.[22] Recent literature, however, has begun to concentrate on this notion as a source of foreign policy motivation.[23] Case studies on Japan, the United States, China, and the Soviet Union have also illustrated how so-called national self-role conceptions can affect policymaking.[24] A self-role conception should include several elements: a description of national mission in the world, analysis of current interstate relationships, a specific notion of world justice, and stability over time. It is quite possible and normal for multiple identities to be held either by the same group of leaders simultaneously or by many different groups competing for access to the policymaking process. Any moral commitment made by the dominant leadership group is no more than pretension in the long run since alternative views can rise up whenever the prevailing one fails to make sense. The cycle of anticapitalism, anticolonialism, antirevisionism, and antihegemonism in China illustrates this point.

Though there are few scholarly works on the typology of national images, they are impressive. Karl Holsti, for example, lists seventeen national conceptions,[25] whereas Martha Cottam suggests only seven.[26] The difference lies in methodology: Holsti's typology is inductive; Cottam's is deductive. Though the richness of human culture makes the work of inductive typology particularly difficult, Holsti's typology, based on a comprehensive survey using data from seventy-one countries, is nevertheless truly sophisticated. His list of national roles concentrates on the categories of moral commitments made by national leaders, not the brands of final justice they are pursuing. His seventeen categories are bastion of revolution–liberator, regional leader, regional protector, active independent, liberator supporter, anti-imperialist agent, defender of the faith, mediator-integrator, regional-subsystem collaborator, developer, bridge, faithful ally, independent, example, internal developer, isolationist, and protectee. (Other role conceptions he mentions are defender of the peace, balancer, antirevisionist, Zionist, and Communist agent). In contrast, Cottam's categorization is based on the logical differentiations among ally, enemy, and neutral; and between puppet and dependant. I propose a vertical-horizontal dichotomy to utilize both approaches. The goal of this dichotomy is threefold: to specify the kinds of role-playing that are more congenial to organizing processes, to simplify the analysis of the degree of congruence among various role conceptions, and to apply Holsti's and Cottam's methodologies to international organization.

The vertical dimension is the time dimension. A role acquires its content by linking the nation either to the "good old days" or to a utopian future. In choosing to highlight the past record of the state, the leaders appeal to the past for state identity, implying that their diplomacy fails to satisfy self-expectations in the contemporary world. So when Sino-Soviet relations were ruptured in the 1960s, antirevisionism began to dominate China's diplomatic rhetoric. The Chinese projected the past into the future and strived to transform the present according to what were perceived to be the good old days under Stalin. They protected the image of Stalin that "revisionists" (meaning Khrushchev) criticized and urged others to embrace this nostalgia. Similarly, when the United States imposed sanctions on China for its crackdown on the 1989 Tiananmen movement, Beijing called on former president Richard Nixon, whose efforts in the early 1970s had ushered in two decades of Sino-U.S. normalization.

To satisfy peoples' notion of historical progress, the present can be seen as a transitional period; in the Chinese vision of anticolonialism, for example, decolonization will eventually lead to the collapse of U.S. imperialism. In the short run, however, the present always needs to be emphasized in order to resolve imminent adversity. A state that, according to its leaders, acquires its sense of self-worth exclusively from the present has to achieve self-fulfillment from interactions with other contemporary states (i.e., on the horizontal dimension). Obviously, this is the diplomacy of states that are satisfied with the international status quo and therefore strive for its maintenance. Imperial China under the Qing dynasty is an excellent example: Chinese emperors struggled to preserve China as the common master of all under heaven. Leaders emphasizing the present may do so also because the state does not have a past that is particularly attractive to them, nor do they have a clear picture of what the world order should eventually be. The rise of neorealism in China after the Cultural Revolution exemplifies this predilection for peaceful coexistence in the status quo (which the Chinese call the new international political order). Peaceful coexistence as an organizing principle had attracted some Chinese leaders in the early 1950s because they believed that China urgently needed to be recognized as a legitimate state. Leaders of this sort thus cherish what the state currently has and adjust international politics to avoid change as much as possible. Consequently, we may find both the hegemonic state and small states striving to maintain the status quo; one enjoys privileges, the others stability.

Finally, an abstract ideological system can guide the role of a state in the future. The role is related to the promise that the state has made, through its leadership, as to its position and proper share in a few generations to come. The reformist state in China in the 1980s, for instance, promised to give China a future of "socialism with Chinese characteristics." Leaders of such states at times label the existing international order exploitative or inappropriate—an evil with historical roots—and strive for its revision or perhaps total replacement; moral commitment to socialism, for example, is thought to be a cure for the evils of capitalism. The value of the Chinese state lies in its commitment to an equitable future world order. Actual plans for the future are contingent upon the estimated relative capability of the states holding this position, hence many Chinese have ruled out the strategy of exporting revolution from an economically weak China. Symbolic actions that dramatize movement toward the future are, generally speaking, necessary to demonstrate that the future is within reach. A utopia is often vaguely sketched so that such an ideal has the chance of being accommodated into other states' worldviews.

On the horizontal dimension, a role is actualized by dealing with other contemporary role players. Leaders confirm their national role by interacting with other states. It is natural for a state to interact directly with its neighbors and international powers, and indirectly with parties that have direct relations with these states. "Power" here refers to a strong state that assertively extends its influence beyond those countries with whom it shares common borders. Specification of roles assists in distinguishing the good power (e.g., the Soviet Union as a socialist leader) from the bad one (e.g., the Soviet Union as a "hegemon") and reveals where and where not to engage in competition. Direct challenge to another power, like the Chinese attack in 1969 on Soviet patrols on Zhenbao Island, dramatizes the devotion of the state to the fulfillment of professed goals. A peaceful relationship with powers (such as Sino-U.S. normalization), however, implies the acceptance of the status quo unless peaceful diplomacy is somehow a camouflage for an ulterior motive based on certain concealed worldviews.

Neighboring countries are even more convenient targets for diplomacy and the most natural place to seek confirmation of one's national self-image. Particular interactive patterns can be found among states with geographical proximity. Role expectations for relationship with neighbors are often less abstract. Enmity like that between China and Japan may continue for generations for no conceptual or ideological reason, while friendship between neighbors like China and North Korea may persist regardless of disputes that would normally have disrupted a relationship between nonneighbors. Changes in historical practices toward neighbors would unambiguously signal a change in worldview and self-expectation. A country like China that has many small neighbors may find it rather easy to manipulate this association to demonstrate the transformation or continuity in its worldview.

The vertical-horizontal dichotomy reconciles Holsti's approach with Cottam's. Holsti's typology is most relevant to the study of national role conceptions that have cultural roots. In contrast, Cottam's typology can help to clarify which states are treated as friends, which enemies, neutrals, and so on. Holsti's in-depth typology further suggests how, for example, enemies should be treated according to historically derived worldviews and role conceptions. Should they be eliminated as revisionists, isolated as hegemons, or ignored as capitalists? One advantage of the vertical-horizontal dichotomy is that one need not examine the content of the role conception to know that nations seeking identity from the past cannot contribute to international organizing. If one is interested in how they are different, one can rely on Holsti's inductive approach.

The inductive approach would be redundant if political actors deliberately avoided using history as guidance. For nations on the horizontal dimension, therefore, Cottam's typology would be sufficient. Since nations of this kind accept the status quo, questions of how enemies should be eliminated or transformed do not arise; for China the question becomes how a revisionist, a hegemon, or a capitalist should be treated as an enemy in general, and how China and that country should coexist. There is no need to explore the historical or cultural implication of the enemy category because enemies are accepted as legitimate actors and enemy relationships are taken as a fact. International organizing occurs here; opponents and allies alike, national leaders agree what causes conflict, how to resolve conflict, and how to keep the current world order within a common range of justice.

Neither utopia nor nostalgia is conducive to coordination in that the current world is seen as lacking justice. Since international organization continues in the contemporary world, those states caught up in nostalgia or utopia are not subject to organizing efforts—on the contrary, they might react vehemently to such efforts. The significance of the vertical-horizontal dichotomy is its implication that states looking for identity in the past and in the future fail to actualize their self-expectation in the contemporary world. International organizing efforts would find the most attentive audience among states that accept the status quo. The dichotomy hence helps simplify the analysis of the degree of congruence among various role expectations. Nations that appeal to either the past or future are not likely to cooperate with the organizing efforts of nations accepting the status quo. It is therefore important to examine if, for example, Chinese leaders feel the world has done justice to China.

Discontented nations might not be able to find an audience in the world, in which case they might withdraw from the ongoing organizational process. China's isolation in the 1960s seemed to be such an outright denial of any contemporary notion of justice. Withdrawal exhibits a resolute psychological break with a decaying environment; it constitutes indulgence in self-cultivation for spiritual purification and physical self-strengthening. This damages international organizing (again, in an amoral sense) because nations are no longer subject to organizing efforts and are, in fact, working to destroy them. The antihegemonic themes coming out of China's isolation illustrate this phenomenon. Conflicts of this kind may be destructive for status quo powers if the self-strengthening of the challenger is a success. A good example is the Axis coalition, whose member states withdrew one by one from the League of Nations in the 1930s; an example of failure is China's Great Leap Forward in the late 1950s.

If a conflict situation involves neither utopia nor nostalgia, it should be subject to resolution through international organizing. Conflicts of this kind are not intended to restructure the international system but serve to confirm and actualize the national role of the conflicting parties. A nation must engage in confrontation with its perceived enemy to make sense of the world for its people; confrontation does not aim at eliminating the enemy as a fact. China's self-restrained military actions against India in 1962 and Vietnam in 1979 illustrate this point. International organizing would therefore help channel this kind of confrontation in an institutionalized fashion. Conflicting parties would not risk escalation of the conflict since both find their identities in the present dimension. The enemy's existence fosters a sense of self-worth for each party to the conflict because national values are highlighted by juxtaposition with the enemy's immoral actions. It is then possible that organizing efforts can establish a consensus on who should confront whom, in what manner, at what time, on what issue, for what reason, and to what extent.

Confrontation does not necessarily represent disorganization in the long run for three reasons. First, confrontation may actually pinpoint incongruities in the worldviews of the parties involved. China-watchers have noted that despite its antihegemonism, China has made efforts to learn in the United Nations. Confrontation thus helps political actors understand how heterogeneous the world really is. When the world is found to be different than originally conceived, a dialectical process between perception and reality leads to the revision of false presumptions.

If it does not change varying notions of justice directly, confrontation may reveal the relative capability of the conflicting countries. This can be conducive to organizing because nations discover the feasibility of their role expectations. It was this discovery that led the Chinese to restrict antihegemonism to the level of rhetoric after the 1969 armed conflict with the Soviet Union. Information concerning relative capability may also be important for the establishment of an international consensus on the status of a superpower, the nature of dependency, and so on.

Finally, confrontation may serve as feedback to national political processes. New political forces within the domestic arena may rise to replace the current leadership and substitute a more practical national role conception for the current worldview. A good example here is China's 1978 replacement of revolutionary diplomacy with the principle of peaceful coexistence. If the leadership insists, however, a discarded worldview may continue to exist even after it has clearly been found to be a failure. Confrontation thus facilitates a domestic process that may bring about a moral version that is more flexible and a notion of justice that is more open to international organizing efforts.

RECONCILIATION

The organizational process of seeking common cause maps has become an intellectual perspective within the field of social psychology. The emphasis on individual actors rather than the organizational entity and on the negotiating aspect of the process seems particularly useful to the study of international organization. The characteristics of the international organizational process are determined by national role conceptions and notions of justice. Cognitive psychology has also been vigorously applied to international politics, especially to the foreign-policymaking process.[27]

Although the normative-cognitive approach by no means negates realism or neorealism, it should be regarded as a complementary rather than a substitutional paradigm, for the notion of organization as entity is useful in some areas of research. An international organization, as an institution, can provide a context in which nations interact, developing its own personality as administrative organs evolve and interests served become more specific and distinct. An analogy can be drawn to the evolution of the state organ within the domestic political process.[28] Thus an international organization as an entity can be seen as a participant in international organization as a process, though the implications for the process are by no means clear. The organizations produce their own worldviews, have their own notions of justice, and compete in negotiations for influence over the interpretations of world events.

Disputes surrounding the analytical utility of neorealist scholarship of international regime can probably be resolved. Stephen Krasner's proposal that regime be seen as an intervening variable, that between power relationship and foreign policy behavior,[29] can be supplemented with another intervening variable, between power relationship and regime: national role conception. While, as Krasner points out, a change in power relationship may not necessarily upset an established normative regime, the change certainly increases the possibility of new self-role conceptions emerging. Regimes do not occur or change directly whenever there are shifts in power relationships; regimes continue after changes in the power matrix because previously negotiated common cause maps persist. The socialist camp, for example, was actually consolidated in 1954 even though China emerged from the Korean War as a new contending power. It is quite possible for an increase or decrease in a nation's power to have no impact on how its leaders interpret events in the world if that nation holds firmly to its identity on the horizontal dimension. Yet there is always the possibility that national role conception will change because of domestic factors and that the balance of power in the world will shift as a result. This logic helps explain Krasner's contention that international regimes can have their own life.

The normative-cognitive perspective and realism can be mutually complementary. Capability calculation and power matrix, both of which are emphasized by realists, are certainly sources of national role conceptions. The approach curbs the extremes of realist thinking by reminding realists of four considerations. First, notions of justice may be based on false perceptions. Some Chinese leaders, for example, honestly thought at one time that the two superpowers were in collusion to contain China's revolution. Second, a certain kind of unrealistic notion of justice may lead to conflict that in turn may change the current power matrix. China's challenge to the Soviet Union in 1969 and the resulting Sino-U.S. normalization illustrate this possibility. Third, given the rigidity of human cognitive structures, a national role conception may linger after the power matrix has changed. Antihegemonism continued to dominate China's diplomatic rhetoric in the 1970s even though earlier attempts at normalizing relations with the "hegemonic" United States had proven successful. Finally, a national role conception may change even if the power matrix doesn't. China's Four Modernizations policy clearly reflects a new national identity that was adopted without the impetus of a significant global power shift. Nevertheless, the realist perspective is still useful in understanding the collapse of justice based on false power calculation. The approach here and the realist approach suit different analytical loci. The former can be applied to the decisionmaking process *before* policy is made while the latter explains the success or failure of the policy *after* it is made.

Neorealists may find the approach here especially useful. One thrust of international organization identified by regime literature is the need to develop norms in a complex world. This book also recognizes the cognitive necessity of simplification and of making sense of the world in ways that are seemingly acceptable to other people. Regimes are built through trial and error, a process of adjustment likewise emphasized in the cognitive approach. The study of national role conception can enrich regime research by giving regimes independent personalities. Regimes continue as long as the cause maps of national actors concerning each issue area in question remain unchanged. This book does not agree, however, with the notion that regime inception is the result of power politics for it emphasizes organization as a consequence rather than a constraint.

It is also possible to reconcile the normative-cognitive approach with the bureaucratic model of foreign policy. Despite the disputes between statism and bureaucratism concerning the integrity of foreign-policymaking organs, all domestic political forces, including government institutions, have to justify the policies they advocate by arguing in terms of national interests. Their arguments make sense only if they are derived from a culturally familiar worldview that carries a tone of justice. For example, Chinese leaders have so far been guided by at least one of the following principles—socialism, peaceful coexistence, and antihegemonism—regardless of which faction is dominant. Domestic political debates, like international political debates, manifest disagreements among various worldviews. If the national role conception is the starting point of research, one must ascertain which national role conception emerges from each domestic political arena, and how international organizing processes feed back to each domestic political process, thus affecting the selection of national role conception in the following round.

Though this normative-cognitive perspective might throw cold water on the possibility of organizing world politics in so heterogeneous a world, it does inspire hope: if we accept perception and motivation as the ultimate source of human behavior, then objective structures do not necessarily determine results and there is still room for maneuvering, communicating, and accommodating. Organizing world politics, in this sense, is still worth the effort.

NOTES

1. James D. Thompson, *Organization in Action* (New York: McGraw-Hill, 1967), pp. 9–13, 159–161.

2. Karl E. Weick, *The Social Psychology of Organizing* (Menlo Park, Calif.: Addison-Wesley, 1969), p. 36.

3. Karl E. Weick, "Enactment Processes in Organization," in B. Staw and G. Salancik (eds.), *New Directions in Organizational Behavior* (Chicago: St. Clair, 1977), p. 278.

4. Peter J. Frost and David C. Hayes, "Having One's Cake and Eating It Too: Middle Range Content and Generalized Process as Ways of Understanding Organization," in C. Pinder and L. Moore (eds.), *Middle Range Theory and the Study of Organization* (Boston: Martinus Nijhoff, 1980), p. 355.

5. David C. Hayes, "An Organizational Perspective on a Psychotechnical System Perspective," *Accounting, Organization, and Society* 5, 1 (1980): 45.

6. George B. Graen and Teni A. Scandura, "Toward a Psychology of Dyadic Organizing," in L. Cummings and B. Staw (eds.), *Research in Organizational Behavior* 9 (London: Jai Press, 1987), pp. 177–186.

7. Weick, *The Social Psychology of Organizing*, p. 43.

8. Arthur Stein, "Coordination and Collaboration: Regimes in an Anarchic World," *International Organization* 36, 2 (Spring 1982): 316.

9. See Viktor Gecas, "The Self-concept," *Annual Review of Sociology* 8 (1982): 1–33.

10. Maxwell Maltz, *Psycho-cybernetics* (New York: Pocket Books, 1966), pp. 28–29.

11. Robert G. Lord, "An Information Processing Approach to Social Perceptions, Leadership and Behavioral Measurement in Organization," in Cummings and Staw (eds.), *Research in Organizational Behavior* 7 (London: Jai Press, 1985), pp. 92–97.

12. Kenneth Boulding, "National Images and International Systems," *Journal of Conflict Resolution* 3 (1959): 120–131.

13. Stuart Albert and David A. Whetten, "Organizational Identity," in Cummings and Staw, *Research in Organizational Behavior* 7, pp. 267–272.

14. William Chandler, *The Science of History: A Cybernetic Approach* (New York: Gordon and Breach, 1984), pp. 65–68.

15. Robert Jervis, "Security Regime," *International Organization* 36, 2 (Spring 1982): 361–362.

16. Roger K. Smith, "Explaining the Non-proliferation Regime," *International Organization* 41, 2 (Spring 1987): 257.

17. For example, see Mark W. Zacher, "Trade Gaps, Analytical Gaps: Regime Analysis and International Commodity Trade Regulation," *International Organization* 41, 2 (Spring 1987): 191, 195; John G. Ruggie, "International Regimes, Transactions, and Change: Embedded Liberalism in the Postwar Economic Order," *International Organization* 36, 2 (Spring 1982): 410–413.

18. For example, see Inis L. Claude, Jr., *Swords and Plowshares* (New York: Random House, 1971), pp. 353–369; Richard Falk, *A Global Approach to National Policy* (Cambridge: Harvard University Press, 1975), pp. 169–196.

19. For example, James A. Caporaso, *The Structure and Function of European Integration* (Pacific Palisades, Calif.: Goodyear, 1974); Karl W. Deutsch et al., *Political Community and the North Atlantic Area* (Princeton: Princeton University Press, 1968).

20. Russel Ackoff, "The Aesthetics of Management," in K. Krippendorff (ed.), *Communications and Control in Society* (New York: Gordon and Breach, 1979), p. 376.

21. Stein, "Coordination and Collaboration," pp. 316–327.

22. Carl W. Backman, "Role Theory and International Relations," *International Studies Quarterly* 14, 3 (September 1970): 310–319; Karl J. Holsti, "National Role Conceptions in the Study of Foreign Policy," *International Studies Quarterly* 14, 3 (September 1970): 233–309; Stephen Walker, "National Role Conceptions and Systemic Outcomes," in L. Falkowski (ed.), *Psychological Models in International Politics* (Boulder: Westview, 1979), pp. 169–210.

23. Richard N. Lebow, *Between War and Peace* (Baltimore: Johns Hopkins University Press, 1981), pp. 192–199; John G. Stoessinger, *Nations in Darkness* (New York: Random House, 1975), pp. 209–233; Stephen Walker and Martin Sampson (eds.), *Role Theory and Foreign Policy Analysis* (Durham, N.C.: Duke University Press, 1987).

24. Nobuya Bamba, *Japanese Diplomacy in a Dilemma* (Kyoto: Minerva Press, 1972); Martha L. Cottam, *Foreign Policy Decision Making: The Influence of Cognition* (Boulder: Westview, 1986); John G. Stoessinger, *Crusaders and Pragmatists* (New York: W. W. Norton, 1979).

25. Holsti, "National Role Conceptions," p. 286.

26. Cottam, *Foreign Policy Decision Making*, pp. 61–109.

27. For a bibliography, see R. Mandel, "Psychological Approaches to International Relations," in M. Hermann (ed.), *Political Psychology* (San Francisco: Jossey-Bass Publishers, 1986).

28. See the discussion in Stephen D. Krasner, *Defending National Interest* (Princeton: Princeton University Press, 1978), pp. 5–34; Theda Skocpol, *State and Social Revolution* (Cambridge: Cambridge University Press, 1979), pp. 24–33.

29. Krasner, "Structural Causes and Regime Consequences," *International Organization* 36, 2 (Spring 1982): 185–205.

3

CHINA'S QUEST FOR JUSTICE

Idealism is relevant not because a utopia is within reach but because the pursuit of justice can go far beyond realist constraints, owing to human ignorance, determination, miscalculation, obsession, animosity, and so on. Nobody, however, can deny the familiar tendency of politics to use idealism for realist purposes and regard it as a semantic game. Nonetheless, this rhetorical pursuit of justice arouses emotions in both politician and constituency from time to time, providing national leaders with a strong motive to engage in some unrealistic venture. The appearance of speaking, analyzing, and evaluating with a sense of justice can therefore create a perception of knowledge and can transform oral power into moral power, and then into political power.

THE CHINESE MORAL REGIME

More than 2,000 years ago, Confucius strived to define the correct order for the warring states during the late Zhou Dynasty. Confucianism did not become the official state ideology until a few hundred years later, during the reign of the Han dynasty's Emperor Wudi. It is interesting to see how an originally irrelevant ideology of interstate relations today underpins modern China's fundamental assumptions in dealing with the rest of the world. The interplay among oral, moral, and political power in a Confucian system has made China's attempts to organize international politics according to its own notion of justice (whatever its contents) dramatic yet genuine. While diplomatic rhetoric is ordinarily considered superficial, the Chinese example provides a different kind of testimony. Before one explores the substance of what the Chinese say they believe, it is important to examine the psychocultural basis of the Chinese style of justice.

Characteristics

A lifetime student of China once argued that the Chinese notion of power is distinctively different from that of the West.[1] In China social status magnetizes power. People of low standing will not command support regardless of how hard they maneuver; people of high standing can safely assume that power will be granted to them by their underlings. Since social status is primarily a result of social consensus, everyone is supposed to know who has power and who does not. There is therefore no need for anyone to seek power actively. Lucian Pye observes, "Power became nothing more than social status, and to exercise power was simply to perform high-status roles. . . . To use power for practical purpose, particularly to advance one's own interests, could compromise the legitimacy of one's own status and thereby turn the whole society against the taboo violator."[2]

This kind of moral regime did not seem to exist at the time of Confucius. Confucius devoted his life to theorizing the moral superiority of the prince of Zhou, who was ideally the head of the family of states. The lords of those warring states were chiefly interested in their own wealth and strength. Confucius then concentrated his efforts on individual lords, trying to convince them that the simplest way of ruling within their own domain was to "rectify names" and exemplify role-playing. He must have hoped that if rectification within each state could succeed, rectification among states would come naturally. The latter kind of rectification would of course give the prince of Zhou, one of the weakest rulers at that time, the power to reign. It seems that Confucius naively believed that morality created power rather than vice versa. Indeed, throughout the Zhou dynasty, Confucianism was ridiculed by proponents of many other schools of thought. In fact, the state that emerged victorious and founded the Qin dynasty was ruled by disciples of legalism, who believed in the use of naked force.

Confucianism nonetheless survived, and the significance of this part of its history is not that it failed in the period of the warring states, but that it spread despite the Confucianists' obvious lack of power. Following the teaching of their sage, Confucianists were determined to "carry on even knowing the impossibility, and carry on without [expecting] to achieve anything."[3] It is perhaps this kind of moral commitment that later made Chinese political behavior dramatic to the point that facts could be ignored, distorted, and imagined (or, more seriously, fabricated) for the sake of a certain belief.[4] In fact, once China was united by Qin Shihuang, legalism proved to be an inadequate instrument of rule because it was virtually impossible for the emperor to amass enough force to control his huge territory. Confucianism was the natural rescue in the sense that a Confucian emperor had only to reign, not to rule, resting on the citizenry's voluntary rather than coerced support.

According to Confucianism, the emperor is the supreme moral symbol of all under heaven. The emperor is the gentleman (*junzi*) and his citizens, little men (*xiaoren*). Confucius said, "The gentleman's virtue is like wind and little men's, weeds. The wind blows over the weeds, the weeds bow."[5] Those who lack morality cannot succeed in ruling because the citizens would lose their sense of direction. Openly seeking power or self-interest is considered a sign of a lack of morality and would actually damage one's power base. A regime collapses when individuals start pursuing their own interests precisely because the emperor is unable to assume real control over the vast land of all under heaven. The Chinese emperor reigned only through a small number of scholar-officials and a cooperative local gentry class, who, in turn, ruled the masses of peasantry whose interest it was to pay their taxes regularly so as to avoid official attention.[6]

Enacting the moral pretension of the regime allowed all to live together harmoniously, although some were better off than others. (Moral pretension in this book refers to the predominance of norm-bound role-playing over other secular considerations, especially material self-interest, in guiding one's deeds and words.) Nevertheless, everyone had something to gain from this moral pretension; citizens knew basically what was expected of them and achieved a sense of security. The gentry class supported the regime to receive tax breaks, to profit from official connections, and to enjoy the respect of the masses. The peasants preserved a considerable freedom and had official protection from bandits. Moral rhetoric has therefore contributed to a collective rationalization process in China. It has allowed people to feel comfortable with taking advantage of the status quo while protecting the regime from challenge. A Chinese moral regime, accordingly, has five characteristics.

First, since leaders are moral beings, their power has no limitation, and defying their wishes implies lack of morality. This is not to say that they can do anything they please but that all their requests in the name of the state are necessarily legitimate. The idea that civil authority should operate like paternalistic power has caused the Chinese to feel that authority should have no precise limits and that its responsibilities are general and cannot be rigorously defined.[7]

Second, the moral character of the regime is expressed through ritualistic, dramatic actions as well as rhetoric. The power of the regime is based upon the integrity of moral pretension. The focus of the "government by goodness" theory—the point that distinguishes Confucianism from its Western counterparts—is the idea of virtue attached to right conduct. To conduct oneself according to the rules of propriety, of *li*, in itself gives one a moral status or prestige. This moral prestige in turn gives one influence over the people.[8]

Third, being told what is morally right but not complying is a sin. The leaders are always the models, but it is believed that all can rise to a higher status if they have the willpower to learn correctly from models. Lack of enthusiasm can be taken as an insult. Reflecting this belief in willpower, Mencius suggested an analogy "The will is of the highest importance; the spirit is subordinate to it. Therefore . . . : 'Hold fast to the will and the spirit will not deviate from it. . . . ' Now chess playing is but a minor art; if a man does not devote his heart to it and concentrate his will on it, he cannot succeed in learning it. . . . Is this because his intelligence is inferior? No . . . , not so."[9]

Fourth, the benefits of the moral regime are shared by elites at all levels. Local leaders should have a real interest in protecting the moral pretension and be supportive of the regime.[10] This ruling pattern is well established: in early Chinese history the gentry families became the dominant class in the towns, which usually doubled as administrative centers. The essential connection between the gentry and officialdom drew the gentry into the towns both as cultural centers and as walled havens against bandits and irate peasants. The gentry family's best security lay not in sole reliance upon landowning but in a union with official prerogatives.[11]

Fifth, and most important, flexibility and realistic adjustment are always essential to the long-term survival of a moral regime, although rhetorical respect must be paid to moral pretension. Confucius, for instance, in his realist analysis of taxation, warned continuously that tax was worse than a tiger to the people and that the people were like water, capable of capsizing a regime like a boat. He urged the prince to feed the people first. This may sound like the legalist advice given by Guanzi: "[People] appreciate propriety only after the granary is full, appreciate honor and shame only after food and clothing are sufficient."[12] The *Analects* records a story reflecting this conventional wisdom: "When the Master went to Wei, Jan Yu acted as the driver of his carriage. The Master said: 'How thriving is the population here!' 'Since it is so thriving,' asked Jan Yu, 'what more shall be done for the people?' 'Enrich them,' the Master replied. 'And when they are enriched, what more shall be done?' 'Educate them!' said the Master."[13]

Moral Rhetoric

The mix of material interests and moral conviction in Chinese politics sheds light on the Chinese obsession with the notion of appearances. On the one hand, if harmony on the surface is questioned, material interests under the surface are put in jeopardy. On the other hand, if underlying material interests are exposed to scrutiny, the moral surface could be denounced as superficial, and this would result in ruthless competition. There is thus a strong tendency in Chinese politics to rhetorically deny the role of personal interests in order to make everyone comfortable with that daily business, which requires flexibility and consideration of material interests. Face is saved whenever rhetorical respect is paid to the regime. In an extreme case, though, material interests can and must be sacrificed to show others that one is sincere, serious, and determined to maintain the proper order in the long run.

The stress on moral rhetoric makes it extremely important to speak with the appearance of authority. In fact, the appearance of being able to speak implies authority in Oriental politics. Scholars have suggested that this phenomenon has something to do with child-rearing practices: children are rarely responded to according to their facial expression.[14] The assumption that children do not know anything requires them to listen and not talk; they are supposed to "take in" and never "talk back."[15] In politics, of course, authority always claims that it is taking good care of citizens: authority is expected to know what is just and good for society. This monopoly of moral rhetoric gives leaders a tremendous advantage in making moral judgments on political affairs for society. Different voices would understandably shock leaders and citizens alike with the potential chaos such a challenge could instill.

Oral evaluation of one's role performance by other members of society or authority serves as the first test of one's social conformity. Oral power becomes the equivalent of moral power in this sense. One acquires an identity in society and is allowed to share social benefits with others only if one's role enactment is orally confirmed by other members of society; hence the need to save face. One should therefore only speak in a manner that confirms one's social status in the larger social hierarchy. So it becomes imperative to submit to the oral power of authority.[16] Violation of this oral propriety creates anxiety not just because the relation with authority is under challenge but because the individual's identity is denied. Coming from ordinary citizens, this kind of violation would be a show of displeasure toward the regime that the regime, for its part, must rebut and even punish.

Realists tend to overlook the importance of moral rhetoric in politics. Exactly because politics is considered dirty, some mechanism in society must be developed to provide psychological comfort for those who have to deal with power. Especially in China, moral rhetoric enables the regime to consolidate a political system so fictitious that at times reality is hardly relevant. What is more, the separation of rhetoric and reality only reinforces the use of rhetoric to disguise deviant behavior in politics. Eventually, protecting the regime's moral integrity through rhetoric becomes a real end. This desire to achieve a moral order, to monopolize moral judgment, to receive rhetorical respect from others, to arrange compromise only beneath the moral surface, and to engage in rhetorical confrontation to counter a perceived threat constitutes a Chinese style of moral politics composing (as I argue later) a Chinese drama that can affect the formation and deformation of international justice.

The Moral Regime in International Organizational Processes

China's brand of moral politics certainly affects the country's understanding of international politics and justice. Chinese leaders have a tendency to look for some sort of moral hierarchy that defines principles that they can sensibly apply when making moral judgments,[17] and they have historically portrayed China as the supreme being in the moral hierarchy, or at least as a model for the rest of the world.[18] With this moral leadership, China can legitimately guide other countries in fulfilling their destiny, if its leaders choose to do so. Since harmony must be maintained within the confines of the moral hierarchy, conflicts between China and other norm followers are not supposed to arise; conflicts result from the failure of others to comply with norms. China certainly has the legitimate right not only to criticize but to correct such violators, although it may decide not to do so in the short run for various reasons. China always expects that, in the long term violators will become aware of China's determined commitment, appreciate their real interests, and join the Chinese side. The effects of this kind of moral conviction on international organizational processes are likely to be negative. Since Chinese moral principles are presumably based upon China's unique historical experiences, a common cause map can hardly emerge if China insists on the correctness of its singular interpretation.

It is enormously difficult for Chinese leaders to convey their moral conviction in the international arena because there is no universally understood ritual that can be used repeatedly to dramatize the integrity of a certain moral order. With the ritualistic aspect of politics absent, Chinese leaders are compelled to rely on rhetorical expression. The moral conviction to which leaders have presumably committed China can only be dramatized by issuing strong statements so that there will be no confusion about China's principled standing. The lack of common rituals in world politics also disallows others from demonstrating their opposition (withdrawal) or support (participation) in these rituals. Chinese leaders would have to expect them to make verbal commitments to the Chinese vision; lack of response would most likely be taken as an insult. When verbal assurance is given to China, a common cause map seems to be shared to some extent.

Chinese psychoculture does not tolerate nonconformity: being told what is right but not complying is a sin. This psychocultural character connotes the inability of the Chinese regime to appreciate pluralism; the fear of moral chaos is constantly present. If other nations lack the willpower to follow the model, the logic goes, it must be that they are preoccupied with material interests and China might be their next prey. In addition, if there is an alternative moral view, the implication is that China might be on the immoral side. Encountering a different worldview would thus force Chinese leaders to pass through an ordeal in order to demonstrate their willpower and the correctness of their view. The encounter may be initiated by China in order to convert others; it may end up having a disorganizing effect as efforts are often made to highlight differences in causal interpretation and moral judgment of world affairs.

It may appear that the persistence of moral rhetoric damages China's ability to adjust. Yet this persistence may also allude to a psychological need to disguise some ulterior, selfish pursuit of material interests. Conscious irrationality to demonstrate willpower can be used to balance subconscious rationality to protect self-interest; it is therefore possible that rigid moral rhetoric in world politics helps psychologically separate moral internationalism and selfish nationalism. Accordingly, if one reads the Chinese style of moral politics correctly and responds to China's moral call positively, one opens a whole new field of negotiation that may eventually lead to sweeping change in actual policy behavior, despite the previous moral rhetoric. Some reinterpretation that extends the confinement of the Chinese moral hierarchy would presumably legitimize such change later on. This type of extended reinterpretation, as argued in Chapter 2, can set off a process that facilitates the overlapping of cause maps among various political actors.

One psychological function of diplomatic rhetoric by the moral regime in selling its notion of justice internationally is the creation of a sense of meaningful existence. Since Chinese leaders lack the moral monopoly in the international arena that they enjoy internally, strong statements and extreme denouncements serve to deny others the authority to speak. In order to substantiate oral debate, it is sometimes necessary to accuse others of evil intention. Fabricated facts satisfy the belief in a battle of good versus evil and dramatize China's role in rectifying the world order. In the long run, China hopes its value to the world will be appreciated and other countries will embrace China's moral exemplification. Whether or not this theatrical performance in politics can really bring about a more widely shared notion of justice depends on how other countries understand and exploit Chinese realism underneath China's rigid moral surface.

CHINA'S ROLE CONCEPTIONS

Studies of Chinese cultural norms, national role conceptions, and development routes all indicate that the Chinese invariably appear to choose from three alternatives. For example, Green Bennett suggests that in modern

China there are three types of cultural norms: traditional, modern, and revolutionary.[19] Kenneth Liberthal identifies three kinds of Chinese leaders with different approaches to foreign policy: activists, selective modernizers, and technology firsters.[20] I have suggested three types of diplomatic norms in China: asymmetric, symmetric, and rebellious.[21] Peter Van Ness finds a close relationship between foreign policy position and domestic development strategy embodied in three roads: command economy, autarky, and market socialism.[22] Studies of communist systems in general also point out three types of incentive systems: coercive, educative, and material.[23] No author has argued that the three identified are necessarily mutually exclusive. In fact, Chinese statements on foreign policy, too, have always included three principles: socialism, peaceful coexistence, and antihegemonism.

Though these last three principles may seem somewhat contradictory at first, a good number of documents mention them side by side. Zhou Enlai, for example, gave his analysis of the world in 1953:

> The imperialist camp of aggression led by the United States . . . uses the method of war and militarizes its national economy . . . to guarantee maximum capitalist profits. . . . On the other hand, the world peace camp of democracy led by the Soviet Union has been consolidated. . . . The people's democracies of Eastern Europe, with the friendly help of the Soviet people, are smoothly engaging in socialist construction. . . . The people's campaign for peace and anti-war has reached world scale. . . .
>
> The Chinese people are filled with the desire for peaceful construction and the wish to maintain permanent peace. . . . [They] must be prepared to struggle . . . with determination against the imperialist force which blocks China's construction.
>
> . . . We must sincerely learn the Soviet experience, making [private businesses] develop their active nature under the national economic leadership and the national unified plan.[24]

In this quote, socialism, revolution, and peace have equal significance. Ten years later, the theme was repeated. A party document stated: "The anti-imperialist revolutionary struggles of the people in Asia, Africa and Latin America are pounding and undermining the foundations of the rule of imperialism and colonialism, old and new, and are now a mighty force in defence of world peace."[25] As late as the 1980s, a diplomacy textbook published in Beijing still listed peaceful coexistence, antihegemonism, and Marxism, Leninism, and Maoism as China's guiding principles for worldwide political struggle.[26] It appears that for Chinese diplomacy, the ideal is a strong, peaceful, socialist camp that can deter capitalist-imperialist intervention in the developing areas' anticolonial search for freedom.

Of course, Chinese culture is far too rich to be divided simply into three norm complexes. For example, for about 200 years during the warring states period and the Qin dynasty, the ultrarealist legalist world-view attracted a substantial number of adherents throughout China. Then, in the early Han dynasty, a quasi-Taoist, laissez-faire view predominated for a period, while another passive philosophy influenced by Buddhism enjoyed brief popularity in the Liang dynasty during the time of the North and South dynasties. During the late Qing dynasty, the Boxers called on supernatural beings to rid China of the Western "barbarians." Mao Zedong nearly succeeded in establishing a similarly isolationist diplomacy in 1958, but his policy was eventually doomed to failure. And there is always the possibility that new ideas will evolve in the future. In addition to the three most commonly mentioned set of norms, this chapter also discusses the presence of "statist" and "isolationist" roles. It is significant that all these roles and norms have appeared repeatedly between 1950 and 1990: once it has become a part of China's diplomatic rhetoric, a specific set of norms is likely to be a permanent feature of Chinese diplomacy. This is why in later chapters many previously made remarks are quoted in the present tense, as if they might reflect the current policy line anytime in the future.

Socialist Role Conceptions

China's participation in the process of consolidating a socialist camp under Soviet leadership was an important development in the postwar international organizational process. Since the beginning of the Korean War, Chinese leaders have endeavored to establish their own worldview. The notion of socialism provides them with guidelines regarding China's role in pursuing justice in the world. The same notion is also responsible for China's expectation that other socialist countries, primarily the Soviet Union, act in certain ways. Based upon their understanding of Marxism, Leninism, and Maoism, Chinese leaders are able to pass moral judgment on others. The meaning of socialism has evolved and been extended over time because of the failure of many socialist countries to comply with China's role expectations—one reason why China's socialist worldview is filled with strong antagonism. The following sections examine China's socialist role expectations.

Proletarian internationalism. Since the founding of the People's Republic, China has held firm to the proposition that socialism is superior to capitalism. The future of the world, according to this notion, lies in the process of consolidation of the socialist camp and the final collapse of its capitalist counterpart. The ability to avoid the development of hostilities within society is the very essence and superiority of socialism. Although under socialism a certain contradiction between superstructure and economic base still endures that requires periodic adjustment, socialist countries are believed more capable of balancing the relations of production and the forces of production, "adjusting internal contradictions among the people, [and] preventing that contradiction from transforming into an antagonistic contradiction." Only in countries led by the working class can "errors be recognized consciously, [and] mistakes in work be reduced." These features supposedly make socialism "superior to any archaic social system."[27]

Avoiding antagonistic contradictions is also the key to establishing the socialist camp. At one time, China's fundamental principle in world affairs, according to Mao, was to "consolidate unity with the Soviet Union and consolidate unity with all socialist countries."[28] Zhou Enlai portrayed ideal internal relations in the socialist camp as being cemented by common communist ideals and goals, and based upon the principle of "proletarian internationalism." Since each socialist country is considered independent and sovereign, relations should likewise be based upon "the Marxist-Leninist principle of national equality." Hence in theory there is no contradiction or conflict of interests among socialist countries. Zhou believed that contrary to the mutually conquering relations that prevail among imperialist nations, association among socialist countries based on consolidation and mutual help represents a brand new type of international relation. The Soviet Union, for example, "always" provided significant aid to other socialist countries. The "friendly unity" between China and the Soviet Union was, according to Zhou, an extremely important part of the great unity of socialist countries.[29]

Zhou noted, however, that interaction among socialist countries was not without its imperfections. A tendency toward "big-nationism" or "narrow nationalism" in interactions among socialist countries had caused division and misunderstanding within the group. Therefore, Zhou would not go so far as to suggest that socialist countries share common views on all questions. As long as the relationship of unity is cherished, it is "all right" to hold differing opinions.[30]

These views obliged Zhou to protect the image that this new international relation based on socialist brotherhood was "unbreakable." So at the time when Soviet experts were withdrawing from China, Zhou denounced attempts to destroy Sino-Soviet unity as "fantasy." Facing the withdrawal, he continued to emphasize the "simultaneous improvement in national economies" of all socialist countries.[31]

A realist would argue that Zhou's effort to maintain the appearance of socialist unity was indeed crucial to China's survival, assuming that the United States was preparing to take military action against China whenever possible. There is another logic behind the pretended unity Zhou tried to rescue. Later chapters point to the theatrical aspect of Zhou's emphasis on Soviet leadership and the harmonious relationship among socialist countries: if there were no unity within the world proletarian class, China would lose its identity. Proletarian internationalism, which Zhou used to justify all Russian foreign intervention, consists of unselfish economic assistance to socialist or other developing countries and unreserved aid in destroying counterrevolution (ie., Hungary in 1956). China is an even better model in this category: although China's aid is rather limited in terms of quantity, "it has no strings attached," demonstrating a sincere wish to help these countries "develop independently."[32]

The Chinese felt that they had successfully displayed their internationalist character. All realist attempts to improve the power status of the socialist camp have to be rationalized and legitimized by such internationalism. This pretense of internationalism deprives the Chinese of a motive to examine socialist unity critically and constrains them from questioning the validity of belonging to the socialist camp even though the camp has never functioned well in the first place.

This obsession with the notion of unity made its collapse in the 1960s all the more drastic and irrevocable, even though the threat from the United States still existed and had in fact increased. This collapse is discussed in greater detail in Chapter 4, but it is worth mentioning here that the break with the Soviet Union made it imperative for the Chinese to denounce the Soviets without reservation. In order to make sense to the military of the socialist camp's demise, Mao then rationalized that U.S. moves in Vietnam were the death throes of an imperialism that posed no danger to China.[33] This stands in vivid contrast with pre–Korean War calculations that labeled the U.S. threat as omnipotent. Instead of realism guiding ideology, this case suggests quite the opposite: the need to demonstrate ideological purity constrains national interest calculation.

The break, however, could be made sensible from a socialist perspective only if there had been socialist countries that had failed to perform their roles correctly. The collapse of socialist unity occurred so abruptly that from then on China criticized Russia at every opportunity to make it perfectly clear that China was on the moral side. The Chinese leaders must have been deeply shocked to realize that China's contribution to the new socialist world order had come to naught. Chinese leaders were unable to achieve a sense of self-actualization because China's role was not respected, the environment for socialist unity was obliterated, China's expectations were not met, and China's moral commitment was ridiculed to a certain extent. The harmonious socialist relationship was thus challenged, and when it became clear that the challenge could not be disguised with rhetorical commitment to unity, it had to be thoroughly denounced so that China's commitment to its own version of socialist order could still appear sensible. Thorough denunciation precipitated the process of disorganization among socialist countries to which China had to assign new meaning.

Antirevisionism. Once the collapse of unity in the socialist camp was recognized, the role of true socialist country had to include the struggle against revisionist socialism. The rise of revisionism was said to be a consequence of incomplete revolution within such countries as the Soviet Union and Yugoslavia, where the working class was not in full control. The charge of revisionism hence completely denied the legitimacy of the revisionist regime. The *Renmin Ribao* (People's daily) quoted Mao as having said that revisionism erased the distinction between socialism and capitalism and that between proletarian dictatorship and bourgeois dictatorship.[34] It was expected, as a result, that "the people" should play a more active role, as a revisionist regime would certainly refuse to acknowledge classes and class struggle and engage in revitalizing capitalism. One lesson Mao hoped the people would learn from the Great Proletarian Cultural Revolution was how to rise up against the revisionists and deprive them of their power.[35]

Chinese leaders may have maintained the moral integrity of their notion of a socialist camp but at the same time the disorganizing effects of their principles should be obvious. But this was not the concern; the concern was to demonstrate that China was a model socialist country and that the revisionist regime was a negative prototype. A true socialist country must act to oppose revisionist regimes, who by their very nature are destined for popular overthrow.

Anti-imperialism. One natural result of antirevisionism is that China has had to draw allies from other parts of the socialist camp: the proletarian class around the world. According to a textbook writer in China, the main revolutionary force should be formed by the working class in each capitalist country and its major revolutionary target should be imperialism. For although the proletarian revolutionary victory has established socialism to oppose capitalism, the major opponent of the international proletariat in this age is imperialism, not general capitalism. Imperialism is the strongest determining part of capitalism,[36] otherwise capitalism could not have threatened socialism as in Europe in 1989. So in addition to solidarity among socialist countries, the future of socialism relies largely on the proletariat's rising up in each country.[37]

One interesting point of argument in anti-imperialism is that socialist countries are not responsible for bringing about revolution in capitalist countries. A socialist country is not expected to play a direct role in the global anti-imperialist revolution. No one can externally impose revolution on another country if there is no demand for revolution among the people; revolution cannot be carried out according to a shopping list or negotiation. Most of the time, China has insisted that revolution cannot be exported—which can stop someone who is "nominally socialist" but actually "an imperialist and chauvinist nationalist" from engaging in aggressive expansion with legitimacy.[38]

The positive yet indirect role of the socialist countries is to demonstrate the superiority of socialism. Chinese leaders envisage final victory because socialism is perceived as a popular movement. Echoing Zhou's theory, one can still insist that in terms of the people's sense of belonging, population, and the speed of productive development, the socialist camp has achieved an absolute advantage over the imperialist camp. Zhou himself believed that the day when socialism would achieve critical victory in its "peaceful competition" with capitalism was not too far off.[39]

Overconfidence justifies China's devotion to socialism and (before its demise) the Soviet-dominated socialist camp, and it was certainly expected that all the other socialist countries would express a similar brand of enthusiasm. But most socialist countries kept their distance from China from the early 1960s onwards. In protecting the meaningfulness of their socialist world order, Chinese leaders appealed to another source of strength: anticolonialism.

Anticolonialism. Zhou portrayed colonialism in a manner consistent with mainstream Marxist interpretation: colonialism is the product of capitalism, and it is in the nature of capitalist countries to carry out "raids and exploitation" of underdeveloped countries in order to monopolize their markets and force them into the position as supplier of raw materials, investment target, and strategic military base site. From this point on, capitalist countries would hinder the development of the forces of production, leaving the underdeveloped country in a state of "perpetual stagnation, extreme poverty, and bankruptcy."[40]

Colonies should be extremely important contributors to the struggle for a socialist world order, according to Xie Yixian, because colonies and dependent countries "suppressed and exploited" by financial capital provide colossal backing for imperialists and are a significant source of their strength. This noted, liberation movements in colonies and semicolonies would most certainly inflict a serious blow on the imperialists and thus render aid to proletarian socialist revolution in capitalist countries. In order for colonies to become independent, Chinese leaders stress economic independence. A socialist country should aid the countries of Asia and Africa just as the Soviet Union aided China in the 1950s.[41] There should be no strings attached to any of this aid. As Mao remarked to Indonesian president Sukarno, a socialist country ought to "strengthen cooperation" with all people in Asia, Africa, and Latin America in response to the colonialists' expectation that "we do not unite, cooperate, or befriend [one another]."[42] In other words, the social systems in these countries should not be an issue. This gesture presumably manifests a socialist country's commitment to anticolonialism, since an oppressed nation in the capitalist camp should be treated as a member of the socialist camp.

Accordingly, the enactment of China's socialist roles depends not just on China as a model but also on colonies, oppressed nations, the proletariat in capitalist and revisionist countries, and other true socialist nations. These socialist norms can certainly be understood from the realist perspective: antirevisionism as a power struggle for socialist leadership; antiimperialism and anticolonialism as political expedients to facilitate alliances with reactionary underdeveloped countries. The realist consideration may be important but so is the capacity of China's socialist worldview to attract only illusory allies for China. In reality, China's obsession with internationalism, harmonious relationships, and socialist commitment has contributed in large part to antagonism. Antirevisionism not only brought about the collapse of the socialist camp but also succeeded in alienating China from many potentially revolutionary nations. Few countries can satisfy China's model of socialist foreign policy; feasible goals are made irrelevant by socialist pretension in its extreme form. Exaggerated, apparently irrational rhetoric has contributed to the misunderstanding of China's true intention (of peace, perhaps). Therefore, in addition to reflecting ulterior realist calculations, socialist norms also help Chinese leaders make sense of the world, specify China's role therein, and establish moral standards to judge other countries. The Chinese style of moral politics makes leaders serve these norms rather than the other way around.

Peaceful Coexistence Role Conceptions

In the diplomatic history of the PRC, Chinese leaders have consistently advocated peaceful coexistence among countries with dissimilar social systems. An abundance of evidence, however, suggests a gap beween China's peaceful policy and reality. Many observers have pointed out that China's criticism of Khrushchev's approach to peaceful coexistence in the early 1960s was a major source of Sino-Soviet friction. During the Cultural Revolution, China was involved in plots to overthrow regimes throughout Indochina.[43] Even today, Chinese leaders occasionally reveal concern that the sources of war are still present and that China should be prepared for war's onslaught. In fact, China is the only country that has fought both superpowers since World War II, and China has had armed conflicts with almost all its major neighbors, including Japan, Korea, Taiwan, India, Russia, and Vietnam. Realists can legitimately contend that China's diplomatic peace offensive is a smoke screen to confuse its enemies.

China's rhetorical commitment to peace seems so irrevocable that it's hard to imagine its being a facade for the exact opposite. In fact, the author of a typical textbook on diplomacy regards peace as a natural state and war as a policy option at best. According to this writer, the overthrow of a domestic exploitative system could destroy the economic roots of aggressive external expansion, and this would imply that socialist countries "need and necessarily execute" a peaceful foreign policy. He maintains that imperialist external aggression is an international phenomenon socialist countries must oppose—even by "using the method of war." This does not contradict peaceful foreign policy; on the contrary, "this is what peaceful foreign policy is."[44] It thus appears that the continuation of imperialist, capitalist systems logically denies the possibility of peace. A closer look, however, may reveal the logic behind China's peace calculus.

The five principles of peaceful coexistence, which Chinese leaders hold to be the norms of world affairs—mutual respect for sovereignty and territorial integrity, mutual nonaggression, mutual nonintervention, mutual benefit and equality, and peaceful coexistence—are targeted at the developing nations. Zhou highlighted these principles in 1955 when he suggested that countries in Asia and Africa with different social systems should have no reason to fear and suspect one another. The expectation was that developing countries could win the Chinese people's friendship as long as they agreed to coexist peacefully with China's communist regime. Therefore, Asian and African countries should, based upon their "common interests in the first place," seek mutual friendship and cooperation and establish affable and neighborly relations. At one time Zhou reminded his audience that the peace process included all countries: because China does not intend to make Asian and African countries and countries in other areas oppose one another, China also "needs to establish a peaceful cooperative relationship with countries in other areas."[45]

Coexistence with countries under differing systems should not compromise China's struggle against capitalism and imperialism; socialist countries' ability to deter imperialist aggression will help bring to maturation those conditions conducive to socialist revolution. Nor should peaceful coexistence imply unity. Mao instructed that China should talk about unity with all Marxists, revolutionaries, and peoples but never with "imperialists and national reactionaries opposed to communism and the people." China may still establish diplomatic relations with them but must strive for peaceful coexistence on the basis of the five principles. This and unity with the people in those countries are "two different matters."[46]

If China can tolerate countries with different social and political systems, then it follows that all other countries, presumably including China's enemies, should tolerate China's communist system. Zhou believed that history would eventually prove that all activities incompatible with the five principles and "attempts to impose one's will upon others are ultimately unfeasible" in contemporary international relations.[47] What is implied in all these remarks is a potential accusation: China can legitimately

castigate all capitalist countries that have conflicts with China because
China has demonstrated its own peaceful intent.

The role of a superpower in peaceful coexistence, accordingly, should
not merely be to negotiate for a superficial peace based on the status quo:
this could quite possibly facilitate even greater supremacy over the rest of
the world. Simply arresting conflict, therefore, is not the most pressing
task. Although superpower confrontation could reinforce the need for increased control, superpower collusion would invariably strengthen the
ability to dominate. To ensure that the superpowers do give up political
control, the priority should be arms reduction. One veteran diplomat has
suggested that peace be achieved through overall arms reduction, antihegemonism, South-South cooperation, and an improvement in North-
South relations.[48] The success of arms reductions depends unambiguously
upon the good intention of the superpowers. Nothing is clearer to the
Chinese than that the superpowers create injustice and immorality when
conflict does occur.

China should act as a role model for all. Chinese scholars insist that
"the five principles of peaceful coexistence be applied not only to countries with different social systems, but also to different socialist countries."[49] As a model for the nuclear club, the Chinese government re-
nounces first use of nuclear weapons and promises not to use these
weapons against countries with no nuclear capability. Following the Confucian tradition, China also treats international relations like interpersonal
relations:

> In short, the saying that "friends have trust" is indeed the principle fol-
> lowed by the Chinese people in dealing with friends in normal, private
> interactions. It is also indeed the principle followed in actuality in our
> national diplomatic activities. . . . Also the saying, "do not impose on
> others what I do not desire" has become a principle followed by every
> household in private relations, and it is the principle actually followed in
> our external activities . . . and we do not "desire" a country to engage in
> armed threat and to launch a war of aggression. . . . [There] is the princi-
> ple of "[if] people do not offend me, I do not offend them, if people of-
> fend me, I must offend them," which is not contradictory with the afore-
> mentioned principle.[50]

A stronger China should therefore be beneficial to all because it would
provide an alternative to and a check on the superpowers. Chinese leaders
can thus comfortably claim that China's purpose in developing its own
nuclear weapons is to destroy nuclear weapons.[51]

Observers of China need treat the issues of development and peaceful
coexistence as two sides of the same coin. In official documents China
supports the idea of the new international economic order (NIEO) pro-

posed by the developing nations as a whole. China advises people in the developed world not to view the NIEO as a threat to peace yet at the same time warns them that without a peaceful environment, development is unimaginable—a peaceful environment refers to "peace and stability in the whole world." Peace and development have an intimate mutual relationship: development can protect and strengthen peace, while only peace can ensure development.[52] To fulfill the mission of a role model, China would like to present a successful development paradigm to persuade other socialist countries to adopt an open-door policy, facilitate peaceful coexistence with capitalist countries, and serve as a paradigm of development for the developing countries.[53]

While socialist role norms provide for intrasocialist bloc relations, peaceful coexistence norms should govern interstate relations. Peaceful coexistence norms may look confusing because there is really no guarantee of peace per se. All countries, socialist or capitalist, developing or developed, are expected to employ peaceful methods in their foreign policy. Peace is conducive to international organization in the Chinese sense because victory belongs to socialism; the strength of socialist countries will be demonstrated, the developing world will achieve development, and the proletarian class will assume control in the developed world. This long-term goal, however, cannot be agreed upon by many other countries. As a result, China's peace offensive may actually sound threatening. In addition, since the norms do not rule out the use of war, peace rhetoric is empty of the intention of maintaining peace in the short run. Peaceful coexistence is therefore a transitional strategy. Its final justification lies in confidence in a promising future. Politics among countries coexisting peacefully does not necessarily become more organized. For the Chinese, though, the important thing is that the process of history should ensure the eventual failure of imperialism.

Antihegemonic Role Conceptions

The third normative element in China's foreign policy is antihegemonism. Not only do capitalist-imperialist countries seek hegemony, but any other country that "executes control, subversion, intervention, and aggression in another country, attempting to force the other to submit to its will" is a hegemonic state. So hegemonism can be broken down into global hegemonism and regional hegemonism. Regional hegemonism denotes international politics, economics, and a military state within a certain region. A regional hegemonic state always looks for a patron and colludes with one or more global counterparts. One example frequently quoted is Vietnamese regional hegemonism and its collusion with Soviet hegemonism. Political hegemonism is therefore always associated with a war of aggression. From the point of view of China's "overall" goal of international struggle, so-called antihegemonism is aimed at "opposing American and Soviet global hegemonism."[54]

The Chinese also called Soviet hegemonism social imperialism because it behaves in much the same way as does capitalist imperialism; earlier analysis suggests that the Chinese believed revisionists had slunk back to revitalize imperialism in the Soviet Union. The most obtuse example of this brand of hegemonism was the 1968 invasion of Czechoslovakia made under the Brezhnev Doctrine's espousal of "limited sovereignty" in the socialist bloc. A *Renmin Ribao* commentator wrote that the Soviet revisionist doctrine of "bullying and dominating" in its "big family" and invading other countries was "shameless!" The writer encouraged the people to uncover "big-country chauvinism" that strived to establish world hegemony, he identified the parallel between the U.S. urge to "limit national sovereignty and establish international sovereignty" and the Soviet advocacy of "limited sovereignty." He concluded that Soviet revisionism and the U.S. imperialism proved to be "products of exactly the same nature."[55]

Collusion between the superpowers to contain China would be the worst nightmare for a realist. Nevertheless, courageous opposition to both at the same time actually creates the sense of being a true revolutionary: "This is China's honor."[56] China's antihegemonism cannot be better dramatized otherwise.

In essence, antihegemonism should target the expansion policy, not the expanding state itself. In the early 1950s, for example, even though the United States consistently carried out a realist policy of armed expansion in order to "seek world hegemony," China's task was to strive together with other countries to ensure the "thorough effectuation" of all resolutions of the Geneva conference regarding the restoration of peace in Indochina and to consolidate and develop peaceful cooperative relations between China and other countries.[57] This posture of self-restraint does not mean, however, that the Chinese simply pay lip service to antihegemonism. The main thrust of antihegemonism ought to be containment of hegemonic policy repercussions by China and all other victims of hegemonism.

Antihegemonism is a test of China's own attitude. When China became a strong nation, Mao warned, it should rid itself of big-nationism "determinedly, thoroughly, cleanly, and completely" in dealing with international affairs.[58] He admonished China to avoid the arrogant attitude of big-nationism and never to posture for achievements in revolutionary victory and construction. Mao noted that nations big and small all had strengths and weaknesses, and he reminded his people that being moderate made one progress whereas being arrogant made one lag behind.[59] As a socialist country, moreover, China would have no need to engage in worldwide economic exploitation; according to Mao, China should never have the motive to expand.

Antihegemonic rhetoric can also serve to remind one of the nature of the enemy. During the Cultural Revolution, for example, revolutionary people around the world had to stay highly alert to these "fierce fascist bandits" and "Soviet revisionists." Revolutionary people should cope with them just as they cope with imperialists: the only method is to organize one's forces and "struggle with them, completely unmask them, ruthlessly strike them, until they are thoroughly destroyed."[60] This extreme rhetoric makes any thought of doing otherwise appear utterly immoral. It is also to be expected that this rhetoric would inspire revolutionary people around the world with more confidence in their struggle for independence.

A more active way to enact antihegemonism is to prepare to fight a war (not actually fight one) against hegemonic invasion. In the case of China, constantly faced with imperialist threat, the people must make full preparations against the enemy "launching a big war . . . , a conventional war or a large-scale nuclear war." By the end of the 1960s, for example, Lin Biao urged the people to be armed with Mao Zedong Thought, tempered in the Great Proletarian Cultural Revolution, and with full confidence in victory in order to "wipe out all aggressors who dare to come."[61]

Those who in fact face invasion should persist in their struggle and not surrender. They can expect the Chinese people to support all revolutionary people in the world to rise up to overthrow the "reactionary rule of the imperialists, the revisionists and their running-dogs." The most important thing is to "adhere to the principle of permanent war and oppose compromise or surrender."[62] This was said during the Vietnam War; China's support may sound hypocritical to an outside observer because China never became directly involved. Nonetheless, if China's call not to surrender were to be met with an enthusiastic response from every nation under hegemonic control, the Chinese leaders could of course expect an end to hegemonism.

In some instances, China's antihegemonic norms can cause China to back out of ongoing negotiations if a potentially friendly country refuses to commit itself rhetorically to antihegemonism. The best illustration of this is China's insistence on the inclusion of an antihegemonism clause in the 1978 Sino-Japanese friendship treaty, an insistence that delayed the signing of the treaty for a considerable time. The Soviet Union's attempt to normalize relations with China in the late 1980s was similarly impeded by China's adamant demands that the Soviet Union withdraw from Afghanistan, Vietnam, and Mongolia. The call for Soviet withdrawal from Vietnam and Mongolia was understandable, but the insistence on Afghanistan appeared to be symbolic. Still, Chinese leaders refused to let this issue pass (even though the Afghan rebels whom China praised had been associated with Muslim riots in Xinjiang). In short, Chinese leaders could opt for noncooperation to dramatize their antihegemonic commitment just as they had done in the case of anti-imperialism, anticolonialism, and anti-revisionism. China expected the same symbolic commitment from other countries.

To ensure that antihegemonism would end up producing isolated, sporadic struggles, Mao formulated the strategy of a united front in his "three-worlds" theory. The First World consists of the United States and the Soviet Union, other developed countries make up the Second World, and the developing countries of Asia, Africa, and Latin America are the Third World. Deng Xiaoping elaborated Mao's theory at the United Nations in 1974, and parts of this view are still held as valid today. Within this theory, the United States is accused of being the largest contemporary international exploiter and oppressor and the source of a new world war. The United States incessantly engages in control, subversion, intervention, and aggression. It carries out economic exploitation by raiding the national wealth and procuring the resources of others. The mass of developing countries suffer most, and their need to resist oppression and seek liberation and development is strongest. To a certain degree, even some developed countries suffer control, intimidation, and exploitation by the superpowers. According to this notion, these nations all seek to release themselves from slavery and control by the United States and to maintain national independence and absolute sovereignty.[63] The appropriate strategy for antihegemonism should be to strike at the First World by uniting the Third World and accommodating the Second World. Third World countries should thus continue their policy of nonalignment, and the people of the Second World their peace and antiwar movements.[64]

Like peaceful coexistence norms, antihegemonic norms provide universal guidance to every country and people except the two hegemons. Antihegemonism serves to remind the Chinese people as well as their potential allies around the globe of the intention behind China's peaceful coexistence rhetoric. It clarifies China's position in world affairs by highlighting who the Chinese leaders believe to be the source of problems. By revealing its moral judgment through rhetoric and risking conflict with both superpowers at the same time, China makes a dramatic show of its commitment. Peaceful coexistence as a diplomatic strategy, then, should not damage China's credit.

Isolationist Role Conceptions

It is apparent that not all countries appreciate China's perplexing role conceptions. At times, China's perspective diverges from the collective approach of striving to organize world politics. Although peaceful coexistence norms may serve as a useful guideline for Chinese leaders, China's occasional isolation may well become a source of psychological comfort to the extent that such isolation is conceptualized as testimony to the Chinese people's determination. For an isolationist idea to emerge, three preconditions must be filled. First, China's role play must be externally denied—China must consider no friend worth making. Second, the ideological commitment that is externally denied must continue to dominate domestic politics—the commitment must be politically irrevocable in the short run. Finally, leaders must decide that it is psychologically and politically necessary to reinforce the commitment to rectify world order. The isolationist gesture therefore implies that working for future justice requires a denial of the status quo. Normal relations can be sacrificed for normative ideologies!

In Chinese history the isolationist tendency has always been dramatized by some sort of self-strengthening movement; justice is always portrayed as within reach in the near future. During the Qing dynasty, for example, this type of movement was accepted by the court conservatives because they thought China could thus stave off Western intervention. When Taiwan lost its UN seat to China in 1971 and became indisputably isolated, Chiang Kai-shek's Nationalist regime stressed the need to "stay calm during the shock" in order to "solemnly strengthen itself." After a series of maneuvers by Khrushchev to de-Stalinize the Soviet Union, peacefully coexist with the U.S. imperialists, and dissuade China from attempting to recover Taiwan, an isolationist tendency emerged in China in 1958. In that year the *Renmin Ribao* editorial department republished an earlier statement by Mao:

> To popularize the line of the Congress is to inspire the whole Party and the whole people with confidence that the victory of the revolution is certain. First of all, we must inspire the vanguard of the revolution so that, resolute and ready for self-sacrifice, they will overcome all difficulties in the struggle for victory. This, however, is not enough; we must also inspire the mass of the people throughout the country so that they too will wholeheartedly join us in the common struggle for victory. . . . We must persevere and work unceasingly, and we too may touch the heart of the God in heaven.[65]

In that same year, in the midst of the Great Leap Forward that mobilized the masses to build socialism independently, Mao's praise of humankind was quoted again: "it is man and not material that is decisive, a contest of forces is not only a contest of military and economic power, but also one of the power and morale of man. Military and economic power must be controlled by man."[66] Self-strengthening is expected to make up for everything else while the country is isolated.

This isolationist role play primarily reflects self-concepts. The international organizational process is logically irrelevant since only self-strengthening is under consideration, even though this may actually damage China's ability to rectify the world order in the long run. Rhetorical commitment to a self-strengthening movement can be regarded as inconsistent with the notion of peaceful coexistence. As a result, a statement of self-strengthening made by Mao in the 1950s may sound much more threatening than was intended. For example, Mao once claimed that U.S. dominance in the world is a "transient" phenomenon and China's predicament as a poor country denied its rights in international affairs would be changed. Mao envisioned a poor country becoming a rich country, a country denied its rights becoming a country enjoying its rights—a transformation of things "into their opposites."[67]

In reality, China's rhetorical commitment to the unity of the socialist bloc did not fade in the slightest during her period of isolation. Chinese leaders are ambivalent toward isolation because on the one hand it is psychologically appealing to be the only country in the world that is morally committed to anti-imperialism and on the other it is unnerving to be left alone to deal with the imperialist (the United States). The isolationist role thus may be conducive to the international organizational process in the long term after Chinese leaders realize that it does not work. Later, in 1983, it was argued that China should not deal with foreign affairs from the class perspective because that is the policy of a "lonely person in a solitary household."[68] Isolation is accepted with the conviction that it will eventually end. Facing international condemnation after the 1989 Beijing Massacre in Tiananmen Square, for example, Chinese leaders repeatedly affirmed during the first weeks of actual isolation that China would never adopt an isolationist policy as it did during the Cultural Revolution. Indeed, isolation is a drama when it becomes clear that what is always important in isolationist statements are China's sincerity of moral commitment and the pretension that such commitment can be fulfilled through China's self-purification as a role model for others.

Statist Role Conceptions

At times, a realist assessment of world politics may lead China to recognize certain constraints on its own moral commitment. Notably when there is some degree of moral decline in the world or in China, national strength may achieve predominant policy attention. The surest sign of moral decline is a tendency toward the use of force rather than negotiation in international affairs, the use of coercion instead of indoctrination in domestic politics. Statism acknowledges a nation's material interests. It serves to legitimize attempts to protect every attribute that belongs to the modern nation-state—chiefly sovereignty, development, and defense. While statism may have been constantly present in China's worldview, there has usually been some ideological pretension that made it morally sensible. However, the socialist bloc has collapsed, the vision of world revolution has perished, and domestic socialist development has stagnated; under such circumstances, statism may come forward to justify peaceful coexistence norms that are supposedly instrumental. Henceforth, compromise of principles in the short run would not hurt the rhetorical legitimacy of the moral regime, and therefore the Chinese people, temporarily at least, do not have to worry about the meaning of the state.

Legalism. The essence of Chinese legalism is wealth and strength. Legalists, in contrast to Confucianists, assume that politics is amoral and recognize the necessity of using rewards and coercion. The *Zhangguoce* records the achievements of two noted Qin legalists, Shang Yang and Bai Qi, the spiritual precursors of the modern legalists:

> Lord Shang, under Shiao-Kung, made equal the beams of the steel-yard, corrected their measures, adjusted their weights, tore down the dikes of the paddy fields and taught his subjects only war and farming. When weapons were wielded territory increased and when they were still the country prosper[ed]. . . .
>
> In Ch'u where pikemen numbered hundreds of thousands, Po Ch'i [Bai Qi], commanding a few thousand, fought Ch'u once and took Yen and Ying again, and burned Yi-ling. To the south he annexed Shu-Han, leapt across Han and Wei to attack mighty Chao. In [the] north he buried Ma Fu and slaughtered his host of four hundred thousands—blood ran in rivers and the sound of sobbing echoed like thunder. He founded the empire in [Qin]; from that time forth Chao and Ch'u submitted, faint of heart, and dared not do battle again with [Qin].[69]

Legalism as a method is not necessarily incompatible with moral commitment. Indeed, the legalist approach to politics has been justified throughout history by the Confucian end it allegedly serves. Before Confucianism became the official doctrine, legalism itself was regarded as a legitimate philosophy. The ruler of the state of Qin, the final victor of the warring states period, was a disciple of legalism.

When a threat is perceived, the leaders of modern China have been known to appeal to legalism for a solution; this has been the case in domestic politics since the Great Leap Forward. Since that time there appears to have been steady moral decline as evidenced by worsening official corruption and factionalism, collapse of a moral consensus within the party, and a predisposition toward using coercion. Society has witnessed calls for a system of checks and balances and a shift of attention from collective interests to individual material interests.[70] The same tendency to use punishment as a diplomatic tool can be seen clearly in China's punitive war against Vietnam. Deng Xiaoping's oft-quoted speech to the United States in February 1979 reads in part, "If you don't teach them some necessary lessons, it just won't do."[71] The Chinese labeled their attack "self-defensive retaliation." Their statement nonetheless emphasized that "after completing the mission . . . , the Chinese border troops withdrew back to the Chinese territory."[72] To maintain China's right to punish Vietnam again, the Chinese have consistently rejected any proposal of a demilitarized zone.

One may wonder if statism and peaceful coexistence are reconcilable. Because peaceful coexistence norms allow self-defense, legalist actions can be legitimate. The question turns on how to determine if there is hegemonic threat to China. The judgment is certainly subjective. While the Chinese rejected the proposal of a demilitarized zone in 1979, they had entertained the same idea in their 1962 border conflict with India. Of course, India in 1962 was not seen as a hegemony as Vietnam was in 1979, the former being much weaker militarily than the latter. The implication seems to be that realist assessment from the statist perspective should determine the presence or absence of a hegemonic power when it comes to border areas: a threat is there if the neighbor is strong. These two sets of norms seem to have been bound together in Chinese thinking throughout most of the country's post-1949 military engagements. The Chinese believe they must fight a threat to demonstrate China's peaceful intentions. Research on the Chinese use of force suggests that the typical Chinese tactic is to attack massively but with a limited goal after issuing a series of warnings (no surprise); the Chinese forces then withdraw unilaterally. This ensures a quick victory and allows the other side to save face.[73] Beyond neighboring areas, however, peaceful coexistence norms usually apply; never has China fought beyond its border areas. This cooperation between the two sets of role conceptions may make the international organizational process along the Chinese border unstable in the short run, since there is always a tendency to punish, but stable in the long run, since there is no attempt to eliminate a neighboring power. This phenomenon is close to the classic balance-of-power system that Morton Kaplan identifies.[74]

Patriotism. Patriotic emotion contributes to China's strength and wealth and therefore should be an important element in the statist role conception. Patriotism first appeared in the People's Republic during the Korean War. On the one hand, some kind of productive patriotism was called for and later praised by Mao. His hope was that growing patriotism could stimulate increases in production on the industrial and agricultural fronts and generate a new atmosphere in China. Mao learned the lesson that as long as workers and peasants were enthusiastic in developing their patriotism to boost production, China would be all right.[75]

On the other hand, and perhaps more importantly, patriotism should be employed to protect national security. Peng Zhen enthusiastically praised and recommended the continuation of the "patriotic movement of resisting the United States and aiding Korea." The workers and peasants told him, "Now we are thoroughly prepared, when the order arrives, if human resources are needed, we have people, if money is needed, we have money, whatever is needed, we have it."[76] Patriotism was highlighted in all subsequent armed conflicts involving China, most dramatically during the 1958 Nationalist-occupied offshore islands crisis. A state council spokesman asked "the Taiwanese authorities [to] cherish peace and focus on [Chinese] patriotism" so that they "could solve the supply problem by themselves" with Chinese help (while China was shelling and cutting off supplies to the offshore islands) and "not depend on American cruiser protection."[77]

The dilemma facing patriotism in the international organizational process is its natural confusion with nationalism. Nationalism, according to the Chinese, is obsession with one nation, while patriotism is a critical part of internationalism. Proletarian patriotism is consistent with the internationalist requirement because only after a nation is liberated can the proletariat and working class possibly be liberated. If China is victorious and the imperialists invading China are defeated, the people in the foreign countries are "helped simultaneously." Today, the people are urged to strive for the early completion of the Four Modernizations in the homeland. Building the homeland into a highly civilized, democratic, socialist power is the "sacred patriotic responsibility" of the people and in the meantime will provide tremendous support and encouragement to the people of all countries in their "opposition to imperialism, colonialism, and hegemonism, and their struggle for progressive social justice." This makes patriotism consistent with internationalism.[78]

The supreme interest of patriots should therefore be proletarian class interest. If this is understood, then patriotism will not turn into narrow nationalism. Its ultimate function is to oppose hegemonism, not to glorify national chauvinism. International organizational processes that aim at a classless world can benefit if people throughout the world appreciate this refined distinction.

Independent foreign policy. After Sino-U.S. normalization in the late 1970s, certain Chinese leaders were horrified at the idea that China might be ready to submit to the capitalist camp in order to use one superpower against the other. In his speech to the CCP's Twelfth National Congress, General Secretary Hu Yaobang said that China's adherence to an independent foreign policy was in full accordance with discharging its lofty international duty of safeguarding world peace and promoting human progress. In the thirty-three years since the founding of the PRC, China has allegedly "never" attached itself to or yielded to pressure from any big power or group of powers. Hu declared that China's foreign policy followed an overall long-term strategy, and was definitely not swayed by expedience or by anybody's instigation or provocation.[79]

This independent gesture, if respected and followed by every country in the world, should ideally result in peaceful coexistence norms. Again, the difficulty lies in the explanation of the notion of independence, especially since Chinese leaders occasionally charge the superpowers with engaging in exploitation that denies economic independence. And the fine line between cooperation and exploitation is not defined in the same way among the different nations.

Hu's use of "independence" rather than any other moral overture to summarize China's foreign policy may have demoralized China's role in the world to some extent. Although Hu discussed socialist, peaceful coexistence, and antihegemonic role conceptions, all appeared as subcategories under the primary heading "independent foreign policy." No wonder that after Hu and his successor, Zhao Ziyang, were purged, Deng Xiaoping rushed to elaborate the relationship between socialism and independent foreign policy in the summer of 1989:

> The whole Western imperialist world attempts to make each socialist country jettison the socialist road, and eventually accommodate itself to the rule of international monopoly capital. Now, we have to resist this wave, our banner must shine. Because if we do not adhere to socialism, the best we can do is to develop into a dependent country, and even to think of development is not easy at all. Now that the international market is fully occupied it is very difficult to break in. Only socialism can save China, only socialism can develop China. . . . The China-U.S.-USSR triangle would not exist if China did not take the socialist road and [henceforth] not have a future. China was originally a poor country, so why is there such a big triangle? It is because China is an independent and self-sustaining country. Why do we say that China is an independent and self-sustaining country? It is because we adhere to socialism.[80]

Statism is similar to the classic notion of balance of power. Both theories are conducive to the organizational process because they accept the legitimacy of all countries in the world. The Chinese notion is dramatic because this acceptance of the status quo is offset by the moral assessment that global justice has yet to arrive and that internal changes in each capitalist and imperialist country will eventually rectify the world. The Chinese efforts, then, should not be directed toward organizing politics artificially but to preventing others from doing so. Statism is thus moralized by Chinese confidence in proletarian world revolution—a confidence conveyed through strong diplomatic rhetoric. While the rhetoric reveals the evil intentions of hegemons and imperialists, realist statism protects China from being bullied.

SINCERE AMBIVALENCE

China's role in international organization is largely rhetorical, but its rich reservoir of jargon frequently leaves other national leaders with a misconception of China's true intentions. In fact, it is hardly clear whether the Chinese themselves are able to reconcile this implicit inconsistency when applying such moral principles over periods of time. Ironically, political maneuvering by other countries aimed at constraining China's seemingly radical view would psychologically compel Chinese leaders to use even more extreme rhetoric. The atmosphere of confrontation might then escalate to the point where China would feel a need symbolically to demonstrate commitment to its version of a moral world order. The Chinese role in international organizational processes is therefore negative to the extent that the country's extreme rhetoric is overwhelmingly obsessed with self-assertion and detrimental to mutual appreciation.

However, exactly because of its pretension that it is the model for other countries and, in the long run, that the right order will gradually emerge, China rarely attempts to reorganize world politics by force. Realists would point out (and they may be right) that the poverty of the Chinese political economy disallows its leaders from assuming a more active role beyond radical rhetorical expression. Nonetheless, the Chinese themselves are quite sensitive to this type of realist suspicion. Instead of making vain attempts to manipulate world politics, the Chinese are eager only to prove that their points are correct and their notion of justice is within reach. This is probably why the Chinese tend to abuse their relations with the superpowers and their neighbors. Its nerve to challenge the superpowers and terminate good neighborly relations can best dramatize China commitment; its ability to win the friendship of superpowers and neighbors demonstrates that China is not irrevocably isolated and that China can serve as a model.

To illustrate this obsession with the appearance of being correct, a few examples may be helpful. When China signed its treaty of friendship with the Soviet Union in 1950, Zhou Enlai talked about its "especially important meaning" to the new People's Republic of China. This treaty and other agreements made the Chinese people "feel that they are not isolated" and no doubt made the Chinese people feel "extremely elated."[81] During the Korean War, Chinese leaders called the United States a paper tiger even though (or perhaps because) the United States was the sole possessor of nuclear weapons. General Peng Dehuai reported in 1953 what war meant to China: Having successfully held on during the war with inferior equipment, China completely unmasked the lying theory of the omnipotent new weapon used by the U.S. imperialists to bluff, threaten, and scare others.[82]

This need to prove moral purity, bravery, and correctness has lead to impasses because Chinese leaders cannot afford to compromise moral principles for the sake of short-term friendship. They seem unable to find a better way of dramatizing their commitment to justice without sacrificing friendship or risking armed confrontation. Instead of consolidating an anticolonialist united front with India, for example, Chinese leaders felt obliged in their 1962 border war to demonstrate China's ability to maintain independence and peace by blaming India for depending on the superpowers and engaging in a war of aggression. Since normalization of diplomatic relations with Japan, Chinese leaders have continually nitpicked about manifestations of Japanese militarism instead of working constructively toward a fusion of Japan's economic strength with China's political and moral power. Instead of patching up the Sino-Soviet rift for the sake of socialist unity, China attacked the Soviets in 1969 even though the U.S. appeared to be using Vietnam to menace China. Instead of strengthening the antihegemonic front with the United States against the Soviet Union, Chinese leaders have incessantly criticized U.S. policy to show their independence.

When China's will is stymied, realist spectators tend to overestimate the muscle behind peaceful coexistence rhetoric that flexes following periods of radicalism. Peaceful coexistence norms provide a good excuse for the Chinese to take a rest from their impossible pursuit of justice. This break is possible provided that they are not ridiculed for jettisoning some previously held inane doctrine. Unfortunately for the Chinese, their affairs have never been left fully alone by wishful thinkers who predict the fall of Chinese pretension; their expectations are rarely confirmed by reality. In 1978 Deng Xiaoping gave the impression that the reformers were in control, but in 1980 there came retrenchment. In 1982 Hu Yaobang inspired the same hope; another retrenchment followed in 1983. In 1986 Deng, Hu, and Zhao Ziyang provided reason to believe that China had returned to the world; then came the purge of Hu. Confidence was restored when Zhao took over in 1987, but this was followed by the 1989 Tiananmen fiasco. The history of the Four Modernizations is also the history of reasserting socialism. Socialism will never die as long as outsiders let the Chinese know that they foresee its death. The style of Chinese moral politics is embodied in this dilemma: China acts in a certain way simply because others say it cannot afford to do so.

China's quest for justice can be superficial at times when other nations respect its principled stand; the quest becomes genuine when China believes its credibility is in jeopardy. One student of Chinese foreign policy suggests that this cycle is embodied in a cybernetics-like process.[83] There seems to be some self-regulating force in the system so that one set of norms, when encountering difficulties in the world, will be replaced by another almost randomly selected set of norms. This randomness is partially explained by domestic political balance, which in turn is partially explained by how a certain set of norms is observed in the world. This cybernetic process apparently contributes to the ambivalence in China's quest for justice, an ambivalence most significant when it comes to relations with the superpowers, neighbors, and the United Nations—areas in which diplomatic stands are most symbolic and dramatic.

NOTES

1. See Lucian Pye, *Asian Power and Authority* (Cambridge: Harvard University Press, 1985).

2. Ibid., p. 47.

3. The classic expression in Chinese is *zhiqi buke er wei, wei er buyou.*

4. I do not believe that the Confucianists created this style of moral commitment. To make their advice acceptable, the Confucianists may have simply reflected the social belief of a much older tradition in northern China.

5. Confucius, "Confucius," in Ch'u Chai and Weinberg Chai (eds.), *The Sacred Books of Confucius and Other Confucian Classics* (New Hyde Park, N.Y.: University Books, 1965), p. 54.

6. John K. Fairbank, *The United States and China* (Cambridge: Harvard University Press, 1983), pp. 32–46.

7. Pye, *Asian Power and Authority*, p. 66.

8. Fairbank, *The United States and China*, p. 59. One can appreciate this kind of moral pretension by reading the sage's teaching on religion. Confucius suggested that one worship the gods as if the gods did exist (*jishen ru shenzai*). He did not care if the gods really existed—rituals of worship were sufficient.

9. Mencius, "Mencius," in Chai and Chai, *The Sacred Books*, pp. 148, 153–154.

10. For a discussion on the origin of the gentry's moral leadership, see Yu Yingshih, "Between Tao and the Regime," *Chinese Culture Monthly* 60 (October 1984): 102–128.

11. Fairbank, *The United States and China*, p. 51.

12. *Changbing zhu er zhirongru, yishi zhu er zhilijie.*

13. Confucius, "Confucius," p. 55.

14. William Caudill and C. Schooler, "Child Behavior and Child Rearing in Japan and the United States: An Interim Report," *Journal of Nervous and Mental Disease* 157, 5 (November 1973): 323–338.

15. See the discussion in Richard Solomon, *Mao's Revolution and the Chinese Political Culture* (Berkeley: University of California Press, 1971).

16. Chih-yu Shih, "The Drama of Chinese Diplomatic Spokesmanship," *China Quarterly* (Summer 1991): 1–8.

17. Some observers argue that all communist countries have a similar tendency to overdepend on ideological justification. In the case of China, see the discussion by Jean-Luc Domenach, "Ideological Reform," in Gerald Segal (ed.), *Chinese Politics and Foreign Policy Reform* (New York: Kegan Paul International, 1990), pp. 19–36.

18. John Cranmer-Byng, "The Chinese View of Their Place in the World," *China Quarterly* 53 (1973): 78.

19. Green Bennett, "Traditional, Modern and Revolutionary Values on New Social Groups in China," in R. Wilson et al. (eds.), *Value Change in Chinese Society* (New York: Praeger, 1979), pp. 207–229.

20. Kenneth Liberthal, "The Background in Chinese Politics," in H. J. Ellison (ed.), *The Sino-Soviet Conflict: The Global Perspective* (Seattle: University of Washington Press, 1982), p. 5.

21. Chih-yu Shih, *The Spirit of Chinese Foreign Policy: A Psychocultural View* (London: Macmillan, 1990), pp. 38–61.

22. Peter Van Ness, "Three Lines in Chinese Foreign Relations, 1950–1983," in D. Solinger (ed.), *Three Versions of Chinese Socialism* (Boulder: Westview, 1983).

23. Charles Lindblom, *Politics and Market* (New York: Basic Books, 1978); also see Alexander Dallin and George Breslauer, *Political Terror in Communist Systems* (Stanford: Stanford University Press, 1970).

24. Zhou Enlai, "Political Report," in Headquarters of the Great Resisting-America-Aiding Korea Movement (ed.), *The Great Resisting-America-Aiding-Korea Movement* (Beijing: People's Press, 1954), pp. 276–285.

25. "The CCP's Proposal Concerning the General Line of the International Communist Movement, June 14, 1963," in William E. Griffith (ed.), *The Sino-Soviet Rift* (Cambridge: MIT Press, 1964), p. 265.

26. See Xie Yixian, *Basic Theory of International Struggle and Basic Principles of Chinese Foreign Policy* (Beijing: Institute of Diplomacy, 1983).

27. Zhou Enlai, in Center for the Studies of Chinese Issues (ed.), *Special Edition on Zhou Enlai* (Hong Kong: Zilian Press, 1971), p. 304.

28. Mao Zedong, in Guo Zhiming et al. (eds.), *Mao Zedong on the United Front* (Beijing: China Literature and History Press, 1987), p. 308.

29. Zhou, *Special Edition*, p. 305.

30. Ibid., p. 306.

31. Ibid., pp. 350–351.

32. Ibid., p. 320.

33. Jonathan Pollack, *Security, Strategy, and the Logic of Chinese Foreign Policy* (Berkeley: Institute of East Asian Studies, University of California, 1981), pp. 34–35.

34. Red Guards, "The Demise of Soviet Revisionist Theory of Ending Class Struggle," *Renmin Ribao*, March 12, 1967: 5.

35. Ibid.

36. Xie, *Basic Theory of International Struggle*, p. 3.

37. Ibid., p. 14.

38. Ibid., p. 12.

39. Zhou, *Special Edition*, p. 344.

40. Ibid., p. 252.

41. Ibid., p. 257.

42. Mao's remarks with Indonesian president quoted in *Renmin Ribao*, October 3, 1956: 1.

43. See the case studies in J. Armstrong, *Revolutionary Diplomacy* (Berkeley: University of California Press, 1977).

44. Xie, *Basic Theory of International Struggle*, p. 12.

45. Zhou, *Special Edition*, pp. 243–244.

46. Mao, *Mao Zedong on the United Front*, p. 343.

47. Zhou, *Special Edition*, p. 293.

48. Wu Xiuquan, "Struggling for the Defense of World Peace," in Chinese Commission (ed.), *Collections of Scholarly Discussions in International Peace Year* (Beijing: Social Science Literature, 1986), pp. 8–13.

49. Zhang Zhongli et al., "Our Country's Main Direction of Revitalizing Economy Internally and Carrying Out an Open Policy Externally and World

Peace," in Chinese Commission, *Collections of Scholarly Discussions*, pp. 187–188.

50. Kuang Yaming, "On Confucian Peace Thought and World Peace," in Chinese Commission, *Collections of Scholarly Discussions*, pp. 174–183.

51. Ni Liyu, "China and World Peace," in Chinese Commission, *Collections of Scholarly Discussions*, p. 194.

52. Su Zhengxing, "Peace and Development," in Chinese Commission, *Collections of Scholarly Discussions*, p. 73.

53. Gao Jingdian, Jiang Lingfei, and Zou Zhengyuan, *Peace and Development: The Agenda of the Modern World* (Beijing: People's Liberation Army Press, 1989), p. 94.

54. Xie, *Basic Theory of International Struggle*, pp. 29–30.

55. Xiangyang Qi, "New Tsar's Theory of Limited Sovereignty," *Renmin Ribao*, May 11, 1969: 1.

56. Lin Biao, "The Report to the Ninth National Congress of the Communist Party of China," in K. Fan (ed.), *Mao Tse-tung and Lin Piao* (Garden City, N.Y.: Anchor Books, 1972), p. 463.

57. Zhou, *Special Edition*, p. 228.

58. Mao, *Mao Zedong on the United Front*, p. 346.

59. *Renmin Ribao*, September 16, 1959, quoted in *Mao Zedong on the United Front*, p. 346.

60. "Use Chairman Mao's New Instructions as Our Weapon . . . ," *Renmin Ribao*, March 17, 1969: 1.

61. Lin Biao, "The Report to the Ninth National Congress," p. 464.

62. "Soviet Revisionist Renegades Are the World's Enemy," *Renmin Ribao*, August 30, 1968: 5.

63. Xie, *Basic Theory of International Struggle*, p. 22.

64. Xing Shugang, "Oppose Hegemonism to Defend World Peace," in Chinese Commission, *Collections of Scholarly Discussions*, p. 115

65. Mao, *Mao Zedong on the United Front*, pp. 226–227.

66. Ibid., p. 230.

67. Ibid., p. 242.

68. Xie, *Basic Theory of International Struggle*, p. 24.

69. See J. I. Crump, Jr., *Intrigues, Studies of the Chan-kuo Ts'e* (Ann Arbor: University of Michigan Press, 1964).

70. Chih-yu Shih, "The Demise of a Moral Regime: The Great Leap Forward in Retrospect," paper presented at the Northeastern Political Science Association annual meeting, November 26, 1989, Philadelphia.

71. Fox Butterfield, "Deng Again Says Chinese May Move Against Vietnam," *New York Times*, February 1, 1979, p. A16.

72. New China News Agency, "Rebutting the Vietnamese Charges on Border Disputes," *Renmin Ribao*, April 7, 1979: 1.

73. See Allen Whiting, *The Chinese Calculus of Deterrence* (Ann Arbor: University of Michigan Press, 1974); Steven Chan, "Chinese Conflict Calculus and Behavior," *World Politics* 30 (April 1978): 391–410.

74. Morton Kaplan, *System and Process in International Politics* (New York: John Wiley and Sons, 1957).

75. Mao Zedong, "Opening Remarks at the First Conference of Chinese People's Political Consultative Conference," in *The Great Resisting-America-Aiding-Korea Movement*, pp. 139–141.

76. Peng Zhen, "Report on Resisting-America-Aiding-Korea-Protecting-Families-Defending-the-Nation Movement," in *The Great Resisting-America-Aiding-Korea Movement*, p. 160.

77. See *Literature on Foreign Relations of the People's Republic of China* 5 (Beijing: World Knowledge Press, 1959), pp. 176–177.

78. Xie, *Basic Theory of International Struggle*, p. 38.

79. Hu Yaobang, "Create a New Situation in All Fields of Socialist Modernization," *Beijing Review* (September 1, 1982): 29.

80. Deng's remark to members of the Central Committee of the CCP quoted in *World Journal*, July 15, 1989: 12.

81. Zhou Enlai, "Speech on Sino-Soviet Treaty of Friendship," *Literature on Foreign Relations of the People's Republic of China* 1 (Beijing: World Knowledge Press, 1957), p. 82.

82. Peng Dehuai, "Report on Chinese Voluntary Troops Resisting America and Aiding Korea," in *The Great Resisting-America-Aiding-Korea Movement*, p. 392.

83. See Shih, *The Spirit of Chinese Foreign Policy*.

4

ANTAGONISTIC COMRADESHIP: CHINA'S SOVIET SCRIPT

The Soviet Union's demise in 1991 has raised expectations that study of Sino-Soviet conflict can finally move beyond vague modes of analysis toward a new study of motivation. Literature on Sino-Soviet relations often concentrates on differences between the two countries in terms of their history of expansion (China during the century under the Mongols, czarist Russia at the time of China's Qing dynasty), revolutionary experience, strategic interest, military prowess, ideological polemics, and level of economic development. The conclusion: the two peoples disliked each other, the two societies distrusted each other, the two Communist parties despised each other, and the two countries impeded each other.[1] There has been little worth celebrating in their bilateral relations, and while their conflict often appears inherent and unavoidable, many an observer has come to the conclusion that the Soviet threat to China was genuine and the Chinese obsession with "social imperialism" understandable.

The history of conflict between the People's Republic of China and the Soviet Union dates back to a string of failures on the part of Stalin regarding China.[2] In 1927 the Soviet dictator sided with the Nationalist Party at the expense of Chinese communism hoping that Nationalist China could prove an effective check on Japan. Later the Soviet leaders failed to appreciate Mao's style of peasant revolution—the Soviets had first gained control in the cities and faced resistance in the countryside.[3] Throughout World War II, Stalin ignored communism in China. During the Chinese civil war, Stalin avoided giving complete support to either side and allegedly suggested that China be divided along the Yangzi River, presumably to ensure Communist China's dependence on the Soviet Union.[4]

Against this background, any political commentator could, in hindsight, explain the conflicts that erupted between the two countries only a few years after a treaty of mutual friendship was signed in 1950. The question is, however, whether the Chinese perceived bilateral conflict from the same structural (strategic, economic, and historical) point of view. Would it have been psychologically feasible for leaders of a moral regime to engage in conflict solely because the other party had infringed upon its interests? A strategic argument would imply the importance of a power calculus that suggests a lack of confidence in China's moral strength; an economic argument would imply concern over material interests that hints at moral impurity; a historical argument would imply China-centered logic that means narrow-minded selfishness. The Chinese moral regime has so far proved to be incapable of justifying its foreign policy purely in terms of national interests that appear selfish on the surface. Would it not be typical of a moral regime to cloak its policy behavior in some universal moral argument? It is therefore interesting to see how the Chinese conceptualized bilateral conflict as the result of Soviet violation of a universal moral code, not Chinese interests.

For the Chinese, the process of bilateral relations since conflict erupted in the late 1950s involved continuous reevaluation of the nature of the Soviet state. To do so unselfishly, the Chinese were obliged to look at the issue from the much larger perspective of the world communist movement, and the Soviet and Chinese roles within that context. On the one hand, the Chinese had to avoid bringing up historical animosity or Stalin's failures lest this signal a nationalist (or selfish) instead of internationalist (or moral) position. On the other hand, to prove that the Soviets lacked morality, the Chinese highlighted the Soviets' position of responsibility in world communism in order to illustrate how the Soviet Union had failed the litmus test of socialism. Once the rhetorical war started and the Chinese made sense of the polemics through their unique notion of antirevisionism and antihegemonism, the confrontation gained a momentum of its own and any structural factors that may have bred the atmosphere of controversy fell into oblivion.

The realist perspective would stress the factor of mutual fear in the Sino-Soviet conflict. The normative-cognitive approach, in contrast, puts emphasis on the factors of frustration, contempt, and anger. The Chinese strived to convince the world that they opposed the Soviet Union for the sake of preserving socialism. Correct role-playing and adherence to moral principles ideally gives one strength and courage. Accordingly, it must be asked to what extent the Chinese feared a genuine or imagined Soviet threat. If, for the Chinese, the alternative to Soviet socialism was the Chinese model, if social imperialism was doomed to fail, and if the Chinese had proved the Soviet Union to be a social imperialist, what was there to fear? China's difficulties in evaluating the Soviet state centered on the Soviet Union's rank as the first socialist state in the world, a state whose founders were raised to near demigod status in China. Could China denounce the Soviet Union without simultaneously undermining its own legitimacy and future? In other words, despite Stalin's failures in China, the Chinese continued to praise him and, before his death, to safeguard his image—quite an unselfish move. De-Stalinization in the Soviet Union, then, could only be taken as the most lucid sign of revisionism. Hence, the question boils down to whether China's Soviet policy was a product of fear or anger. Fearful policymakers saw the Soviet Union as just another state; angry policymakers saw it as a recalcitrant role player in world communism.

It is argued in this book that there was a cognitive need for China to perceive a threat from the Soviet Union after it had portrayed the USSR as a revisionist regime. A more serious threat entailed a purer Chinese socialism and a more dramatic Chinese resistance. This chapter examines the deliberate Chinese creation of the perception of a Soviet threat. Since the late 1950s, we have witnessed China's efforts to shame the Soviets by uncovering their erroneous role-playing in the world communist movement, defining the Soviet threat, and then dramatizing Chinese moral commitment in the face of that threat. The use of this shaming technique implies that contrary to the popular impression, the Chinese *never* seriously entertained the possibility of a Soviet invasion.

THE ORIGIN OF SOVIET LEADERSHIP

From the very creation of the Soviet Union, the Chinese had difficulty in defining the proper relationship between China and the Soviet Union. The postwar world was far from being neatly divided along socialist and capitalist lines; it was an antagonistic world equipped with a friendship treaty between the Soviet Union and Nationalist China that granted the Soviets special privileges in Manchuria, including treaty ports and railroads. The Soviet Union was therefore not necessarily on the communist side, and there seemed to exist the real possibility that Soviet-Nationalist association could jeopardize the Communists' position in the civil war.

Other matters gave Mao and his followers cause for anxiety. Although Soviet troops in Manchuria had handed over Japanese arms to the Communists for use in the civil war, they had dismantled and shipped home entire industrial plants and facilities. Two months before the founding of the People's Republic, Stalin received Gao Gang, the Chinese political commissar charged with taking back Manchuria from Japan.[5] Gao was later purged for allegedly attempting to establish an independent kingdom in Manchuria. Finally, the Soviet ambassador retreated with the Nationalist troops during the civil war while the U.S. ambassador waited for the dust to settle in Nanjing.

As the Communists advanced during the civil war, Europe was being divided into East and West. It was to make sense of this emerging bipolar system that Mao formulated his theory of capitalist and socialist camps fighting for control over an intermediate zone. Though the theory finalized the Soviet Union's position as leader of the socialist camp, China's role was not clearly specified. While the civil war continued, China appeared to belong to the intermediate zone. This failure to mention China's role implied that a unified China might not necessarily belong to the socialist camp.[6]

Nevertheless, toward the end of the civil war Mao declared the lean-to-one-side policy. The rationale behind the policy may well have been strategic: the United States was clearly unhappy with the pending loss of China. If China was going to rely on the Soviets, it had better do so early and without reservation in order to win Stalin's trust. After prolonged negotiation between Mao and Stalin, the Sino-Soviet treaty of friendship, which specified socialism to be the common goal of the two countries, was finally signed in 1950. The outbreak of the Korean War proved Mao's wisdom: the U.S. military encircled China via Vietnam (aiding French troops), the Philippines, Taiwan (dispatching the Seventh Fleet), and Korea. The Chinese decision to intervene directly in Korea cleared up any remaining doubt about China's membership in the Soviet bloc.

Stalin's lukewarm treatment of Mao in 1950 and Mao's final acceptance of a friendship treaty that contained provisions for exploitative joint-stock companies and special rights in Manchuria and Guangdong suggested that Mao had made a realistic assessment of the world situation. Yet to justify national sacrifice for the sake of survival, Mao had to praise Stalin as the Great Teacher despite his errors in the 1920s and preference for the Nationalists in the 1930s and 1940s. The drama of the Great Teacher not only constrained the Chinese from challenging Stalin but also imposed (from the Chinese perspective) certain moral obligations on Stalin's regime to treat China well. Conflict with Stalin would hurt Mao's legitimacy; errors by Stalin would imply Mao's imprudence.

QUESTIONING THE SOVIET LEADERSHIP

Reviewing the history of the October Revolution as well as China's own experience, Chinese leaders later concluded that "the communist movement needs no 'center of leadership' or 'leading party.'" They were especially sensitive to the Soviet role in the world communist movement:

> No Party, no matter how long its history, how early its revolutionary success, or how rich its experience, has any privilege to place itself above other Parties.
> . . . [The] proletariat and its political party of this or that country will, at different historical [moments] temporarily stand at the "forefront" of the international movement and find itself in a "pioneer position."

> The Chinese Communist Party suffered from the attempt of one self-proclaimed patriarchal Party to keep us under control. It was through resisting such control that our independent foreign policy won success.[7]

Before we examine the contents of China's Soviet policy, a few general observations are in order. From the Chinese perspective, development of Sino-Soviet relations following Khrushchev's secret de-Stalinization speech of 1956 centered on the nature of Soviet leadership in the communist movement. In terms of socialist leadership the Soviet Union had fallen far short of China's expectations. Khrushchev's speech later proved to be only the thin edge of the wedge. The more the Chinese discussed the nature of the Soviet regime, the more pessimistic they became and the more awkward their position appeared to be. Mao had struggled to finalize and justify China's place in the socialist bloc only to discover that the Soviet Union was not prepared to lead the fight for world communism as expected. The denial of the Chinese normative expectation put pressure on the Chinese leaders to make sense of the change with a new self-image, hence a new code of norms. This, in turn, triggered the process of reassessment of the Soviet Union in the 1960s and the emergence of the perception of a Soviet threat in the 1970s.

Initially, the Chinese felt obliged to shroud Soviet mistakes, and only when a confrontation could better demonstrate China's moral commitment to socialism was the torrent of conflict finally let loose. Looking carefully at polemical documents, one notes that the issue at hand was really the search for moral meaning of China's existence. At one time, meaning was grounded in world socialism under Soviet leadership. Polemics became a dominant approach for China after it became clear that Soviet betrayal was irrevocable. The whole purpose of China's Soviet policy was to draw a sharp contrast between their styles and persuade the world that global communism was still possible with the support of Chinese moral power. In addition, the perception of a Soviet threat and the notion of betrayal (i.e., revisionism) were mutually reinforcing and together footnoted China's moral status in world communism.

Peaceful Coexistence

A review of Soviet documents often leads to a misunderstanding of China's criticism of Khrushchev's peaceful coexistence policy. It is generally held that China advocated world war and revolution and therefore wished to perpetuate confrontation between the Soviet Union and the United States. In other words, the Chinese strived to prevent superpower collaboration. However, nowhere in Chinese documents can one detect concrete signs of alarm that détente would entail security risks for China. In fact, in 1958 China shelled the offshore islands defended by U.S.-

supported Nationalist troops *without* Soviet consent. In 1962 China attacked India, though India was supplied with Soviet arms. Nevertheless,
the Chinese repeatedly stated their adherence to the principles of peaceful
coexistence throughout this period of polemics. The Chinese were neither
threatened by the likelihood of a world war nor likely to start one.

Without a sizable audience, the Chinese struggled to distinguish their
concept of peaceful coexistence from Khrushchev's. China's peaceful coexistence existed between nations while Khrushchev's required "all-round
co-operation":

> It is necessary for the socialist countries to engage in negotiations of one
> kind or another with the imperialist countries. It is possible to reach cer
> tain agreements through negotiation by relying on the correct policies of
> the socialist countries and on the pressure of the people of all countries.
> But necessary compromises between socialist countries and the imperi
> alist countries do not require the oppressed peoples and nations to follow
> suit and compromise with imperialism and its lackeys. No one should
> ever demand in the name of peaceful coexistence that the oppressed peo
> ples and nations should give up their revolutionary struggles.[8]

The Chinese agreed that a world war could be avoided. By no means,
however, was peace the only possibility, as "there is no historical precedent for peaceful transition from capitalism to socialism."[9] The Chinese
warned that a true proletarian party would never "base its thinking, its
policies for revolution and its entire work on the assumption that the imperialists and reactionaries will accept peaceful transformation." Otherwise, the Chinese continued, "The proletarian party will paralyse the revolutionary will of the proletariat, disarm itself ideologically and sink into a
totally passive state of unpreparedness both politically and organizationally, and the result will be to bury the proletarian revolutionary cause."[10]

In short, the principle of peaceful coexistence was acceptable because
it restrained imperialist interference in areas ripe for revolution. The application of the principle should have a limit, but Khrushchev made peaceful transition "a new world wide strategic principle for the international
communist movement." This was "absolutely" wrong. To show the absurdity of the Soviet peace approach, China described the Sino-Indian border
war in 1962 as a result of U.S. manipulation of India (which it was not).[11]
Since the Soviet Union shipped supplies to India during the war, Chinese
theory must have been aimed precisely at showing the capitulatory nature
of Soviet policy.

Khrushchev's opposition to armed conflict with the imperialists made
China's advocacy of revolution by oppressed people and its position on the
Taiwan issue rather awkward. China could either redefine its role or reinterpret the nature of the Soviet state. Because China had followed the

Great Teacher faithfully since 1949, the task of reinterpretation had to be primarily an explanation of the changing nature of the Soviet state. Chinese polemics were concerned precisely with showing Khrushchev's capitulationism, and this China did without alluding to its own (i.e., selfish) interests—this required an international perspective. The Chinese repeatedly stressed that the proletarian party had to have confidence in the strength of the world masses (even though China had no intention of taking advantage of said strength). The connotation was that Khrushchev's peaceful coexistence was reactionary in that it was evidence of a lack of faith in the world proletarian revolution.

The Chinese carefully portrayed for the world the inconsistency between Soviet strength and Soviet retreat from socialist leadership. In 1957 Mao formulated the notion of the East wind prevailing over the West wind to celebrate the launch of Sputnik. In the following year, he demonstrated China's determination to fight solo against the imperialist in the Taiwan Straits and later charged the Soviets with rendering oral support only after the Taiwan Straits crisis was over.[12] China's assessment of the Cuban missile crisis included criticism of Soviet adventurism before the crisis and contempt for its capitulationism afterwards.[13] China denounced the 1963 test ban treaty as an agreement that allowed the imperialists monopolization of nuclear weapons. In the words of the Chinese government, the Soviet leaders "brought disgrace to the Soviet people, the Cuban people, the people of the countries in the Socialist camp and the people of the whole world."[14] China was not mentioned. The message was that China did everything for the socialist cause and not Chinese self-interest.

Nowadays, China contends that peaceful coexistence leads to worrisome developments because there is no concomitant alert to the dangers of bourgeois subversion. According to the Chinese, "even though tense U.S.-Soviet relations will be eased, the United States, with its economic, scientific and technological superiority," will continue to prevail over the Soviet Union. The situation in 1989 proved that their worries were well founded. The Chinese once warned Mikhail Gorbachev that the United States would take

> its rival's economic and political deterioration as a golden opportunity to carry out its policy of "beyond containment" toward the Soviet Union. . . . Washington is enhancing its measures of "peaceful evolution" and encouraging Moscow to evolve into [a] "reopened society." The White House is forcing the Kremlin to "integrate into the international community."
>
> [In the] future, infiltration activities, whether blatant or covert, as well as "peaceful evolution" and "anti-peaceful evolution" activities between the two countries will continue, occasionally reaching dangerous levels.[15]

In the final analysis, Khrushchev's (and, more recently, Gorbachev's) peaceful coexistence was defection because it embraced imperialism; the Chinese worldview, received almost a knock-out strike. Not only had the two-camp theory become irrelevant, but China's own role had become muddled. Following Khrushchev meant compromising anti-imperialism; defying him meant splitting the socialist camp. Why would China want to protect anti-imperialism? For a realist, anti-imperialism may have meant one of two things. First, it may have reflected China's fear of the United States. If this had been true, China would not have started antirevisionism, thereby jeopardizing its own security. Then again, anti-imperialism may have been a reflection of China's acquisitive desire for power through confrontation with the United States. However, China had never possessed the capability nor the will to challenge the imperialist directly. In short, China did not protect anti-imperialism for the sake of power struggle with the United States. Its insistence on antirevisionism at the expense of socialist unity must have been the result of a cognitive need for consistency on anti-imperialist logic, not an effort to gather strength to actually engage in anti-imperialism. Anti-imperialism was therefore a drama that dictated China's role-playing. Consequently, China applied all possible shaming techniques to most of the remaining components of Sino-Soviet polemics in order to distinguish itself from a decaying leadership and evidence its undeviating commitment to socialism. This is contrary to the realist view that China had to depend on at least one superpower to feel safe.[16]

Comradeship

As comrades in the socialist bloc, the Chinese were understandably worried about Soviet policy mistakes: "As a member in the ranks of the international communist movement, how could we be indifferent, and keep silent about these errors? If we should do that, would not we be abandoning our duty to defend Marxism-Leninism and proletarian internationalism?"[17] A critical stand was thus deemed necessary and appropriate to assist fraternal parties; in this way the international proletarian parties could strengthen themselves. There should be no reason to worry about imperialist interference in private intrabloc consultation because a party-to-party dispute should not be extended to the state-to-state relationship. Even though socialist parties may disagree about the proper route to communism, their interstate relations should always be friendly and peaceful.

Many Western analysts fail to note the significance of withdrawal of Soviet advisers from China in 1960 when they discuss the "point of no return" in Sino-Soviet conflict.[18] For the Chinese, the withdrawal was a serious mistake because it escalated an interparty dispute into an interstate dispute. The Chinese later recalled that they had always borne in mind the "high prestige in the international communist movement" enjoyed by the Communist Party of the Soviet Union (CPSU) and therefore had, "for the sake of unity against the enemy and out of consideration for the difficult position the leaders of the CPSU were then in . . . , refrained in those days from open criticism of the errors of the 20th Congress, because the imperialists and the reactionaries of all countries were exploiting these errors and carrying on frenzied activities against the Soviet Union, against Communism and against the people."[19]

In contrast, as the Chinese charged, the Soviet Union had made public attacks on the Albanian Party of Labor and severed diplomatic ties with Albania. National (i.e., state-to-state) instead of international (i.e., party-to-party) concern prevailed in the CPSU.

As a result, according to the Chinese, Soviet attempts to lead fraternal parties in other countries reflected big-power chauvinism. The first sign of this was in 1957 when the Soviet Union considered suppressing Polish comrades. Later, when the Soviets pounced on Albania, the Chinese ridiculed the Soviet approach. Chinese commentators pointed to the irony that "a certain party" had criticized the Albanians in public and demanded the latter scrap their original positions. This was said to be unadulterated chauvinism because the Albanians were not permitted a defense of positions after being publicly denounced. Once again, Chinese opinion of the Soviet Union was revealed within the context of China's observation of the international communist movement as if from the point of view of an objective bystander.

In state-to-state relations, "socialism in one country" was by then a dead principle according to the Chinese. Socialist comradeship was embodied by principles of equality and democracy, hence Khrushchev's alleged attempt in 1958 to put China under Soviet military control stood in stark violation of these principles. This testifies to the earlier suggestion that China's shelling of offshore islands three weeks after Khrushchev's visit was, to a large extent, a furious response to Soviet betrayal. Nonetheless, the denouncement of socialism in one country as a guiding principle had never been presented within the context of Chinese national interest. The Chinese argued in the 1960s that because there were thirteen socialist states (not counting Yugoslavia) in the world, unity, not the preservation of any specific leadership, should be of primary concern. Compared with the communiqué of the Moscow conference that proclaimed the Soviet Union as the "universally recognized vanguard" of the world communist movement, the following CCP statement hit the nail on the head: "If anybody . . . does not defend the unity of the socialist camp . . . then he is betraying [communism]. . . . If anybody . . . following in the footsteps of others, defends the erroneous opportunist line and policies pursued by a certain socialist country . . . then he is departing from Marxism-Leninism and proletarian internationalism."[20]

In a much worse situation, "a certain country" with predominant power and status could also exploit other bloc members to achieve its own economic prosperity. This sort of exploitation might take several distinct forms. The Soviet Union, for example, forced China to repay loans that had financed China's Korean War effort, which, according to the Chinese, was a war aimed at defending the socialist bloc. As usual, for the Chinese to make legitimate (i.e., unselfish) complaints, they would have to identify points of contention elsewhere.

To uncover the exploitative nature of intrabloc economic relationships, the Chinese first laid down their correct principles. Equality among socialist countries should not be affected by the level of economic development in each country; the Chinese contended that each must depend on "the diligent labor and talents of its own people" in accordance with "its own concrete conditions." The strength of the entire socialist camp could only be increased by each country's enhancing its capacity to assist the revolutionary cause of the international proletariat; the Chinese thus argued that "to observe the principle of mainly relying on oneself in construction is to apply proletarian internationalism concretely."[21]

The Soviet Union had pressured China to join the Soviet-led Council for Mutual Economic Assistance (COMECON), but the Chinese refused to comply with such a notion of socialist division of labor.[22] Khrushchev allegedly suggested a division of labor between the two countries whereby China would provide agricultural products and the Soviet Union industrial goods. China's reaction was reportedly negative.[23] The Chinese gave this appraisal of COMECON:

> It would be great power chauvinism to deny [the] principles and, in the name of "international division of labor" or "specialization," to impose one's own will on others, infringe on the independence and sovereignty of fraternal countries or harm the interests of their people.
>
> In relations among socialist countries it would be preposterous to follow the practice of gaining profit for oneself at the expense of others, a practice characteristic of relations among capitalist countries . . . as examples which socialist countries ought to follow in their economic cooperation and mutual assistance.[24]

On the whole, comradeship among fraternal parties and among socialist states is fundamentally similar from the Chinese perspective. If one compares documents from the 1960s and 1980s, one can see that the Chinese have been consistently advocating the five principles of peaceful coexistence among all countries including socialist countries. The same principles, with the exception of mutual respect for territorial integrity (irrelevant here), should be applied to interparty relations. The Soviet Union finally gave public consent to them for the first time in 1989. Only then did Deng Xiaoping declare that relations between the two countries had been normalized.[25]

It is difficult to see how the Chinese notion of comradeship protected their national interests. Refusal to join COMECON and deterioration of Sino-Soviet trade relations (the Chinese argued this was the result of the withdrawal of Soviet advisers and unilateral scrapping of bilateral agreements)[26] probably hurt China more than the Soviet Union both economically and politically. China received not a penny of desperately needed economic assistance from fraternal parties during the disastrous period of 1959–1962, and the Soviet Union sided with India in the Sino-Indian War. Later, in 1982, the Chinese refused to normalize relations with the Soviet Union, even though such a move would have substantiated an "independent foreign policy," promulgated to blunt pro-U.S. expectations during the height of Sino-U.S. relations.

The implication is that the Chinese triumphantly highlighted these principles of comradeship because they proved the Soviet Union a bad comrade. The Chinese made the point that they were on the right side; they demonstrated their determination to stay there by sacrificing those so-called national interests so conspicuous to everyone else. The process of conflict was thus not quite a consequence of a sense of mutual threat, historical animosity, racism, nationalism (however defined), and dissimilar economic strategy. Instead, it was a process of escalation involving initially consultative advice, rejection and anxiety, publicity of polemics, discovery of self-justification, and finally breakdown of comradeship and dramatization of moral distinction. The whole process started with Chinese surprise at Khrushchev's secret de-Stalinization speech in 1956, to which this chapter now turns.

De-Stalinization

China received mid-1950s de-Stalinization and mid-1980s de-Stalinization very differently: de-Stalinization in the 1950s directly challenged China's worldview, whereas in the 1980s it was basically regarded as a component of internal Soviet reform. The challenge of 1950s de-Stalinization had nothing to do with national security, economic development, or ideology. In fact, at the beginning of de-Stalinization, China felt more puzzled than threatened. Stalin had been praised in China as one of the Great Teachers, second only in stature to Marx, Engels, and Lenin; the heretical denial of the mentor inescapably harbored criticism of the disciple. This 1956 challenge to the Chinese prescription for proper management of world com-

munism was raised against the backdrop of unreserved Chinese praise for
Stalin as an essential player in the October Revolution and father of Stalinism—key to international proletarianism. By the 1980s, the world communist movement no longer existed in China's worldview, so de-Staliniz-
ization was not pertinent.

After de-Stalinization began in the Soviet Union, the Chinese continued to portray all four Great Teachers together (even as Mao himself was
targeted during the 1957 Hundred Flowers movement). It would have been
impossible for the Chinese to de-Stalinize at this time precisely because it
would have flown in the face of China's worldview. Just how far China
would go in defending Stalin was not clear at the beginning. As the Chinese themselves later admitted, they were not sure what Khrushchev's
speech actually meant at that stage, and they refrained from openly resisting the campaign. In his discourse with Anastas Mikoyan, president of the
Presidium, Mao emphasized that Stalin's "merits outweighed his faults."[27]
According to the Chinese account, high officials including Liu Shaoqi,
Zhou Enlai, and other Central Committee members consulted with the
Soviets about Stalin's historical role on several occasions.

Later Chinese interpretations of de-Stalinization concentrated on its
impact on the unity of the world communist movement:

> Without any prior consultation with the fraternal Parties, the leadership
> of the CPSU drew arbitrary conclusions; it forced the fraternal Parties to
> accept a *fait accompli* and, on the pretext of "combating the personality
> cult," crudely interfered in the internal affairs of fraternal Parties and
> countries and subverted their leadership, thus pushing its policy of sec-
> tarianism and splittism in the international Communist movement.
>
>   Subsequent developments show with increasing clarity that the re-
> vision and betrayal of Marxism-Leninism and proletarian international-
> ism by the leaders of the CPSU have grown out of the above errors.[28]

In their counterattack, the Chinese aimed at shaming Khrushchev. De-
Stalinization was portrayed as an abuse of Stalin that brought "a gross insult . . . to the dictatorship of the proletariat and to the socialist system."
Who did Khrushchev think he was to criticize Stalin and Stalinism? "In
what position does Khrushchev, who participated in the leadership of the
Party and the state during Stalin's period, place himself when he beats his
breast, pounds the table and shouts abuse of Stalin at the top of his voice?
In the position of an accomplice to a 'murderer' or a 'bandit'? Or in the
same position as a 'fool' or an 'idiot'?"[29] The Chinese then quoted
Khrushchev's support of Stalin in 1937 when he criticized all those who
attacked Stalin and said that Stalin had been like a father to him. Finally,
the Chinese accused him of actively supporting and carrying out a policy

of suppressing counterrevolutionaries. The Chinese concluded that he had made a "180-degree turn."[30]

Scholars have paid a great deal of attention to the substance of Sino-Soviet polemics but have largely ignored their style. While we know that the two sides disagreed on de-Stalinization, why did the campaign upset the Chinese so much? The polemics reached a level hardly comprehensible from a realist point of view, but even so, no armed conflict broke out between the two as a result. According to the Soviet account, public polemics were started by China in April 1960 with the publication of the well-known *Hongqi* (Red flag) article entitled "Long Live Leninism." What did the Chinese think they could achieve by publicly exposing revisionism and deriding Khrushchev? If they just wanted to shame him and nothing more, the obsession with pretended moral integrity must indeed be deeply embedded in the Chinese moral regime. Did they actually hope to get rid of Khrushchev in this way? If so, only a moral regime could have been so confident in its moral strength. In either case, realism was irrelevant.

Indeed, there is an inner, cognitive need for the moral regime to rationalize away inconsistency between its worldview and reality; there is a tendency to employ shaming techniques when inconsistency is perceived to be irreconcilable. Shaming would be effective if the Chinese could prove that the Soviets had victimized other socialist countries in addition to China, thus introducing the context of the world communist movement. That the Chinese viewed Stalinism as representing the world communist movement does not mean that China would have organized the socialist bloc in the same manner Stalin did. Anyway, Stalin as a symbol of China's moral commitment to world communism was intact despite the mistakes he might have committed. That is why when Stalinism (whatever its true meaning) was denied as a guiding principle (even though this was done but rhetorically in front of the Chinese delegation at the Twentieth Congress of the CPSU), China's role in the world communist movement was unmistakably challenged.

REVISIONISM

Exactly what did Khrushchev do to make his de-Stalinization campaign a sign of revisionism for the Chinese? But first, was revisionism in fact a threat to the Chinese? Although it might have caused an internal legitimacy problem, revisionism in the late 1980s and early 1990s presented no external threat to China. This is because the most recent outbreak of "revisionism" in Eastern Europe and the Soviet Union did not deny China's role in the world, which is grounded primarily in the notions of independent foreign policy and peaceful coexistence.[31] In comparison, China saw its role in the 1950s as a contributing member of the socialist bloc. This was especially true after China successfully held off UN forces during the Korean War. By the 1980s, the Chinese recognized that the world communist movement still had a long way to go and that the pressing task was antihegemonism. (In fact, in 1979 the Chinese decided that the Soviet Union was not a revisionist country but still a social imperialist). For those living in the 1950s, world communism was the only meaningful goal that the moral regime could possibly aim for in world politics.

Yugoslavia

Confusion about de-Stalinization was clarified not only by Khrushchev's "all-round peaceful coexistence" but also, as the Chinese perceived it, by his changing approach to Yugoslavia. Yugoslavia was specified as a revisionist country at the 1957 Moscow conference and its Communist Party was never regarded as a fraternal party by the Chinese. In fact, the author of the article "Long Live Leninism" attacked Khrushchev's policy without naming him, using Yugoslavia as a vicarious target. Conceding to mounting public pressure from China, the CPSU included the same charge of revisionism against Yugoslavia in the 1960 Moscow statement. The Chinese strategy was to force Khrushchev to jettison policy that China publicly associated with Yugoslavian revisionism. The belief was that Khrushchev would strive to avoid public embarrassment over his lack of moral consistency on the issue of revisionism—a typical Chinese assumption.

The Soviets counterattacked by specifying Albania as a vicarious target. The polemics between China and the Soviet Union thus concentrated on the nature of these two states. The moral implication was strong for China: the loser of the polemical battle would be denied a proper role in the world communist movement. To prove that revisionism had been evolving in the Soviet Union, the Chinese took pains to list twelve similarities between Khrushchev and Marshal Tito and then contended that capitalism had made a recovery in Yugoslavia. How could this possibly be? The Chinese explained:

> When the working class seizes power, struggle continues between the bourgeoisie and the proletariat, struggle for victory continues between the two roads of capitalism and socialism. . . .
>
> The restoration of capitalism in a socialist country can be achieved not necessarily through a counter-revolutionary coup d'état or armed imperialist invasion . . . [but] it can also be achieved through *the degradation of the leading group in that country.* . . .
>
> Imperialism has now extended the scope of its operations and is buying over leading groups in socialist countries and pursues through them its desired policy of peaceful evolution.[32]

This theory of Yugoslavian revisionism was later elaborated upon in the famous "Ninth Comment" on the Open Letter of the Central Committee of the CPSU and applied to the emergence of renegades in the Khrushchev regime.[33] Perhaps the most interesting aspect of the argument is its stress on the personal degeneration of the individual leaders in Yugoslavia and the Soviet Union and how this affects socialism (not China). This is similar to the direct personal attacks that occurred repeatedly during China's internal political struggles. It is quite possible the Chinese believed that direct denouncement of Khrushchev would contribute to his fall by eroding respect for him in Soviet society; Khrushchev's removal in 1964 apparently testifies to the effectiveness of such reasoning (but when the Chinese employed the same tactics later, charging Leonid Brezhnev with "Khrushchevism without Khrushchev," the effect on the Soviet regime was obviously negligible).

Social Imperialism

China's appraisal of the Vietnam situation likewise attempted to shame the Soviet Union. According to Mao, the Vietnam War was a classic case of imperialist decline. There was no need for China to intervene directly, for the people's war in the Vietnamese jungle would eventually prove too much for the imperialists. Though the Chinese continued to supply Vietnam throughout the mid-1970s, there is no doubt that Beijing felt much easier about this situation than it had about Korea. In fact, China utilized its geographical position to slow down or obstruct the flow of Soviet military supplies to Vietnam; China was concerned that Vietnam might become more dependent on the Soviet Union. According to Mao, Vietnam could win the war by its own devices, and a quick victory would not be worth the price of Soviet involvement.

In this context, the Cultural Revolution theme of superpower collusion over Vietnam was obviously formulated for the sake of argument. One may interpret the theory as an indicator of China's fear of collusion. If China had believed in its own theory of superpower collusion, the Vietnam War should have been a greater threat to China. Besides, it was China that tried to curb Soviet involvement. The collusion theme was so dominant that it appeared in the Chinese mass media almost every day. What would shame the revisionist more than revelation of evil intentions behind the "united action" of the Soviet Union and the United States?

The Soviet invasion of Czechoslovakia in 1968 could only be welcomed by China because from the Chinese perspective it conclusively proved the collusion theory—the United States did no more than express regret over the invasion! Almost elatedly the Chinese described the exchange of Vietnam for Czechoslovakia between the superpowers:

This is an unprecedented, great exposure of the horrible face behind the imperialist power politics madly enforced by the Soviet renegade clique, it is the most shameless show of dog-eat-dog struggle between the Soviet renegade clique and Czechoslovakian renegade clique, it is a result of the Soviet . . . attempt to collude with the U.S. imperialist in redividing the world, it is the stroke before death carried out by the Soviet renegade clique to rescue the whole contemporary revisionist bloc from the crisis of collapse, split and annihilation, it has exposed the paper-tiger character of the Soviet revisionism.[34]

Between 1968 and 1973, Soviet revisionism was also called social imperialism. The terminology here is significant because imperialism is theoretically a phenomenon of capitalism. "Social imperialism," (*shehui diguozhuyi*) is defined as imperialism with a socialist label. A better translation might be "socialist imperialism" since the Chinese meant to emphasize the self-contradiction within the term. Accordingly, China's assessment of the world communist movement did *not* change as a result of the Soviet invasion, as many observers have described. The struggle between socialism and capitalism continued. The only difference between today's struggle and yesterday's is that China proved the Soviet Union to be on the other side. With this change in Soviet identity, instead of coming from the existing socialist states, the final victory should come from the people (as always). The Soviet Union was not on the people's side. The shaming implication was once again apparent here since no serious impact on Soviet politics could really have been expected.

A popular assessment of the 1968 invasion is that it created a sense of danger inside China. However, imperialism is not supposed to pose a serious threat in the long run. The invasion was described as evidence of "total bankruptcy," "extreme weakness," "sharpening of internal contradiction," and so on.[35] Yet the term "social imperialism" proved the collusion theory and therefore proved the existence of revisionism. The collusion was then conceptualized as a natural result of weakness. Otherwise, why would the superpowers collude? Would it not have been more sensible for the Chinese to have come up with an alternative, or at least a supplementary, theory or term to connote the Soviet threat if Mao and the cultural revolutionaries has truly believed in the existence of such a threat? Instead, they depended on terms that connoted the weakness of the enemy, not the threat it might pose. There were no new troop deployments on the Chinese side after the 1968 invasion. If the menace was perceived, the Chinese coped with it morally, not militarily.

Peaceful Evolution

Another aspect of revisionism regards the theory of peaceful evolution. The Chinese criticize those who seek to achieve socialism through a peaceful transition from capitalism and believe this would distract vigilance from Western attempts to achieve capitalism through a peaceful evolution of socialism. Again, of interest here is the source of concern and its expression rather than its form. Since the Chinese advocate peaceful coexistence among socialist countries as well as among countries with different social systems, it should hardly matter if any particular country were to attempt peaceful transition and, presumably, fail. The Chinese contend that socialism can neither be exported nor imported. Therefore attempts at peaceful evolution by others should not endanger China's national security or its internal development. In fact, the more aggressive European "revisionism" of the 1990s never distracted China from peaceful coexistence. It was not until 1991 that China openly criticized the theory of peaceful evolution, doing so only within the bounds of China. In comparison, China's reaction to the theory in the 1960s seems absurd.

Overreaction must be understood in terms of the cognitive needs of leaders of a moral regime. Although the theory of peaceful evolution had scant implications for China's actual level of power, it confirmed China's anxiety about Soviet betrayal. The theory was a sign of the revisionism that threatened to demoralize world communism in the 1960s. On the one hand, it was psychologically comforting to completely unmask Khrushchev's treachery. On the other hand, it would be morally useful to establish China as a sharply contrasting model–and, as we have seen, in China being morally useful implies being politically useful. The Chinese thus continued to stress the need for proletarian dictatorship led by the Communist Party. The theory of peaceful evolution, in contrast, invites pluralism. The Communist Party should not be a democratic party: it belongs only to the working class and not to all the people, as Khrushchev had asserted. Since the party created socialism, the party is irreplaceable, and giving up the historical role of the party is proof of revisionism. Criticism of peaceful evolution is therefore an instrument for drawing distinction between moral and immoral, progressive and reactionary, socialist and bourgeois—distinctions essential to highlighting the betrayal of the Soviet revisionists.

When the theory of peaceful evolution actually constituted an internal threat in the 1990s (thanks to the 1980s prodemocracy movement in China), the Chinese were less assertive and more defensive in discussing pluralism in other socialist countries. Without the larger context of the world communist movement, the Chinese nonetheless reiterated in 1990 the principle of exclusive leadership by the party; fraternal democratic parties are welcome to share power only if they accept such leadership.[36] The same principle is not used to judge other socialist countries, though. For example, having taken a very different route of reform, Russia is not perceived as negating China's moral status in the current decade. Criticizing peaceful evolution on the world stage is irrelevant because this does not help clarify role obligations for socialist states in the 1990s. (The power of the new Russian state is seen to be declining; fraternal parties in Eastern Europe have collapsed one after another; peaceful evolution is acknowledged and openly praised there!) The real danger comes from the imperialist capitalist camp.[37] Besides, shaming Gorbachev might actually have had a negative political and psychological effect, as he once sought to learn from China's economic reforms and complied properly with China's antihegemonic requests.

ANTIHEGEMONISM

Deng Xiaoping's 1974 elaboration at the United Nations of Mao's three-worlds theory marked a significant change in China's assessment of the Soviet state. According to the theory, both the United States and the Soviet Union sought hegemony. The implication is that the two superpowers were competing rather than colluding; the collusion theme during the Cultural Revolution was thus proved to be only polemic. The pronouncement of the three-worlds theory buried the previous world communist movement and initiated a new one. Socialism would have to evolve from the unity of the Third World countries in their struggle against hegemonism. By encouraging the oppressed to rise up, the theory is consistent with the tone of the Cultural Revolution.

Before 1974, hegemony or hegemonism was occasionally mentioned, but the theoretical meaning of the term was vague at best. In contrast, "social imperialism" continued to be a part of China's diplomatic rhetoric into the 1970s. The function of this term was more to prove the existence of hegemony than to prove the existence of revisionism (as in the 1960s). Revisionism became a lesser concern apparently because the process of global détente had outdated the original two-camps theory. Being a good socialist state was less relevant during détente. According to the three-worlds theory, China should have a new mission as everyone else did. The industrialized societies of the two camps, for example, were victims of the First World and hence good allies in the united front against it. Since hegemonism could exist in either socialist or capitalist states, antihegemonism was the responsibility of all regardless of ideology.

Did the three-worlds theory or antihegemonism further China's national interests? The Chinese present the theory in such a way that China appears to be serving antihegemonism rather than vice versa. For example, China could decide to purchase mineral resources from a Third World country simply to help the latter be independent from a North American buyer; China could also give a zero-interest loan to that country. The Chinese understood that they must convince other countries that either Soviet hegemonism is dangerous or that the Chinese themselves are friendly. The immediate goal was clearly to persuade the world to cut all Soviet connections. Why would this be important to the Chinese? For a realist, this type of foreign policy would inevitably escalate conflict and competition not only in other parts of the world but also along the Sino-Soviet borders *without* really enhancing China's power. Anyway, China was not a global power; it had no interest in overseas military bases or mineral resources. The Soviet military connection around the world did not create additional problems for China in any sense of realpolitik. But China still went about denouncing the Soviet Union. Such reckless agitation of the Soviets hardly seems rational.

The implication is that China had used its three-worlds theory to shame the Soviets, not to compete with them. One only has to look closely at the manner in which the Chinese divided the world into three parts to appreciate their philosophy. Devoid of strictly logical connotations, divisions were not drawn along lines of power because, for example, Brazil was in the Third World whereas Sweden was in the Second; nor was it along economic lines since Japan was in the Second World whereas the Soviet Union was in the First; nor was it along ideological lines since there were capitalist as well as socialist countries in all three worlds. The sole purpose of the theory was to single out the Soviet Union as the primary target for what was presumably a world united front. Once the Soviet Union was singled out, all that remained was to show that China was on the other side through symbolic aid and rhetorical support for the Third World's struggle for independence. The Chinese were more interested in selling their way of interpreting world affairs than toppling the hegemonic regime in the Soviet Union. They wanted to be the enemy of the Soviet Union.

The Role of the United States

There are two familiar themes in China's triangular policy. One concentrates on China's security needs, the other on its development needs. The first theme is concerned with external constraints and argues that China needs the United States to counter the Soviet Union. The second is interested in internal constraints and contends that the moderate faction, apprehensive about economic development, is responsible for China's pro-U.S. posture. Both make sense but neither tells the complete story.

China seriously considered the possibility of a Soviet surprise attack after border clashes in March and June 1969. More troops were deployed around Beijing and in Manchuria. As Liberthal has argued, however, it is not clear whether such troop movements were not actually part of Lin Biao's 1971 coup attempt.[38] Besides, the most popular domestic slogan at that time was "grasp revolution, promote production" (*zhua geming cu shengchan*), a sign that domestic production took priority over Soviet threat. As to internal constraints, development needs may have played a more important role in the 1980s than the 1970s. How could anyone have said outright that socialist development required assistance from the United States during the course of the Cultural Revolution and before Mao's death?

Was it still possible that antihegemonism supplied ex post facto justification for China's semialliance with the United States? If a united front was formed with the United States to oppose the Soviet Union militarily, at least one of the following three possibilities must be true: China was prepared to assist the United States to offset the Soviet Union on the battlefield, China relied on the United States to do the same, or China expected a united front to lead to a higher-level confrontation between the two hegemonies. Was China to help the United States if the latter lost in the Third World battlefield? Some observers have pointed out China's tone of regret whenever the United States appeared to be soft on the Soviet Union. But in no way would China get involved in superpower confrontation. China lacked the economic, technological, and military capabilities significantly to alter the balance between the two superpowers; it had, though, the most eloquent and morally cloaked spokesman. China's tone of regret had more to do with occasional U.S. failure to counter Soviet hegemonism than with China's desire for an alliance.

Did China expect war to break out between the two superpowers? Possibly, but China could not deliberately bring this about since it would obviously have disastrous global effects. Nonetheless, China noted a decline in the power of both superpowers during the 1980s. Although the danger of war continues to exist, the Chinese believe that the chance of its occurrence has dropped dramatically. In 1990 China referred to hegemony only in connection with the United States, not the Soviet Union. How could China ever expect the United States to risk war to save China from a Soviet invasion? The United States certainly did not believe in such a commitment. In view of the continuous criticism of U.S. imperialism that accompanied the process of Sino-U.S. normalization (discussed in Chapter 5), no one should miss the message that China would not consciously choose to depend on the United States. Normalization with the United States combined with incessant criticism of the United States thus strongly smacked of indirect but severe criticism of the Soviet Union: the imperialist is terrible, but you are worse. This is one of the most typical shaming techniques used in daily Chinese life (especially when dealing with mischievous children).

In short, China's normalization with the United States was not intended as the formation of a military or economic front against the Soviet

Union; what was intended was a moral front. Antihegemonism was aimed at building up U.S. morale in the competition with the Soviet Union. This has to be seen more as a psychological technique than as an instrument for power struggle. Antihegemonism, according to this psychological explanation, shifted the battlefield from intrabloc polemics (the socialist bloc no longer exists) to interworld competition. Shaming within the socialist bloc lost attraction given Soviet hegemonic control over most socialist countries. The three-worlds theory and antihegemonism created a whole new field of competition. China was willing to deal with outsiders in order to clean up the socialist family. China's willingness, not fear, is the focus here.

It should be clear now that the earlier theory of superpower collusion was more a matter of polemical tactics and shaming than a genuine perception. If the idea of collusion was seriously entertained, how could any rational Chinese leader risk sending erroneous signals to the United States that China needed its help in dealing with the Soviet Union and that China still believed a united front with the United States could be rewarding? If China was to lure the United States out of alleged collusion, how could any rational Chinese stubbornly denounce U.S. imperialism at the time negotiations were in progress? The United States was simply used in the collusion theory in the 1960s to prove the revisionist nature of the Soviet Union. Similarly, it was probably used in the three-worlds theory to show that the Soviet Union was the world's worst hegemon. Henry Kissinger's analysis that China was playing a balance-of-power game was, to some extent, wishful thinking.[39]

The Role of the Third World

China's continuous opposition to imperialism was demonstrated in the Third World, where China competed with the Soviet Union for popularity among anticolonial forces. In ideological terms, both were committed to the overthrow of colonial power; in psychological terms, neither considered the other an ideological comrade. Sometimes, China would even support a reactionary regime like that of Zaire for the sake of antihegemonism's establishing a parallel to China's U.S. policy: the reactionary regime was bad but Soviet hegemony was worse. One principal mission of China's Third World aid and work teams was invariably to demonstrate the hypocrisy of Soviet aid (discussed in Chapter 7). Again, China's criticism here made sense only through the enactment of a Third World movement.

Just as Sino-U.S. normalization revealed the contentious nature of the superpower collusion theory, the notion of Soviet hegemonism busily expanding its sphere of influence contradicted previous charges of cowardice against Khrushchev. Massive Soviet intervention in the Third World was criticized as if all-inclusive peace had never been a Soviet policy goal (keep in mind China's criticism of such a peace policy for sacrificing Third World revolution). This implicit inconsistency in rhetoric may mean one of two things: a change in China's shaming technique or a change in China's perception of the nature of the Soviet threat.

One has to wonder if the Soviets ever posed a real threat to China in, for example, Africa. Also, with its limited resources and the poor reception its cultural revolutionary image received, was China really capable of competing with the Soviets in the Third World? China's leverage in the Third World was its alleged moral strength. Antihegemonism was the theoretical version of that moral strength. And yet Third World countries did not appreciate the language of revisionism. China's search for anti-Soviet allies depended to a large extent on which—the revisionist or the hegemonist—was more threatening. If hegemonism was more dangerous to the Third World, then China must depict itself as a victim of hegemonism to be on the popular, moral side. Therefore, the use of the three-worlds theory represented a change in the shaming technique, not in the perception of the Soviet threat. The jargon of shaming shaped the image of threat. Ironically, once China proved this image, the need to cope with that threat was no longer urgent.

Therefore, when the Soviet Union invaded Afghanistan in 1980, China only indirectly supported the Afghan rebels through Pakistan. Afghanistan is much closer to China than Africa and more important strategically. However, China reacted to the invasion more like it had to the invasion of Czechoslovakia in 1968. The former proved the danger of hegemonism just as the latter proved the presence of revisionism. Nonetheless, China's support leaned chiefly to the rhetorical, moral, and philosophical side.

This moral support later constrained China's foreign policy options. During the process of normalization in the 1980s, China could not help but remind the Soviets of their hegemonism in Vietnam, Mongolia, and Afghanistan; normalization was slowed down as a result. If China had been threatened, it should have done more than just fight a symbolic war with Vietnam and then withdraw unilaterally in 1979, or just render moderate support to the Afghan rebels. Antihegemonism compelled China to pretend interest in areas where it lacked leverage or a real stake. Yet because it had not been threatened, it could presumably have speeded up the normalization process with the Soviet Union but chose instead not to do so. In this sense, antihegemonism held China back where it may have advanced. Whether or not the world at large accepted the vision of the three-worlds theory is irrelevant.

Dramatization

China's 1971 entry into the United Nations must have suggested to the Chinese that they had much to gain in the Third World. If the Third World could provide a bigger audience, why not shift the battlefield there? Antihegemonism was a continuation of an ongoing shaming effort with a different theoretical outlook. If China could not mobilize the socialist bloc, it would mobilize the Third World. Both the spirit of the Cultural Revolution and the triumph of UN membership contributed to the emergence of antihegemonism.

It is certainly hard to accept that China's attempts to organize world politics were principally aimed at shaming the Soviet Union. The strategy, however, is not necessarily irrational. China's military capability in comparison to that of the Soviet Union was truly crude, so China had to depend on moral power—and the Chinese traditionally have a solid conviction of their own moral power. Antihegemonism shifted the tension to the Third World, where China had no direct stake and any failure on China's part would ironically demonstrate Soviet hegemonism. Besides, shaming was consistent with the historical belief (mentioned in Chapter 1) that people without moral respect would not command power; power was something to which subordinates would voluntarily submit.

There is an intriguing interaction between the creation of moral power and the image of threat. While it is rational to depend on moral power to cope with the Soviet threat, the consolidation of moral power in turn relies on threat by an evil force. That encourages the tendency of the moral regime to escalate an existing dispute and create an enemy, hence satisfying the obsession with its own moral commitment against the enemy. Looking for a more receptive audience in what was previously the enemy camp (i.e., reactionary regimes in the capitalist camp) is just such a dramatic expression of disgust toward a powerful defector.

The drama of antihegemonism satisfied the search for a threat, the self-image of being victimized. It justified the struggle against a former ally and ideological comrade, it enabled China to make a show of moral strength, and it gave China a sense of popularity. As a result, the world communist movement suffered. Socialism fared much worse under antihegemonism because revisionism was no longer the point of contention or the target of attack. This is the irony of dramatization. The two comrades fought over appropriate strategy for world communism and proper interpretation of their ideology. When the Chinese lost their audience in this battle, they had to save their moral status by discrediting the other party through excessively personal incriminations. Escalation reached such a degree that the moral regime eventually looked for a different battleground to demonstrate the evil nature of its adversary. Once the battleground had shifted to the Third World, socialism became relatively inconsequential.

THE MYTH OF REALISM

The shaming argument presented in this chapter depends on one premise: either the Chinese had not seriously considered the Soviet threat or the Chinese were not interested in preparing for that threat. Contrary to most observers' impression that China's foreign policy since the 1970s had been mainly a response to the Soviet "threat," I believe that the ultimate motivation of Chinese foreign policy had been the protection of a moral pretension—there is a correct world order worth pursuing, and there is a positive role for China to play in it. In short, the Chinese deliberately created the image of a threat to satisfy their cognitive need for a sense that politics was meaningful.

The 1969 Border Conflict

Authors like Richard Wich, Gerald Segal, Steve Chan, Melvin Gurtov and Byng-Moo Hwang believe Chinese military moves on March 2, 1969 were a strike of deterrence.[40] Shocked by the Soviet invasion of Czechoslovakia and afraid that Moscow would take advantage of China's domestic chaos, the Chinese finally decided to launch a limited attack on Soviet patrols on Zhenbao Island. The rationale was that this would test the Soviets' intentions or give a signal that the Chinese were ready to defend their territory if invaded.

Intriguing questions of logic remain. If the Chinese were so worried about a Soviet attack, why did they not think their limited strike would give the Soviet Union an excuse to escalate the conflict? That the Chinese had no intention of turning these exchanges of fire into total war is clear from their rapid disengagement from Zhenbao Island after nine hours of conflict. What if China's attack had failed to achieve a surprise effect or make any significant impression? Would the Chinese have risked exposing how out-of-date their military technology and equipment were? Would the Chinese encourage superpower collusion with the United States in Vietnam? Even if the Chinese had successfully deterred a perceived possible attack, wouldn't this limited war have worsened China's strategic position in the long run by inviting in more Soviet troops along its borders (or were the Soviet troops along the border exactly what they desired)? In short, the deterrence theory does not make perfect sense in this case.

The conflict must be understood within the context of the Cultural Revolution. The cultural revolutionary viewed the status quo as corrupt, for it provided opportunities for revisionism. A note dropped off at the

Soviet embassy in Beijing on October 27, 1966, charged that "you unite with the United States to oppose China, with India to oppose China, and with Japan to oppose China. . . . you have moved much further than Khrushchev on the road to revisionism."[41] Zhou Enlai proclaimed the next month that "at the present time . . . the situation looks great for the revolutionary people of the whole world to oppose imperialism and revisionism."[42] The Soviet Union became the target of world revolution. By early 1968 Mao was already calling for action against the Soviet revisionist regime. The *Renmin Ribao* quoted Mao's earlier analysis that "all reactionary forces would inevitably take military risks and perform politically deceptive actions to rescue themselves from annihilation."[43] One editorial explicitly called for the overthrow of the "reactionary regime of the Soviet revisionists."[44]

The question is not the validity of Chinese perception or even the sincerity of Chinese analysis of superpower collusion and potential Soviet military threat. The question is how urgently China did need a threat. The Soviet Union was the only sensible external target of the Cultural Revolution because it was a strong, revisionist defector. As the internal revolution was approaching its final phase, some external target had to be found for permanent revolution for both political and psychological reasons. The drama of the Cultural Revolution simply did not allow Chinese leaders to translate their individual sense of fear (if it existed) to foreign policy. They had to behave as if people's war could make up for military weaknesses on the Chinese side.

Indeed, in contrast to China's obsolete equipment and logistics, lack of long-range strategic bombers and missiles, and no modern nuclear weapon delivery system,[45] ten of the fifteen to seventeen Soviet combat divisions east of Lake Baikal were in a high state of combat readiness. The Soviet army enjoyed qualitative superiority in planes, tanks, and armored personnel carriers; it had better logistics and major air and military bases along vital railroads. The Chinese forces had only a numerical advantage, thirty-five to forty divisions, and certain geographic and topographic advantages. Morale was strong and the population would support the People's Liberation Army (PLA) against a Soviet invasion.[46]

What would the Soviet Union gain by invading China? Only an immense, hostile population to its south and all sorts of ethnic troubles along their common border. Would war with China prove to the United States the Soviets' peaceful intentions? No. Would the Soviet Union use nuclear weapons, whose danger its leaders had bitterly acknowledged in 1962? No. Did the Soviet Union need to demonstrate its supreme leadership over the socialist bloc by "Czech-mating" China now that Eastern Europe was under its firm control? No. Would war with China help convince the Chinese that the Soviet Union was not revisionist? No. There was no reason, sane or otherwise, to invade, and Mao surely knew this. In Zhou Enlai's speech to the Tenth Party Congress in 1973, China's confidence was revealed. He proclaimed that China was like a delicious piece of meat loaf that everyone desired but no one was tough enough to bite and digest.[47]

However, according to China's antirevisionist logic, it was imperative that revisionism be depicted as springing from warlike intentions. The deterrence theory makes sense only within the context of the Chinese theme of revisionism. China had to deter the alleged Soviet threat to complete the story of Soviet revisionism. China's deterrence calculus was not a response to Soviet threat but a drama that provoked the sense of danger. In this case, the drama of deterrence enacted the threat, not the other way around. The artificially created menace was not feared, of course. The Chinese were perfectly prepared for the clashes of March 2nd. According to the official Chinese tally sheet, 260 million people joined in demonstrations against the Soviet Union in the following days—a good sign of prewar preparation. Such preparation was clearly for shaming, not for fighting.

It was not until the March 15 rematch and later clashes over Xinjiang in the summer that China took the Soviet threat more seriously. According to the Chinese, Soviet shells reached Chinese targets 7 kilometers inside the border during the March 15 incident, and Soviet troops moved several kilometers into Chinese territory during the course of June. But the sense of threat was soon dissolved after Aleksey Kosygin's visit to China toward the end of 1969; confrontation between the two was then shifted to other parts of the world. In fact, the Chinese mass media depicted the Soviet Union more favorably than it did the United States in the early 1970s.[48]

The 1970s

Analysts tend to see the Sino-U.S. normalization in 1972 as laying the foundation for a big triangle in world politics. China reentered the world arena determined to utilize the existing bipolar structure to protect itself against Soviet aggression. No one could blame the Chinese for their anxiety because the military balance between China and the Soviet Union was overwhelmingly in favor of the latter. Its attempt to recruit the United States into the united front seemed so obvious to everyone else. But how worried were the Chinese really?

A sensible strategy when facing a formidable enemy on one's border is to quietly strengthen oneself without provoking the enemy into premature showdown. The Chinese did exactly the opposite: they incessantly provoked the enemy around the globe without making strategic improvements (or even preparations). The Chinese made no serious internal effort to upgrade military capability to match their competitive behavior. The enemy was shamed and provoked but undefeated. The Chinese way of recruiting public moral forces in the world forum is a kind of defense unheard of in military history.

The implication is that there was no need to defend. During the ten years following the Zhenbao Island incident, the military balance worsened for the Chinese. In the 1979 punitive war against Vietnam, it became widely known that Chinese military equipment was not only out of date but also poorly maintained. Notwithstanding its antihegemonic rhetoric, defense modernization has been given lowest priority among China's Four Modernizations. Close to a quarter of PLA manpower was scheduled for pruning at a time when China was criticizing Soviet hegemonism in Afghanistan. A substantial part of military resources was shifted to profit-oriented business in the 1980s. As one expert on the Chinese military pessimistically concludes:

> The obsolete equipment flown by the PLA air force and deployed by China's ground-based air defense systems would be woefully inadequate against a sustained Soviet attack. Chinese naval forces suffer from the same problem. Although large in size, the PLA navy would be inadequate to challenge Soviet naval units. Chinese anti-submarine warfare (ASW) capabilities are crude at best and could be easily defeated, and the navy's surface combatants lack the necessary weapons to successfully engage the Soviet navy in anything but a limited coastal defense action. In any sustained combat, it may be assumed that the USSR could quickly gain both air and naval superiority.[49]

But the Chinese did continue their involvement in Third World guerrilla activities. Although the Chinese contribution was minor compared to that of the Soviet Union, they competed with style. Occasionally, the Chinese and Soviet client met eye to eye in direct confrontation. What was the rationale behind competing elsewhere in the world but relaxing at home? The answer lies in cognitive psychology. The revolutionary, moral regime relied on the perception of hegemonic threat to survive. Hegemonism had to be proved to exist all over the world, otherwise antihegemonism would be dismissed as the selfish concern of the Chinese. Demonstrating the existence of the threat was psychologically more significant than dealing with it.

Antihegemonism has to be seen as drama because the Chinese showed no serious interest in responding to the perception of hegemonic threat. The threat concocted by the theme of antihegemonism did not enable the Chinese to achieve political unity in the 1970s. Nor was their relationship with the United States in the 1970s particularly warm. The Chinese defense industry did not respond enthusiastically to the theme either. On the domestic front, no one took antihegemonism seriously enough in terms of behavioral adjustment; the theme nevertheless dominated foreign policy norms and occupied the time of most professional diplomats.

This lack of real security concern but obsession with antihegemonic rhetoric can be fully appreciated only if one understands the style of foreign policy of the moral regime. The Chinese have continuously been preoccupied with defining their proper role in the world. Once Khrushchev denied this role in the 1960s, the Chinese geared up to denounce Khrushchev and his successors. Analysis in this chapter so far suggests that ultimate motivation behind China's Soviet policy derives not from security concerns but from the need to moralize China's role in the world. There is thus a strong predilection to employ shaming techniques to the point that China's realpolitik interests can be ignored. In the changing world the Chinese used various dramatic statements, mainly antirevisionism and antihegemonism, to demonstrate the Soviet threat to the outside. The united front was in the end an act of shaming, although in effect it may have looked like flawed realism.

REFORMIST COMRADESHIP

When the two socialist giants first expressed different views on the path to communism, their comradeship ran into bitter difficulties. In the late 1980s and early 1990s, however, comradeship between the two appeared destined for renewal. New comradeship was not based on achieving a specific notion of socialism with consensus; it reemerged because neither side claimed to know the truth of socialism and each acknowledged a degree of ignorance in its respective approach to reaching communism.

The consensus was that each socialist country had to rely on itself and the will of its own people in building socialism. No country has the right to impose its particular vision of socialism on others; every socialist party is completely independent. The Chinese restated the principle in 1983: "The correctness of a Party's domestic line and policies can only be tested by practice or judged by its own people, no foreign Party has any right whatsoever to intervene. In the course of its prolonged struggle, any party will unavoidably commit some errors. Once a Party makes mistakes, they should be corrected by the Party itself after recognizing the mistakes and drawing lessons from them. Open criticism by a foreign Party will not achieve desirable results even if the criticism is correct." There was a provision, though: "However, it is a different matter if a Party and the government it leads practice hegemonism, issue orders to, [and] attempt to manipulate and control another Party, interfere in others' internal affairs, [and] subvert and invade other countries. Such acts must be strongly repudiated."[50]

China's anxieties about hegemonism were alleviated in the mid-1980s.

Deng Xiaoping's three conditions for normalizing relations with the Soviet Union—-withdrawal of Soviet troops from both Afghanistan and Mongolia and withdrawal of Vietnamese troops from Cambodia—elicited a favorable response from the Soviet Union. In 1986 Gorbachev promised to initiate troop pullouts from Mongolia and Afghanistan. A year later, 12,000 Soviet troops headed home from Mongolia, and the withdrawal of three quarters of Soviet troops there commenced the day Gorbachev arrived in Beijing in May 1989. In early 1989, Soviet troop extraction from Afghanistan was completed. Tension along the border was alleviated during Premier Li Peng's visit to Moscow in 1990. Since the beginning of the decade, Soviet hegemonism has become a historical term: the Soviets permitted (or even encouraged) political changes in Eastern Europe. The Soviet Union was no longer interested in keeping Eastern Europe within the socialist bloc; in fact, the bloc ceased to exist.

The Soviet government was forced to deal with a barrage of domestic challenges, ranging from economic stagnation and political disintegration to ideological breakdown and escalating ethnic conflict. Gorbachev cranked out a slew of slogans, including *glasnost, perestroika*, and "new thinking" in an effort to rescue socialism in the Soviet Union. Despite the shocking similarities of his policies to Khrushchev's revisionism (Gorbachev was actually more revisionist than Khrushchev), Gorbachev was adamant in declaring himself to be a true Communist.

In the face of such rapid change north of the border, Chinese reformist leaders needed to evaluate the new world and the new decade. On the one hand, China faced a similar combination of economic, political, and ideological problems for which it was seeking its own solution. On the other, Chinese leaders repeatedly trumpeted their determination to adhere to socialism, Marxism-Leninism, Mao Zedong Thought, the party's leadership, and proletarian dictatorship. Like the Soviet Union, China maintained a socialist self-image and yet was unable to explain its meaning. The situation was dramatically different from the 1960s, when both claimed to be socialists and each insisted that it alone held the key to truth. In the 1990s, although both asserted a similar identity, neither claimed to know the truth. The possibility of new comradeship thus increased.

Learning from Each Other

Most observers have held that it was impossible for Sino-Soviet relations to return to their level of the early 1950s. The reasons they give are primarily historical. One ought to remember that the intimacy of the early 1950s existed within the context of a high level of mutual distrust. However, these important reasons alone would be insufficient to impede the complete resuscitation of bilateral relations. What truly hindered the formation of close relations was that the two sides lacked meaningful role expectations for each other. China saw the Soviet Union as another reformist socialist state looking for the true meaning of socialism. The function and the meaning of bilateral relations therefore had to be viewed as the exchange of reform experiences.

There were signs that the two had developed different perspectives on key issues related to the meaning of socialism. One issue concerned the role of the party. The Chinese criticized Khrushchev for seeing the party as a party of all people and instead insisted on its proletarian and exclusive nature. Gorbachev moved a step further by allowing the East European Communist parties to disintegrate one after another, a significant concession compared with Khrushchev's and Brezhnev's relatively coercive measures in that area. Democracy in the Soviet Union itself became a passion; Li Peng's 1990 visit to the Kremlin witnessed Moscow's first demonstration against him as a top-level foreign official. In sharp contrast, China mercilessly crushed student demonstrations in 1989 and allowed "democratic parties" to share power only if they submitted to the leadership of the Chinese Communist Party.

The Chinese were certainly unnerved by the collapse of Communist party leadership in Eastern Europe and the Soviet Union. They have nonetheless stuck to their declared principle of noninterference and have refrained from open criticism of the internal affairs of other socialist countries.[51] But few positive comments have been heard on the situation in the Eastern bloc. The Chinese see uncertainty at best: "East European countries have achieved some results in economic and political reforms, but face many difficulties. Because long-standing issues in these countries could not be resolved at once, and there is no experience to fall back on, it is unavoidable to make mistakes. New thinking in the Soviet Union has caused quarrels at home and abroad. Some East European countries are carrying out some political reforms too quickly, and this has led to unrest and instability."[52] On the Soviet Union, the Chinese comments were even less sanguine:

> The political and economic reforms in the Soviet Union, as well as the problems and difficulties that have cropped up in the course of the reform, have aroused the attention of the world. The Soviet Union's extensive economy and unreasonable production structure, caused by the arms race, will not be improved quickly. The accumulated political, economic, ethnic, democratic and legal problems have become more intense, causing increased economic difficulties, a lack of supplies, repeated strikes and ethnic unrest. As a result, opinions toward Gorbachev's new thinking differ.[53]

What would have hurt bilateral relations and encouraged uncertainty was the tendency of the Chinese to fall back on the moral interpretation of Soviet politics and policy. If the Chinese continued their pretension regarding the party's moral leadership, they would be unlikely to allow the Sino-Soviet relationship to develop fully without worrying about the moral implications of the Soviet democratic experiment. The regime faced a moral dilemma: developing full-fledged relations with the Soviet Union or its successor (which had scrapped socialism in deed as well as in word) would jeopardize the moral position of the regime. This moral vulnerability would be utilized eventually by more radical reformers. However, the moral regime could not shame Russia for jettisoning socialism since world communist standards no longer exist that could make sense of this kind of charge. A relatively isolationist tendency would make better sense.

Another issue is the role of ideology. The Chinese understand the feeling of triumph in the West at the apparent collapse of socialism. The Chinese foreign minister explains the Chinese view:

> [Because] the socialist countries met with difficulties in the reform and development process and made some errors in policy decisions, the superiority of the socialist system was not fully realized. There appeared an ideological trend that socialism has suffered a "big failure" and that capitalism could "win without a fight."
>
> In fact, socialism has not failed and there is no ground to claim a success of capitalism. . . .
>
> With the general trend toward détente the struggle between different social systems and different ideologies will become more complicated and more acute.[54]

Accordingly, the nature of reform in socialist society is best characterized by the stage of socialism in history: "The introduction by socialist countries of reforms and opening is not because there are inherent and insurmountable defects in their socialist systems which therefore require fundamental transformation, but instead, because socialism is constantly developing and improving. . . . Socialism is not an isolated system, but rather, a member of the world economic system and so socialist countries need to develop economic and technological relations with the various countries around the world."[55]

In contrast to the Soviet Union, ideological problems seem to cause a substantial stir in China. Ironically, political control has been more successful and complete in reformist China than in Gorbachev's Soviet Union. The question is whether or not China is able or willing to learn from the fall of a fellow reformist state. If not, can the Chinese still regard Russia as a reformist state? The implication would be that the Soviet Union took the wrong path. Unless the Chinese cease viewing the world with some type of moral pretension in the 1990s (this is discussed in Chapter 8), the prospects for an intimate bilateral relationship with Russia do not look promising.

New Socialist Role Conceptions

Socialist states in the 1990s do not have the classic responsibilities of anti-imperialism and anticolonialism. The nature of the world has changed, and there is now more room for China and the new states of the former Soviet Union to collaborate. The dominant features of the new world include multipolarity, bipolar competition, new hegemonism, and uncertainty.

Difficulty in China's Russia policy is embedded in the predicament of peaceful coexistence. Russia, for example, joined the United Nations in 1992 in condemning China's human rights record and claimed that human rights standards are universal, much to China's disbelief. It was especially painful for China to recognize the independent republics that emerged from the collapse of the USSR because their existence was viewed as the fruit of peaceful evolution. How could China officially acknowledge that fact? China therefore did not rush to establish diplomatic relations with these states. After days of reflection, China found a rhetorical solution. In its diplomatic communiqué, China agreed to support these newcomers to the international arena in securing national independence and economic development. This suggests that China now conceived of these states as plausible victims of imperialism and hence as friends. According to the Chinese view, the new world powers are the United States, Japan, Germany, and the newly industrialized developing countries. Their relations will be marked by both competition and cooperation. The tendency toward bipolar competition will continue, though, and "the emphasis will shift to seeking superiority in comprehensive national strength, particularly in economics, science and technology."[56] The coexistence of a number of powers and bipolar competition creates instability and uncertainty in the world. The danger of instability is combined with the rise of U.S. hegemony, which is in the process of replacing Soviet hegemony. This is because the drastic change in Eastern Europe has put the United States more "on the offensive" while socialism is "more on the defensive and retreating."[57]

The role of the socialist states is to keep the world peaceful in accordance with China's most cherished five principles of peaceful coexistence. The Chinese analysis of the world shows no signs of optimism, however:

> The United States and other Western countries have also said reform in socialist countries needs Western capital and technology, which they can use as a political lever to exert influence. Of course, the anti-communist forces in these countries have always yearned for the collapse of socialist countries. They have never abandoned their ideology; the only difference is that their tactics are more glaring and brazen during the period of East-West relaxation than in times of tension. . . .
>
> Détente and dialogue have not weakened the struggle between capitalist and socialist systems and ideologies. On the contrary, it is sharper.

The struggle of interference and counter-interference, subversion and counter-subversion and infiltration and counter-infiltration will continue.[58]

In this scenario, the fall of the Soviet Union can also be evaluated according to its successors' policy behavior. If the Soviet Union was seen as a victim of the capitalist conspiracy of peaceful evolution, the shaming technique used against Khrushchev will not be used against the new Russia. However, if Russia is also seen as being on the offensive in competition with the United States, the perception of hegemonic expansion may once again prevail in China's Russia policy. The power status and the nature of the Russian state will be examined against its Third World policy. The earlier Soviet retreat from Afghanistan and the lack of active interest in the defeat of a pro-Soviet regime in Nicaragua and its replacement by a pro-U.S. regime may serve as clues for the Chinese. Realignment within reformist comradeship as an indirect way of shaming the new hegemony in North America could become a possibility.

Since the two comrades' open break in the 1960s, Chinese policy has primarily been dominated by concern for correct moral standing. This moral role is enacted in China's rhetorical world, filled with various classifications of just order. The Chinese depend on an international setting to promote their sense of moral integrity; international organizational processes cannot be understood unless one analyzes the national sources of role conceptions, while national role expectations cannot be appreciated without an international environment. Immediately after the revolution, Chinese moral pretension was focused on their particular vision of the world communist movement. Since the 1970s, charges of revisionism have been replaced by charges of antihegemonism. Despite the similarity in the declared ideological goals of the two countries and their theoretical comradeship, competition between China and the Soviet Union has been more intense than that between either of them and the capitalist world. However, this competition has been only a matter of drama and rhetoric; there has been no serious arms race between the two.

The interesting question remains, How do the Chinese perceive the Soviet retreat from hegemonism since the mid-1980s? Without a hegemonic identity, Russia could, to some extent, be considered a socialist country again. Whether or not this is a positive development is yet to be seen; the Chinese worldview is also in a state of flux. The ultimate clue lies in Russian reaction to Chinese role expectations in the future. That Russia has accepted Western human rights standards may serve as the first negative sign. Although many commentators who assert that the two sides will never return to the kind of relationship they enjoyed in the early 1950s may be guilty of overstating their case, there is a good chance that they will be proved correct.[59]

NOTES

1. For a good summary of literature on the origin of the Sino-Soviet conflict, see Donald W. Treadgold, "Alternative Western Views of the Sino-Soviet Conflict," in H. J. Ellison (ed.), *The Sino-Soviet Conflict: The Global Perspective* (Seattle: University of Washington Press, 1982), pp. 325–355.

2. For a detailed discussion, see Conrad Brandt, *Stalin's Failure in China* (Cambridge: Harvard University Press, 1958).

3. One textbook on comparative communism contains an excellent treatment of this subject. See William G. Rosenberg and Marilyn B. Young, *Transforming Russia and China* (New York: Oxford University Press, 1982).

4. John Gittings, *The World and China, 1922–1972* (New York: Harper & Row, 1974), p. 150.

5. Some Chinese intellectuals compare Gao Gang's relationship with Mao to that between Wang Lun and Chao Gai. Wang was the original bandit leader in *The Water Margin* who received the 108 heroes led by Chao. The old and the new groups developed a conflict of interest, and Chao successfully overthrew Wang Lun. When Mao and his troops reached Yenan after the Long March, Gao was in charge there.

6. Mark Mancall actually argues that Mao put China at the center surrounded by two camps and the intermediate zone. See Mark Mancall, *China at Center: 300 Years of Foreign Policy* (New York: Free Press, 1984), p. 402.

7. Li Ji and Guo Qingshi, "Principles Governing Relations with Foreign Communist Parties," *Beijing Review* (April 25, 1983): 17.

8. "The CCP's Proposal Concerning the General Line of International Communist Movement, June 14, 1963," in William E. Griffith (ed.), *The Sino-Soviet Rift* (Cambridge: MIT Press, 1964), p. 276.

9. Ibid., p. 269.

10. Ibid.

11. For discussion of the Chinese perception during the war, see Jonathan Adelman and Chih-yu Shih, "War East and West," *Annual of Chinese Political Science Association* No. 18 (December 1990): 177–219.

12. "A Comment on the Soviet Government's Statement, August 21, 1963," in Griffith, *The Sino-Soviet Rift*, p. 382.

13. Ibid., pp. 384–385.

14. Ibid., p. 384.

15. Wu Shuqing, "The Course for China's Reform and Opening," *Beijing Review* (January 1–7, 1990): 15.

16. Michael Ng-quinn, "Effects of Bipolarity on Chinese Foreign Policy," *Survey* 26, 2 (1982): 102–130.

17. "The Origin and the Development of the Differences Between the Leadership of the CPSU and Ourselves—Comment on the Open Letter of the Central Committee of the CPSU (1)," in Griffith, *The Sino-Soviet Rift*, p. 413.

18. See the discussion in Treadgold, "Alternative Western Views of the Sino-Soviet Conflict," in Ellison, *The Sino-Soviet Conflict*, pp. 330–347.

19. "The Origin and the Development," pp. 393, 413.

20. The famous June 14, 1963, statement quoted in Griffith, *The Sino-Soviet Rift*, p. 144.

21. "The CCP's Proposal Concerning the General Line of the International Communist Movement, June 14, 1963," in Griffith, *The Sino-Soviet Rift*, p. 281.

22. See Henry W. Schaefer, "The Economic Background and Implications for the USSR," in Ellison, *The Sino-Soviet Conflict*, pp. 113–114.

23. Chun-tu Hsueh, "Introduction," in C. Hsueh (ed.), *China's Foreign Relations: New Perspectives* (New York: Praeger, 1982), p. 3.

24. "The CCP's Proposal Concerning the General Line," p. 281.

25. Ya-chun Chang, "Gorbachev's Visit to Beijing and Sino-Soviet Relations," *Mainland China Studies* 32, 2 (July 1989): 26.

26. Harry Schwartz, *Tsars, Mandarins and Commissars: A History of Chinese-Russian Relations* (Garden City, N.Y.: Doubleday, 1973), p. 242.

27. "The Origin and the Development," p. 392.

28. Ibid.

29. "On the Question of Stalin—Comment on the Open Letter of the Central Committee of the CPSU (2)," in Griffith, *The Sino-Soviet Rift*, p. 423.

30. Ibid., p. 424.

31. Characterizing 1990 Eastern Europe in terms of revisionism may sound bizarre, but some Chinese diplomats actually drew the comparison between 1960s and 1990s in a private conversation.

32. "Is Yugoslavia a Socialist Country?—Comment on the Open Letter of the Central Committee of the CPSU (3)," in Griffith, *The Sino-Soviet Rift*, p. 465 (emphasis added).

33. "On Khrushchev's Phony Communism and Its Historical Lessons for the World," *Renmin Ribao*, July 20, 1964.

34. From the New China News Agency's lengthy comment in *Renmin Ribao*, August 23, 1968.

35. See, for example, Commentator, "The Complete Bankruptcy of Contemporary Soviet Revisionism," *Renmin Ribao*, February 3, 1968.

36. Editorial, *Mainland China Studies* 32, 9 (March 1990): 2.

37. Premier Li Peng's Speech on the National Day, *Renmin Ribao*, October 1, 1989: 1–2, Commentary, "For the 40th Anniversary of the People's Republic," *Guangming Ribao* (Shining daily), September 28, 1989: 1–2.

38. "The Background in Chinese Politics," in Ellison, *The Sino-Soviet Conflict*, p. 14.

39. Kissinger has the impression that Mao was eager to cooperate with the United States in resisting the Soviet Union. He and Mao did not discuss how China wanted to cooperate, though. See Henry Kissinger, *Years of Upheaval* (Boston: Little, Brown, 1982), p. 67.

40. Richard Wich, *Sino-Soviet Crisis Politics* (Cambridge: Harvard University Press, 1980); Gerald Segal, *Defending China* (London: Oxford University Press, 1985); Melvin Gurtov and Byng-Moo Hwang, *China Under Threat* (Baltimore: Johns Hopkins University Press, 1980); Steve Chan, "Chinese Conflict Calculus and Behavior," *World Politics* 30 (April 1978): 391–410; Allen Whiting, *The Chinese Calculus of Deterrence* (Ann Arbor: University of Michigan Press, 1974).

41. *Collection of Original Documents Concerning the Disputes Between the Russians and the Chinese Bandits*, vol. 8 (Taipei: Institute of International Relations, 1968), p. 30.

42. Ibid., p. 49.

43. Ibid., vol. 12 (1970), p. 269.

44. Ibid., p. 271.

45. Gurtov and Hwang, *China Under Threat*, pp. 197–214.

46. Thomas Robinson, *The Sino-Soviet Border Dispute: Background, Development and the March 1969 Clashes* (Santa Monica, Calif.: Rand, 1970), pp. 33–35.

47. Chinese Communist Party, *The Tenth National Congress of the Communist Party of China Documents* (Beijing: Foreign Languages Press, 1973), pp. 24–25.

48. John Garver, *China's Decision for Rapprochement with the United States, 1968–1971* (Boulder: Westview, 1982).

49. Paul H. B. Godwin, "Mao Zedong Revised: Deterrence and Defense in the 1980s," in P. Godwin (ed.), *The Chinese Defense Establishment: Continuity and Change in the 1980s* (Boulder: Westview, 1983), p. 23.

50. Li and Guo, "Principles Governing Relations with Foreign Communist Parties," p. 18.

51. Taiwanese sources suggest that Gorbachev has been severely criticized in the Chinese Communist Party. See Yeh Po-tang, "Communist China Stricken by Changes in East Europe," *Mainland China Studies* 32, 9 (March 1990): 12–25.

52. Chinese foreign minister Qian Qichen on the world situation in *Beijing Review* 33, 3 (January 15-21, 1990): 20.

53. Lin Wang, "Looking Towards the 1990s," *Beijing Review* 33, 1 (January 1-7, 1990): 16–17.

54. Qian Qichen on the world situation, pp. 14–15.

55. Wu Shuqing, "The Course for China's Reform and Opening," *Beijing Review* 33, 1 (January 1-7, 1990): 18–19.

56. Qian Qichen on the world situation, p. 19.

57. Ibid., p. 15.

58. Ibid., p. 20.

59. For a typical analysis, see Gerald Segal, "Sino-Soviet Relations," in Gerald Segal (ed.), *Chinese Politics and Foreign Policy Reform* (New York: Kegan Paul International, 1990), pp. 161–179.

5

PEACEFUL STRUGGLE:
CHINA'S UNITED STATES SCRIPT

In the 1990s, China's primary concerns, viewing Sino-U.S. relations from a balance-of-power perspective, should have been national security and modernization. In pursuit of these goals, China was thought to be constrained by competition between the United States and the Soviet Union and an inevitable dependence on one to resist the other. The China-U.S.-USSR triangle may have been an unequal one, but it was nonetheless a triangle. This realist perspective portrays China's U.S. policy as a reaction to the external situation in the pursuit of a predetermined set of national interests. However, from the Great Leap Forward (1958–1959), through the politics of the Cultural Revolution (1966–1976), the formulation of the three-worlds theory (1974), and the inauguration of an independent foreign policy (1982), to the crackdown on the prodemocracy movement (1989–1990), the Chinese have demonstrated their willingness occasionally to set aside these political and economic interests in favor of ideological ones. It is timely in this sense to see security and modernization needs as constraints rather than goals themselves. There are other, higher goals in China's U.S. policy.

Determining China's goals in the world from the Chinese perspective is impossible unless one examines the moral principles to which China adheres. Of course, one legitimate question to ask before studying principles is whether change in principle reflects change in the balance of power or vice versa. In the case of China, national power status seems to be almost irrelevant in the short run. For one thing, China's U.S. policy seems to be associated with leaders rather than national power. Zhou Enlai, pro-U.S. or otherwise, was a constant force for peaceful coexistence with the United States, while Mao never openly favored a pro-U.S. policy and reproved U.S. treachery throughout his career (even during the period of normalization). The implication is that policy is linked to the visions of individual leaders.

For another, China's national strength vis-à-vis the United States' and the Soviet Union's has scarcely changed since the Korean War. In contrast, its U.S. policy has periodically been altered. Contrary to the likely reaction to the perceived scenario of superpower collusion against China, the Chinese more than once have pledged themselves to opposing both superpowers. Even if global power struggle has occasionally influenced the Chinese mind-set (for example, normalization with the United States in 1972 and 1979 to counter the Soviet Union and Vietnam), it is not clear how China's national power has been increased specifically. More importantly, the Chinese have expended no small effort to demonstrate their independence from existing or proposed alliance with the United States. To view Sino-U.S. rapprochement as pure realpolitik is an oversimplification. That topic is the focus of this chapter.

Broadening the scope of national interests to include modernization does not necessarily enhance the realist perspective, primarily because it is virtually impossible to predict which interest will be dominant in a given period. The United States is supposedly China's most intimate comrade because of its unique ability to assist in the country's modernization and national defense. Both goals were seemingly jettisoned, however, in the aftermath of the Beijing massacre. This event perplexed both observers and the Chinese themselves: which goal should have higher priority—independence, socialism, development, democracy, or stability? Each would most likely assign the United States a somewhat different role. The Chinese style of organizing world politics lies in this continual shift in emphasis in order to claim dedication to each goal in its turn; the United States is always a target of these shifts. Attempts to clarify the ranking of priority are destined to be fruitless because ambiguity is intrinsic to the Chinese moral pretension.

The United States is significant to the Chinese not just because China must deal with widespread U.S. influence but also because the United States' superpower status furnishes China's U.S. policy with visibility and symbolic relevance. Complying with the wishes of a superpower implies confirmation of China's value; defying it signals China's determination to rectify world order. When Chinese leaders conceive of China as a moral model for the world, disciplining a superpower becomes an extremely delicate task. China has to prove that it stands on history's side by making a show of its will and ability to coerce the superpower, while at the same time avoiding actually doing so for want of genuine ability. Dramatization is the natural result.

Another reason the United States is significant to the Chinese centers on a historical friendship with China coupled with ideological enmity. The mutual affection between the two peoples can be traced back to numerous historical instances: Qing dynasty China's first ambassador overseas was an American; "United States" is translated as "beautiful country" in Chinese. The Chinese appreciated the United States' open-door policy at the beginning of the century as it saved China from being carved up by the European powers, but they were then bewildered by Woodrow Wilson's principle of self-determination. Even during the anti-U.S. campaign, Mao maintained a personal friendship with the U.S. reporter Edgar Snow; no Russian ever enjoyed a similar degree of intimacy with any high-level Chinese official. Despite decades of anti-U.S. education, the Chinese people have responded enthusiastically to U.S. friendship since the beginning of the 1980s, a time when the rest of the world tended to hold anti-American sentiments.

On the state-to-state level, however, the U.S. government has alternately been tagged imperialist, colonialist, capitalist, hegemon, target of world revolution, and declining superpower. The Chinese want to launch a struggle against the United States in hopes that the value of the Chinese moral world will eventually be recognized by the American people. China has struggled to draw a distinction between the government and the people, the reactionary and the popular, the short-sighted and the wise.

This love-hate psychology is reinforced by the coexistence of several different principles governing China's foreign policy that define China's goals in the world. In order to organize the world in the correct way, the Chinese assign the United States certain roles and expect to see the United States behave in a certain manner. Although the Chinese definition of the U.S. role in world politics is clearly ambivalent, it is hardly inconsistent, though widely perceived as such. Scholars note the shift in China's U.S. policy from confrontation to cooperation, but few have argued that the change of position can be attributed to a single motivational source: China's desire to prove it can make the world right. Besides, the Chinese always have an explanation for any seeming inconsistency in their principled positions. The self-deceptive effect of dramatization lies exactly in this kind of ambiguity.

What China wants the United States to do tells us what China wants the world to become. This chapter looks into various doctrines involved in China's efforts to specify the U.S. role in the world. The Taiwan factor is discussed to illustrate how the Chinese demonstrate their determination to remain committed to a multifaceted moral vision while moving toward rapprochement with the United States. Finally, the Chinese notion of the united front is analyzed. The conclusion of this chapter draws a parallel with the popular viewpoint that some limited confrontation between the two is inevitable.

DEFINING THE U.S. ROLE

Anti-imperialism

China's anti-imperialist theme with respect to the United States is derived from socialist role conceptions. The imperialist deeds of the United States are intrinsically linked to its being a capitalist society; the imperialist role of the United States is an inevitable part of the historical process. The theme thus portrays what will happen rather than what should be done.

The role of the United States. China's mission in the world was determined in part by unadulterated U.S. imperialist tendencies perceived during the Korean War. The United States' actions were a case of textbook imperialism:

> The United States invaded Korea and, in defiance of China's many warnings, its troops crossed the "38th parallel line," advancing on the Yalu River and the Sino-Korean border. At the same time, it intensified its interference in the Indochinese people's struggle against the French colonialists and sent troops to occupy China's territory, Taiwan and the Taiwan Straits, thus presenting a military threat to China from three directions. The United States also tried to isolate China politically and imposed a trade embargo and blockade in an attempt to strangle New China in its cradle.[1]

Being the primary enemy of a superpower made the Chinese feel honored. Throughout the postwar era, the Chinese have sought opportunities to demonstrate their determination to resist U.S. imperialism, thus proving that China is on the socialist side. It also fosters Chinese contempt toward the imperialist. Imperialist tendencies of the United States are perceived everywhere, though the best testimony that the imperialist will never relinquish efforts to topple the Chinese Communist regime is provided by U.S. support for the Nationalists on Taiwan. Although the Truman Doctrine and Marshall Plan caused "an irreparable rupture between the Soviet Union and the United States" and were potential sources of conflict in the aftermath of World War II,[2] détente was perceived as a device used by the two superpowers to contain China. It is likewise expected that the imperialist will struggle to prevent its own inevitable decline; involvement and eventual defeat in the Vietnam War is one telltale sign.

The tendency to see all U.S. comment on or policy toward China as imperialist interference has continued to this day, fostered by such U.S. actions as selling arms to Taiwan; granting asylum to a Chinese tennis player; criticizing China's population policy, Tibet policy, and arms sales to the Middle East; inviting dissidents to an official U.S. reception in Beijing; and publicizing the prodemocracy movement in the United States. The perception of interference substantiates charges of imperialism and confirms China's socialist status.

Pro-U.S. policy and the emphasis on economic modernization in the past decade do not contradict the anti-imperialist theme. Quoting Lenin's analysis, Deng Xiaoping argues in a recent article that "the pursuit of world domination" by the imperialist is one of the "roots of modern war."[3]

There has been renewed alarm about capitalist and imperialist subversion in China and the danger of "spiritual pollution," and so-called U.S. imperialist interference has been officially condemned for nurturing the pro-democracy movement (which the Chinese label bourgeois liberalization) throughout the 1980s.[4] The Chinese claim that their adherence to socialism is a matter of sovereignty and that they are not responsible for faltering "improvements in Sino-U.S. relations."[5] U.S. sanctions imposed in the wake of the June 4, 1989 crackdown only prove that China is still the ultimate target of imperialism, hence a true socialist country.

According to the anti-imperialism theme, then, the United States is expected to seek dominance through military, political, and economic means. It is inevitable that the country is declining, and it is expected to seek remedy through détente. The U.S. invasions of Grenada in 1983 and Panama in 1989 shocked the Chinese in the sense that they saw that the danger of imperialism was still quite alive.

China's anti-imperialism drama. The Chinese have adopted a three-pronged approach to dealing with imperialism: first it must be uncovered, then it must be criticized, and finally, it must be demonstrated that there has been no compromise, that principles have been preserved. In short, the world forum must be maneuvered to shame the imperialist. Emphasis on clarifying a causal interpretation of international problems for the rest of the world through persuasion is a typical Chinese practice. In reality, the Chinese do indeed show their opposition to the United States. In the United Nations, for example, a U.S. diplomat complained that although the Chinese understood the need to confront the Soviet Union, they actually sided more often with the Soviet Union than with the United States in that particular organization.[6] Except on the Cambodian issue, China and the United States have rarely cooperated.

Because anti-imperialism is sensible only if imperialism exists, it is imperative that the Chinese occasionally bear testimony to its prevalence. China's occasional bursts of anti-imperialism are therefore limited in scope, indirectly targeted, yet strongly worded. That is precisely why the Taiwan issue is so convenient for anti-imperialism, as is discussed later. The commitment to anti-imperialism appears sincere because China protests from a position of weakness. For example, China criticized U.S. imperialism at the same time it put out feelers to reopen bilateral talks in November 1969, just months after military confrontation with the Soviet Union; criticism continued until President Nixon's arrival in China in 1972. The intention was probably to test the seriousness of U.S. anti-Soviet commitment. Any attempt to assess whether China is sincere about anti-imperialism would miss the point because the Chinese never want to see antagonism between anti-imperialism and anti-Sovietism; they would prefer to believe that there is none.

Anti-imperialism is a drama because the Chinese consistently deny that the United States is their direct opponent. The strength of their opposition to U.S. imperialism is born of a moral conviction that the American people are on China's side. The best strategy of opposition is therefore to enhance the American people's awareness of China's greatness. Although U.S. strength may appear to vacillate, the effect on China's anti-imperialist position is minimal. China would never be physically strong enough to take on the United States even at its weakest. Opposition, therefore, is best exercised by sporadic acts of noncooperation, polemics, or simply ignoring the United States, but not by direct confrontation.

Imperialist interference, which China claims has rocked Eastern Europe, will not affect China for five reasons, according to CCP General Secretary Jiang Zemin. First, the Chinese Communist Party, equipped with Marxism, Leninism, and Maoism, has grown strong through armed struggle. Second, the Chinese military is also armed with Maoism and led by the party. Third, Chinese socialism was created by the Chinese themselves—not forced on China by the Soviet Red Army. Fourth, China is not surrounded by capitalist countries. Finally, Marxism has been sinicized by Mao Zedong and Deng Xiaoping and therefore is not subject to the Soviet reform movement.[7] This adherence to socialism also makes Deng Xiaoping confident that China's open-door policy will not make the country dependent on a capitalist-dominated world market. Jiang's portrayal of this closed system is the best testimony of the dramatic nature of China's anti-imperialism. It is more important for the Chinese simply to prove that the imperialist has unsuccessfully attempted to meddle in China than to overthrow the imperialist.

Peaceful Coexistence

Unlike anti-imperialism, peaceful coexistence role conceptions are not formed from an objective analysis of the imperialist's role in history. Instead, peaceful coexistence is a general principle specifying how nations should behave. Although the Chinese do not expect the United States to follow this principle, advocating it helps the Chinese uncover the deviant aspect of the imperialist's actions and supplies convenient targets for attack.

The role of the United States. The United States, like any nation, has a responsibility for maintaining peace. That the United States is an imperialist country is not an important factor in determining its state-to-state relations with China. One significant element of the principle of peaceful coexistence is respect for national sovereignty and noninterference in others' domestic affairs. The Chinese contend that the United States constantly violates this element: one example being the Taiwan issue, a more recent one the U.S. involvement in the prodemocracy movement between 1986 and 1989. The Chinese believe that deterioration in Sino-U.S. relations is caused by the United States' efforts to make China's willingness to accept U.S. political and social values a precondition for peaceful coexistence.[8] Since early 1990 the Communist Party has repeatedly warned comrades of the conspiracy to bring about "peaceful evolution" that lies behind Washington's China policy.[9]

The United States is expected to withdraw troops from overseas, halt intervention in China's domestic affairs, drastically reduce its nuclear arsenal, and negotiate arms control with the Soviet Union. By specifying China's role expectations, we can easily demonstrate how the United States has failed the Chinese test. According to the Chinese, the United States' special responsibility for solving the world's problems derives from its superpower status. But a superpower is evaluated by its policy, not by its national strength. Zhou Enlai once told his American friends, "[A] country should not always think of leading other countries. It was dangerous for a country to force others to see itself as a leader. The United States suffered greatly for attempting this. Morally, it could not lead others. All nations, big or small, are equal regardless of their populations."[10]

The main practical guideline associated with peaceful coexistence norms is to seek common ground but maintain and respect differences.[11] China is ready to deal with the United States any time the latter is ready to recognize that China is different. U.S. predilection for sending troops abroad or resorting to force is a stark violation of this guideline and leaves the United States at odds with rest of the world community. A Maoist reminder is useful here to summarize China's disappointment in the past few decades:

> Who is more afraid of whom? . . . England, America, Germany and France in the West fear us a bit more. . . . It's a question of strength, it's a question of popular support. Popular support means strength, and we have more people on our side than they do. Between the three -isms of communism, nationalism and capitalism, communism and nationalism are rather closer to each other. And the forces of nationalism occupy quite a large area, the three continents of Asia, Africa and Latin America. . . . The hearts of the Americans are hollow; ours are more sincere. For we rely on the people, and they prop up those reactionary rulers.[12]

China's peace drama. The imperialist tendency to violate peaceful coexistence role expectations is well established in history, according to the Chinese. Why, then, would China wish to achieve peace with the United States? One reason mentioned earlier is Chinese confidence that the internal logic of imperialism will eventually lead to its collapse. Chinese adherence to the principle of peaceful coexistence can help stress that people around the world, including the American people, disfavor war. When war does break out, this principle helps resolve the conflict peacefully once it is recognized that the Americans are more afraid of the Chinese than the Chinese are of the Americans. This simple perception of China's strength as well as popular support suggests why peaceful coexistence does not violate the principle of anti-imperialism.

The principle of peaceful coexistence also contributes to long-term peace because of simple pragmatism: peace provides an environment conducive to development.[13] In fact, the theme of peace has prevailed in Chinese diplomacy on several occasions when domestic development was of top priority. This development-through-peace conceptualization is believed to have external repercussions regarding Sino-U.S. relations. Mao, for example, argued that the United States would feel obliged to deal with China and would do so by accepting China's position if China could further develop national strength.[14]

The principle of peaceful coexistence remains a statement of intention in its purest form. To a large extent, the Chinese have manipulated bilateral relations with the United States just to illustrate how the United States violates this principle. For example, it is up to the Chinese to decide unilaterally when Taiwan becomes an issue. The issue of Taiwan is always on hand for the Chinese to show the world and themselves how blatantly the United States has interfered in China's domestic affairs. When military conflict does occur, the Chinese declare their peaceful intent by sending in volunteer troops (not the People's Liberation Army), as in the Korean War, or by refusing to regard the United States as an opponent, as in the various offshore island crises. Force is actually used, but peace is maintained on the surface, and blame can be rightly and squarely placed on the United States. What a manipulation of psychology!

When the Chinese negotiate, they do not necessarily intend to reach an agreement. Maintaining differences but continuing negotiations supposedly signals China's sincere desire for peace yet at the same time demonstrates China's determination to stick to principled positions even as peace is being negotiated. For example, the Chinese felt proud that the United States failed to wring concessions out of them in the course of the Warsaw negotiations.[15] Negotiation thus provides an opportunity for the Chinese to educate the Americans, to shame them, and eventually to convert them.

In short, all attempts to show how the United States has failed the test of peace do not imply that the United States is always an enemy. China has no intention of enforcing peace in addition to uncovering so-called U.S. wrongdoing. Peace is a drama to the extent that the Chinese consciously prevent efforts to cooperate with the United States from undermining many of China's historically held positions. The willingness to employ violent measures is also a reminder to the United States that it should not expect to take advantage of China's peace offensive—one that can be reversed overnight if U.S. policymakers try to interfere in China's domestic affairs. From time to time, the Chinese resort to peace rhetoric to show up U.S. violation of the principle of coexistence. Peace rhetoric thus becomes a shaming technique instead of a constraint, a policy option, or a reality.

Antihegemonism

Although the United States belongs to the First World, the Chinese rarely bring up antihegemonism when dealing with the United States on a one-to-one basis. As is widely known, antihegemonism was originally Chinese shorthand for anti–Soviet hegemonism. As far as the United States is concerned, therefore, this principle is more a specification of what should be rather than what is. This does not mean, however, that the United States is not a target. Chinese antihegemonism targets hegemonic policy, not the hegemonic state. Since the United States is a hegemonic state, it may be expected to act like one. In 1990 the Chinese (for the first time, to my knowledge) discussed U.S. hegemonism without simultaneously mentioning the Soviet Union.

The role of the United States. Once the Soviet Union was identified as the world's most hostile hegemon, China strove to include the United States in its antihegemonic front. Beginning in the early 1970s, China perceived the Soviet Union to be the more dominant power, perhaps owing to the U.S. retreat from Indochina. The United States was expected to close the gap and resume the balance between the two superpowers. For this reason, the Chinese actually welcomed increases in U.S. military strength. They thought that President Ronald Reagan, who increased U.S. defense capability, did a better job than President Jimmy Carter, who appeared to have weakened it.[16] It was imperative for China to encourage the United States to match the Soviet military buildup not necessarily because China wanted to see war but because it wanted to isolate the Soviet Union. Anxiety about U.S. retreat was temporary because, according to Chinese analysis, both superpowers will decline in the long run, a trend that should continue into the twenty-first century.[17]

The Chinese also felt that an arms race would drain the U.S. economy. In order to counter the Soviet Union, the United States was supposed to assist in China's defense modernization (read technology transfer), and indeed exchange of high-level military staff has been carried out since the early 1980s.[18] In terms of antihegemonism, the United States should treat China as an ally. Many U.S. realists like Nixon, Kissinger, and Alexander Haig actually hold this view, and the image of Nixon drinking mao-tai has been used by the Chinese to remind other U.S. politicians of China's strategic value. The Chinese have in fact developed the unusual habit of inviting Nixon to China whenever snags develop between China and the current U.S. administration: in 1976 after Gerald Ford's unsuccessful visit to China, in 1980 amidst Reagan's overtures to Taiwan and criticism of communism, and in 1989 after the Tiananmen incident.

It is expected that the United States will at times engage in hegemonism. One purpose of including the United States in the united front is precisely to prevent the two hegemons from monopolizing world politics. The three-worlds theory (see Chapter 3) was partially aimed at assuring the United States that the Chinese would cooperate in resisting the Soviet Union. If the Americans would only see the world the way the Chinese do, they would want to be a part of the united front, and the world could achieve consensus on who wears the black hat. For this reason, China condemned any form of superpower collusion, whether it be an agreement to halt nuclear proliferation, a test ban treaty, or any small-scale arms regulation, as these actually strengthen the two hegemons' global domination.

Antihegemonic role conceptions involving the United States are thus two-sided: the United States should contribute but it is sure to abrade; the United States should catch up but it is certain to decline. The Chinese may have to discipline the United States into playing the right role, but on the whole it is up to the United States to recognize the historical trend of socialism. The apparent contradiction between what should be done and what eventually happens is intriguing, yet it does permit flexibility in Chinese evaluation. If what should be done is done, China can claim success in organizing world politics; if it is not done, China must continue to struggle and await the decline of the United States.

China's antihegemonism drama. The United States is nonetheless a hegemon, and the Chinese often describe it as such in public forums. This role has three implications. First, the United States is reminded that it is essentially no different from the Soviet Union regardless of inclusion in the popular antihegemonic united front; the United States should be very careful not to repeat the mistakes of the Soviet Union if it doesn't want to be treated in the same manner. In reality, of course, the Chinese united front has never been as popular as they would like it to be, but their vehement antihegemonic rhetoric should serve to scare hegemony-oriented Americans. The Chinese perception that they are on the popular side is derived from the antihegemonic pretension that categorizes China and most countries as the Third World. Even as China criticizes the United States, the combination of cooperation and struggle keeps alive U.S. hopes that China can be won over to its side. Ideally, this should give the United States an incentive to satisfy China's requests.

Second, it is important for the Chinese occasionally to remind themselves that they are dealing with a hegemon. Although they invariably blame the United States as well as the (former) Soviet Union for the world's problems, the latter was considered more dangerous. There are always imperialist agents interested in converting China to capitalism, a perception that was vividly reinforced by prodemocracy movements in the latter half of the 1980s.

Third, since Soviet hegemony no longer exists, the resurgence of U.S. hegemony appears starkly real. The temptation to interfere in China's internal affairs must be strong, and this has been especially true in the aftermath of the Tiananmen incident. According to the Chinese analysis:

> The recent [Summer 1989] summit of the seven leading industrialized nations . . . continued to ignore the realities in China, and made judgments on China's affairs as judges who rely on their own so-called "values. . . ." These groundless charges . . . represent gross interference in China's internal affairs. . . .
>
> Some Western media, the U.S. media in particular, tried their best to exaggerate and distort China's quelling of the rebellion. . . . Some Western governmental figures . . . wilfully denounced and adopted sanctions against China, interfering in China's internal affairs in violation of international norms.[19]

As the antihegemonic front loses currency in the 1990s, China has to decide whether or not to find a new target. Under these circumstances, that target is most likely the United States. The Chinese position is that the United States is responsible for avoiding this possibility since it is the United States that is attempting to convert China. For the peace drama to prevail over a possible new antihegemonic drama against the United States, the United States would have to prove that U.S. hegemony no longer exists. As the Chinese say, the one who ties the bell to the tiger should untie it.

Open-Door Policy

The open-door policy (*kaifang zhengce*), as policy rather than global moral theme, has no guarantee of permanent implementation. The possibility exists, however, that the policy will eventually acquire moral significance for the Chinese and hence become a permanent feature of China's normative foreign policy. The policy contains elements of the principle of peaceful coexistence suggesting that countries of different social systems should coexist peacefully and maintain interactive relations accordingly. It is also a natural derivative of legalist role conceptions that dictate that a country seek wealth and strength.

Although the open-door policy is not yet a moral theme, its advocates have certain role expectations for the United States as well as for China itself. Because it may reflect certain moral themes, it implies both an objective analysis of what will happen and the normative prescription for what should happen; for example, since the policy presumes open access to the international market, China condemns protectionism; peaceful co-existence elements imply that countries that enjoy commercial and cultural opportunities in China should not interfere in the Chinese system. The Chinese thus criticize U.S. attempts at the "spiritual pollution" of Chinese society. The Chinese analysis of the world situation finds that both protectionism and the tendency for imperialist interference in Chinese affairs have continued into the 1990s.

The role of the United States. The open-door policy has swept away many obstacles to commercial and cultural interaction with other nations. The most important obstacle was created by the U.S. freeze on Chinese assets during the Korean War and subsequent Chinese retaliation that prevented direct investment in China by U.S. business. The freeze was lifted immediately after the two sides normalized relations in January 1979, and a comprehensive trade agreement was signed later that year. The agreement includes a most-favored-nation clause reducing U.S. tariffs on Chinese exports from an average of 30 percent to just 6 percent. The two sides established the Commission on Science and Technology Cooperation in 1979, the Joint Economic Committee in 1980, and the Joint Commission on Commerce and Trade in 1982. The United States was clearly fulfilling China's role expectations.

By allowing in the leader of the capitalist camp, Chinese policymakers have sent a clear message of openness. On the one hand, China expects the United States to utilize newly available business opportunities; on the other hand, since the open-door policy presumes mutual benefit, the United States should help China develop high technology to modernize the Chinese economy. The United States has signed a variety of bilateral agreements to assist China in upgrading technology in certain fields specified primarily by China, the most significant help being provided in the energy sector. With respect to its own commercial interests, the United States has assisted in offshore oil exploration. As one U.S. official noted: "Offshore oil is the cutting edge of Sino-U.S. relations for the rest of the century."[20] For strategic as well as commercial reasons, the United States has agreed to export nuclear facilities and technology to China. That deal is still on despite U.S. sanctions imposed on China after June 4, 1989.

Trade with the United States is an equally significant element in the open-door policy. China's trade with Western Europe and Japan began to increase in the early 1970s, but it wasn't until 1978, the year the policy was launched, that Sino-U.S. trade suddenly tripled. Chinese products, especially textile products, have proved popular in the U.S. market. The U.S.

government has also helped develop the Chinese market for U.S. products and investment. Through the Trade and Development Program, the government sponsored forty-six feasibility studies between 1984 and 1987 and provided funding for technological training.[21]

The United States, though, has not fulfilled all Chinese expectations. First of all, China's growing trade surplus with the United States has caused concern, and quota systems have been imposed on Chinese imports that, to China's ire, include Chinese reexports via Hong Kong. Second, the flood of cheap Chinese clothing into the U.S. market has caused serious concern among U.S. apparel manufacturers; both parties dispute proper growth rates for Chinese textile exports to the United States. There are also problems with safety and hygiene standards; in 1988 the United States recalled all Chinese canned mushrooms after staphylococcus was discovered in one batch. The Chinese did not appreciate this "unreasonable" action, claiming the problem originated from but a small number of factories.

Complaints are also aired regarding the slow growth of U.S. investment in China, which represents only about 1 percent of direct U.S. overseas investment. During the first three years of urban reform, 1984 to 1987, less than 16 percent of direct investment in China came from the United States, and less than 5 percent of China's direct investment agreements were with U.S. firms between 1983 and 1987.[22] The United States, for its part, points to the plethora of administrative obstacles. Moreover, it cannot compete with overseas Chinese and the Japanese in sorting out bureaucratic complexities.

Besides failing to satisfy certain demands, the United States seems to be doing other things that it should not: the United States is not supposed to take advantage of the open door to make China dependent, but some feel this is exactly what is happening; the United States should avoid contributing to international perceptions that there is a Sino-U.S. alliance against the Soviet Union; it should avoid using cultural interaction to influence Chinese values; and above all the United States should refrain from trying to influence China's internal political development. The 1989 congressional resolution imposing sanctions on China because of a poor human rights record was in direct conflict with China's expectations for the United States.

These sanctions covered a broad range of activities: the Trade and Development Program, for example, was asked to stop financing economic activities in China; the government was requested to refuse export licenses for military goods; and more importantly the government was forbidden to export satellite facilities and was asked to reevaluate an agreement with China on transferring nuclear technology. The administration of George Bush is concerned that such sanctions will encourage an isolationist tendency in China despite repeated Chinese assurances that the door will remain open and efforts will be made to circumvent the resolution. The Chinese thus pin the blame for a deterioration in bilateral relations on a few malicious (*bieyou yongxin*) individuals.

China's open-door drama. The open-door policy has evolved into a symbol of reform in China. Although different political forces disagree on specific measures and the pace of reform, continuation is seen to be an inevitable phase of socialist development—regardless of how it is defined. Chinese analysis of the Romanian revolution—the popular overthrow of a Communist regime—underscores reluctance on the part of the Romanian regime to carry out reform. Reform is the key to legitimacy, and the open-door policy is the key to reform. In this sense, recognition by the industrial nations, especially the United States, of the value of China in the world market is psychologically significant to China's sense of its future. Chinese theory of an interdependent, unitary world market suggests to U.S. and other Western businesspeople that China must not be left out of the process of world development.[23]

The open-door policy has become such a drama that reformist leaders view any and all maladies associated with the policy as necessary evils. Aware that most Chinese students traveling to the United States take great pains to avoid returning to China, the initial Chinese reaction was to strengthen incentives for the students to return rather than reduce the number sent in the first place. When stories in Western magazines mar China's image, authorities rip out the pages instead of banning the magazines. Voice of America has been permitted to send a representative back to China after being condemned and banned for triggering the 1989 Tiananmen protests. Delegation after delegation is sent to the United States to study how to improve a Chinese investment climate that the United States has severely criticized. Only when exchanges are clearly inconsistent with China's historical image will there be problems. One example is the cancellation of a July 1987 art exhibition because the Chinese refused to permit portraits of Douglas MacArthur and Golda Meir to enter the country.

Although people-to-people relations have expanded rapidly, they are restricted when the Chinese blame U.S. connections for contributing to domestic unrest. In 1987 China decided that a smaller proportion of students should be sent to the United States, and in 1989, according to a Taiwanese source, doctoral students had to wait three years after graduation, masters students five years, and undergraduates eight years before being allowed to study overseas.[24] (A different source suggests the only new constraint is five years for college students.) The government also began the recentralization of previously decentralized financial controls and was expected to limit the international activities of Chinese corporations. Despite such moves, the Chinese claimed that the open-door policy was still in effect and would remain so.

The theatrical aspect of the open-door policy has been obvious since its inception. Admittedly dissatisfied with the speed of technology transfer, the Chinese clearly benefit from U.S. high technology, yet they continue to deemphasize its importance. For example, China canceled a major military cooperation project in 1990 on the pretext that it was too expensive.[25] Inconsistency with notions of self-reliance still cherished by a good number of conservatives makes dependence on U.S. technology a politically ignominious policy. More aggressive reformers of the Zhao Ziyang mold tend to ignore reform's immediate negative aspects and urge patience for its positive, long-term fruits. Meanwhile, China suffers from inflation, trade deficits, international debt, skewed income distribution, and, most significantly, corruption and spiritual pollution. It is not clear to what extent economic growth can even be attributed to the open-door policy.

As a consequence, while aggressive reformers have not yet been able to reap benefits from this policy, conservative reformers have already politicized its uglier aspects. When the latter took center stage in 1989, they confirmed the validity of the policy but slowed its tempo. The open door has become a statement of intention because political debates about it center exclusively on philosophical implications and rarely on detailed implementation. The open-door policy itself was apparently decided upon before anyone knew how it would be implemented. Almost overnight China seemed to open up—thousands of delegations were received and dispatched over a short period; the number of sister-city and sister-province agreements mushroomed; higher educational institutions scrambled to establish exchange relationships of all sorts. Before the exact context of the policy was comprehended, the Chinese were rushing to open up.

Declaring the open-door policy before the door was actually opened was done primarily to satisfy the desire for change after the Cultural Revolution and the purge of the Gang of Four. The irony is that the policy had become official before its advocates could effectively structure it, and it is still official even though opponents have succeeded in reversing it to a certain degree. How the door should be opened is de facto determined by the most active outsiders—overseas Chinese, Japanese, and Americans. Since 1989 the Chinese seem to have come to the conclusion that these outsiders, not the policy itself, ought to shoulder the blame for the problems it has spawned. The actual contents of the policy have never been clear despite the government's repeated expressions of its intention to open up. The originally rational policy of enhancing national wealth and strength has hence become a drama of reform considered essential to the regime's survival.

Dramatization

It is difficult to be consistent with the notions of anti-imperialism, peaceful coexistence, antihegemonism, and the open-door policy all at the same time. How can the United States be treated simultaneously as a hostile imperialist, a friendly state, an undeclared pseudo ally against Soviet hegemony, and a source of technology and capital? At times the Chinese emphasize one of these roles at the expense of the others without actually knowing it. At other times bothersome observers and Chinese ideologues point out cynical aspects of Chinese foreign policy and force adjustments in policy gestures to satisfy several principles simultaneously.

It is possible to struggle with the United States in a way that dramatizes U.S. imperialist inclinations and at the same time permits U.S. belief that China might be won over to its side. The Chinese continuously remind Americans that their government is an imperialist and a hegemon; Americans are eager to placate China in order to establish a united front. This accomplished, the open-door policy can then be used to attract those Americans anxious to prove their value. It is inevitable that despite government maneuvering, some Chinese, notably the young and the well connected, will either adapt to the U.S. value system or take advantage of their U.S. connections, legally or illegally. Is this then not a reminder to the Chinese that imperialist interference is still alive and hence vital to the apparently forgotten theme of anti-imperialism?

Just as Deng Xiaoping predicted when Congress imposed sanctions in 1989, the United States has once again returned to China. Deng's prediction was actually a dramatic declaration that the open-door policy would continue—China was still open; it was only that the United States had decided not to come. Deng understands the importance of maintaining the element of struggle in the Sino-U.S. relationship. In fact, it is this gesture of anti-imperialism and readiness to sacrifice the relationship that has made the open-door policy and peaceful coexistence so dramatic that the Chinese have been able to maintain moral consistency. Indeed, only through this policy can China demonstrate that peaceful coexistence between countries with different social systems is rewarding and that China is welcome in the world.

In fact, Sino-U.S. relations have been developed upon the same psychological imperative: peace is valuable only within the context of political struggle. It is a political art to struggle with the United States to a degree that maintains peace without losing dignity. The next section discusses how the Chinese have utilized the Taiwan issue to strive for exactly this effect.

THE TAIWAN FACTOR IN CHINA'S U.S. POLICY

The Significance of the Taiwan Issue

Since neither superpower openly declared a preference during the Chinese civil war, Mao and his cohorts remained hopeful of U.S. recognition throughout the war. But the Communists probably understood that in seeking U.S. support they risked antagonizing the Soviet Union and making themselves dependent on a United States whose backing was lukewarm at best. In the end, the victorious Communists announced that China would "lean" toward the Soviet Union; the debate over "who lost China" evidently illustrated upon which side of the fence the United States sat.

Meanwhile, the defeated Nationalists fled to Taiwan to establish their rival regime. Immediately after the outbreak of the Korean War, the Taiwan Straits were neutralized by the arrival of the U.S. Seventh Fleet, and after the war the United States included Taiwan in its global scheme of containment. In 1954 the two sides signed a mutual defense treaty that inevitably carried the legal implication that the United States recognized the Nationalists' claim to be the legitimate rulers of China. For the Chinese, U.S.-Taiwan relations have always represented imperialist intervention in their internal affairs.

Since the 1950s relations between the United States and Taiwan have experienced all-round development. The Nationalists depended heavily on the United States for direct military support before 1979 and for military supplies and technology after 1980. Taiwan's economy has benefited immensely from U.S. aid and a relatively unfettered U.S. market for its exports. Nationalist politics, sensitive as they are to U.S. influence, have prompted some to label Taiwan's economic "miracle" in part a U.S. achievement.[26] Taiwan's peaceful democratization in the 1980s was well (though quietly) received in Washington, which has given continuous encouragement for such development through political and moral pressure. Taiwan is the star pupil in the U.S. school of development, demonstrating for a global audience that U.S. aid can produce development, equity, stability, and democracy all at the same time. (This creates an ironic moral dilemma for the United States because any official recognition of Taiwan's achievement would run counter to its pro-China policy).[27]

In 1979 the Carter administration concluded that Sino-U.S. normalization was essential to U.S. national interests. This prompted the United States to sever diplomatic relations with Taiwan and cleared the last stumbling block to normalization with Beijing. Politically and psychologically unable to disrupt the Taiwan miracle, the U.S. Congress passed the Taiwan Relations Act to preserve bilateral relations as far as possible and extend official protection to nongovernmental relations with Taiwan; even arms sales have continued. In the 1980s Taiwan became the United States' fifth largest trade partner. Toward the end of the 1980s, the two cooperated closely in arranging Taiwanese financial support for a number of U.S. allies to whom the United States was politically incapable of providing sufficient aid, including the Nicaraguan Contras and Panama.

As mentioned before, if China is to recruit the United States into its antihegemonic united front without losing sight of U.S. imperialism, maintain peaceful relations with the United States without giving the green light to U.S. hegemonic policy, and open the door to the United States without damaging the pretension of self-reliance, it is imperative for the Chinese to demonstrate their willingness to sacrifice alliance, peace, and high technology for the sake of principled stands on anti-imperialism, antihegemonism, and self-reliance. The delicate task for the Chinese is to do this symbolically so that it is always possible for the United States to come back to renew the relationship.

The Taiwan issue is a perfect locus for such a demonstration. U.S.-Taiwan relations are developed to the extent that this is an almost permanent issue. It is easier to maintain rhetorical consistency on one issue only and choose the occasion if the issue is always there to be exploited. The issue is relevant from the Chinese point of view because it involves the legitimacy of the Communist regime and hence a perfect test of U.S. sincerity in befriending China. If the United States is unwilling to give in on an insignificant symbolic issue that involves extreme loss of face for the Chinese, then what sort of friend is it?

It is not necessarily true that China deliberately utilizes the Taiwan issue to blackmail the United States. It may look like a Chinese bluff if the United States complies rhetorically and cajoles the Chinese into dropping the issue. The relationship would genuinely deteriorate, however, if the United States failed the test of friendship at the rhetorical level. On the whole, China has not really tried to struggle directly against the imperialist on the Taiwan issue. To do that would give the impression that China's anti-imperialism was to serve China's own (i.e., selfish) interests. The Taiwan factor serves two rational purposes within the Chinese context: to present China as a victim of imperialism and to demonstrate China's moral strength by fearlessly denouncing imperialism.

It is interesting to examine the timing of the Chinese use of the Taiwan issue and the reasons the Chinese find it necessary to use this issue. As argued later, the timing has to do with a perception that China's declared positions on anti-imperialism, independent foreign policy, and self-reliance are being challenged. It is almost essential for China to use the issue because no other issue better demonstrates U.S. imperialism to the Chinese people, at least before the United States was blamed for spiritual pollution in 1983.

Selected Analyses

Immediately following normalization of Sino-U.S. diplomatic relations in 1979, there was renewed interest in the role of Taiwan in China's U.S. policy.[28] For years China insisted that U.S.-Taiwan relations were the main obstacle to the improvement of Sino-U.S. relations. Studies that deal with the triangular relationship are for the most part policy-oriented. Four outstanding works that analyze the Chinese strategic calculus all assume that there is a rational actor, although the assumption is, to various degrees, conditional. As rationality analyses, they assume that decisionmakers consciously examine the pros and cons of any action and that policymaking is based on such calculation. Before we move to the psychological interpretation of China's security policy in the Taiwan Straits, let us first examine how the rational actor paradigm sees the issue.

Three of the four works noted here discuss the offshore islands incidents in the period prior to Sino-U.S. normalization. While their arguments differ, they all attempt to unearth the rationale behind China's aggressive use of force in the 1954–1955 and 1958 crises. For example, Gurtov and Hwang argue that the 1958 use of force in the Taiwan Straits manifests the Chinese strategic constant that dictates vehement reaction to a perceived danger when domestic chaos leaves the nation vulnerable to external threat or exploitation.[29] In 1958 domestic vulnerability refers, of course, to the Great Leap Forward, while external threat designates the U.S. military presence in Taiwan. In deterrence terminology, hostility is designed to deter external forces from exploiting domestic vulnerability.

Thomas Stolper, in contrast, sees a more aggressive line of thinking behind Mao's strategic moves in 1958.[30] He contends that China's ultimate goal was Taiwan's recovery. Since the United States was guarding Taiwan, it was rational for China to undermine U.S. commitment to the Nationalists. China knew that the United States was both reluctant to defend the offshore islands and unwilling to go to war with China. The Chinese, therefore, cleverly designed a limited provocative strategy. They used a restrained military attack to remind the United States that there would always be conflict over the islands but that the Chinese would not take them. In so doing, the Chinese signaled that the ultimate objective was the island of Taiwan. This way, the United States could avoid war with China only if it withdrew its military forces from Taiwan. According to Stolper, this was the strategic logic of both crises in the 1950s.

Segal also finds that the offshore islands incidents were unique in terms of strategic thinking. But in contrast to the other writers he argues that Chinese objectives were to test U.S. intentions in the Taiwan Straits and also possibly to take over the offshore islands of Quemoy and

Matsu.[31] Segal maintains, as does Stolper, that the Chinese strategy in the 1954–1955 crisis targeted the new mutual defense treaty between the United States and Taiwan. Unlike Stolper, however, Segal suggests that the use of force by China at that time was initially a protest, later an effort to break through the U.S. encirclement and in the end an attempt to seize some of the small islands; the action was not just a reminder of the Quemoy-Taiwan link.[32]

Robert Ross looks into post–Shanghai communiqué bargaining between the United States and China from the international system perspective.[33] He argues that although reunification is China's national goal, China has not consistently pushed the Taiwan issue in its dealings with the United States. The importance of the issue varies according to China's bargaining power, which in turn is a function of the global balance of power among the United States, the Soviet Union, and China. China pushes this issue harder whenever it assumes the role of balance between the superpowers, and it backs out a little when the United States becomes a counterbalance between China and the Soviet Union. Accordingly, Ross contends, the Shanghai communiqué and the 1979 joint communiqué represented a compromise of China's position on the Taiwan issue. China's insistence on independent diplomacy in the 1980s and its success in forcing the United States to agree to cut arms sales to Taiwan is the result of China's position as balance.

The Taiwan issue, then, has been used to save the regime from its legitimacy crisis (Gurtov and Hwang), to discourage U.S. commitment to Taiwan (Stolper), and to achieve opportunist goals (Segal). For Ross, recovering Taiwan itself is a goal secondary to China's power relationship with the two superpowers; power is considered either as the major concern or as the ultimate goal. Ross may be correct in explaining the timing of China's moves on the Taiwan issue. However, it is not clear how goals and their relative priority are determined. In fact, the changing structure of the world political system since the mid-1980s has not yet been reflected in China's U.S. and Taiwan policies. The above authors obviously imply that China's moral position is irrelevant and that the United States and China are involved in a zero-sum game. No author deals with China's attempt to discipline the United States into playing the correct role. Normative concerns in world politics are really not an issue at all.

It is difficult to prove or disprove conclusively the relevance of power concern. One author acknowledges that he has to reject certain information because it does not accord with the goal he identifies for China.[34] It is useful to point out, though, that certain moral assumptions are pertinent to goal setting. For one, anti-imperialism makes sense of the assumption that the United States was treated as a threatening enemy in Gurtov and Hwang's work. For another, antihegemonism makes sense of Ross's assertion that China treats Taiwan as a secondary issue.

These authors also assume China's ability to control or adapt. The Chinese (or any nation for that matter) could experience little sense of control during a legitimacy crisis (Gurtov and Hwang), stagnation on the battlefield (Stolper and Segal), or contention with the Soviet Union (Ross). In fact, no rational actor assumes control in world politics. Manipulating power to adjust to changing reality without alluding to legitimacy, consistency, and justification (as China seems to be doing with ease) is an overdrawn conceptualization. There is a lack of appreciation of the Chinese style of manipulating power through manipulating words. That China has rarely had control over the result makes its policy no more than a drama. The following pages introduce a different perspective: how the Taiwan issue has been used to express Chinese criticism and tolerance of U.S. wrongdoing in world politics.

Taiwan and Anti-imperialism

In order to persuade others to accept China's worldview, it is necessary to convince them of the existence of an imperialist threat. The Taiwan issue is the one ready example: U.S. support for the Nationalists on Taiwan provides ample evidence of imperialism. The Chinese regard such support as a violation of China's territorial integrity and the presence of U.S. troops in Taiwan as an outright act of imperialism and military interference in China's domestic affairs. Since the end of the Chinese civil war, the Taiwan issue has been continuously stressed, albeit to varying degrees. The Taiwan issue is particularly important when the Chinese feel a need to demonstrate their independence and unbending opposition to imperialism.

When negotiating a cease-fire in the course of the Korean War, for example, the Chinese demanded that the United States withdraw its troops from Taiwan as a condition to any settlement. Because the armistice could be misconstrued as compromise with imperialism, the Chinese used the Taiwan issue to demonstrate their steadfast opposition to imperialism. Stolper quotes Zhou Enlai as saying in August 1954: "If any foreign aggressors dare to try to hinder the Chinese people from liberating Taiwan, if they dare to infringe upon our sovereignty and violate our territorial integrity, if they dare to interfere in our internal affairs, they must take all the grave consequences of such acts of aggression upon themselves."[35] When the United States and Taiwan were negotiating their defense treaty, the Chinese began shelling the offshore islands in September 1954. The military confrontation escalated after the treaty was signed in December. Upon the recommendation of the United States, the Nationalists withdrew from Dachen Island, which was immediately recovered by the Communists.[36]

This military show of determination to liberate Taiwan was for U.S. consumption, and Zhou later made it clear that peaceful "liberation" of

Taiwan depended upon noninterference by the United States; imperialist interference would only invite violence. The Chinese have repeatedly drawn this conceptual link between U.S. withdrawal and a peaceful solution, as conveyed during ambassadorial talks in Geneva and Warsaw. During the 1958 offshore islands crisis, the link was made dramatically clear when Marshal Peng Dehuai offered to supply the offshore islands to assist their defense against China's own shelling if the Nationalists agreed to give up U.S. supplies for the sake of anti-imperialism.[37] Large-scale shelling of the offshore islands during Dwight Eisenhower's 1960 visit to Taiwan was one more Chinese demonstration against U.S. imperialism.[38]

The Chinese remind the United States of its imperialist nature whenever they fear that the world may mistake China's policy for compromise. This happened during the early 1970s when the two sides negotiated normalization. In the Shanghai communiqué, for example, the Chinese reemphasized their opposition to "foreign aggression, interference, control and subversion" and asserted that "all foreign troops should withdraw to their own countries." They then went on to tell the United States that it must not support "the creation of 'one China, one Taiwan,' 'one China, two governments,' 'two Chinas,' or an 'independent Taiwan,' or insist that 'the status of Taiwan remains to be determined.'"[39] In the meantime, they felt obliged to arm their people spiritually against any misinterpretation of the communiqué:

> Because of the forcible occupation of Taiwan by U.S. imperialism, the Taiwan question has become a question of international dimensions. The *Shanghai Communique* released during the visit of Nixon to China has forced U.S. imperialism to take cognizance of the fact that Taiwan is a part of Chinese territory and that the ultimate objective is the withdrawal of all U.S. forces and military installations from Taiwan. This keeps U.S. imperialism from making a further intervention in Taiwan. . . . The Chiang [Kai-shek] gang, when formerly banking on the support of U.S. imperialism, appeared to be quite tough. Now . . . , the Chiang gang is no longer able to get tough.[40]

Similar reassurances appeared a year before the final round of normalization talks in 1979. U.S. interference in Taiwan was said to be a smoke screen: the United States didn't really want to fulfill its obligations under the defense treaty with Taiwan. Chinese opposition nonetheless continued because this was "a question of principle, on which [China could] not accept any compromise." Therefore, the U.S.-Taiwan defense treaty was "one of the obstacles to the solution of China-U.S. relations."[41] China thus laid down three preconditions for normalization: cutting diplomatic relations with Taiwan, withdrawing troops from the island, and terminating the treaty. According to the Chinese, President Ford had failed to meet these preconditions. Contrary to many observers' impression that China backed down on these preconditions, the final joint communiqué signed by the Carter administration in 1979 met all three.[42]

The biggest remaining problem is U.S. insistence of its right to sell defensive arms to Taiwan. While this issue does not logically conflict with the three preconditions, China "absolutely" opposes the sales because they are "detrimental to the peaceful liberation of Taiwan."[43] Within this context, the Chinese once blamed both imperialism and social imperialism for being a potential source of war. Chinese citizens were reminded that "even the skin of a dead tiger carries some of its prowess," and if the United States continued "to play the role of international gendarme in world affairs," others "will still be daunted by the tiger's prowess and will have no peace in mind."[44]

The Chinese side started pushing on the arms sale issue in October 1981, when Premier Zhao Ziyang met President Reagan in Mexico. The subsequent discussion continued between Foreign Minister Huang Hua and Secretary of State Haig in Washington. Vice-President Bush visited Beijing in May 1982 and held discussions on the same subject. The two sides finally reached an agreement on August 17, 1982, that "over a period of time," the two governments would adopt measures for a "final settlement of the question of United States arms sales to Taiwan."[45]

The 1982 communiqué actually created false expectations and led to a subsequent Chinese perception that Washington continued to interfere in China's domestic affairs. In 1983 Foreign Minister Wu Xueqian spoke in Chicago on U.S. arms sales to Taiwan, which he said were an obstacle to the unification of China. The arms sales, he claimed, were not only a violation of China's sovereignty and interference in China's internal affairs but were actually an encouragement to Taiwan to refuse talks.[46] Zhao Ziyang, in a 1984 interview in San Francisco, also asked the United States not to obstruct Taiwan's peaceful return to the homeland.[47] State President Li Xiannian addressed the issue before U.S. audiences again in 1985 and Foreign Minister Wu Xueqian in 1987.

Anti-imperialism and its legacy will continue to be a theme in China's diplomacy simply because the Taiwan issue can easily symbolize China's anti-imperialist position. It is true, however, that during the Vietnam War the Taiwan issue received measurably less attention, probably because U.S. imperialism was much more obvious in Vietnam; similarly, in the mid-1980s the focus shifted to alleged U.S. involvement in the prodemocracy movement. In 1989 and 1990 China mentioned on several occasions that Taiwanese agents and the U.S. imperialists were behind the prodemocracy protests of 1989. Although the Taiwan issue had clearly become less significant, its importance may be dramatized again in the future to remind the Chinese people of the dangers of imperialism.

One attack appeared in the September 25, 1989, issue of *Liaowang Zhoukan* (Outlook weekly):

> The U.S. "two-track policy" is the important international cause of the existence and development of the Taiwan independence movement. The U.S.-made Taiwan Relations Act *de facto* acknowledges Taiwan as an independent political entity. In recent years, moves by the United States to exert pressure on the Taiwan authorities to speed up "Taiwanizing the Taiwan regime" all give extreme encouragement to those advocating Taiwan independence. . . . A few American politicians and research institutions even support "self-determination by residents" and the "independence" of Taiwan.[48]

The article criticizes the idea that the United States should help Taiwan to become a fully independent sovereign state if China attacks Taiwan. The strongly worded conclusion that China must react vehemently to those who encourage Taiwan's independence is a new reminder that the Taiwan issue is far from disappearing in future Sino-U.S. relations.

Taiwan and Peaceful Coexistence

The Chinese argue that they have never wanted a war with the United States. China's request that the United States withdraw from Taiwan is a component of the peaceful coexistence principle that includes noninterference and respect for territorial integrity. China struggles to prove that there is no contradiction between anti-imperialism and peaceful coexistence.

During the offshore island crises in 1954–1955 and 1958, China claimed that it was not treating the United States as its opponent. The military confrontation was purely an internal Chinese affair, and Zhou Enlai expressed willingness to discuss with Washington the peaceful solution of the Taiwan issue. The solution was for the United States to withdraw its troops from Taiwan so that China and the United States could peacefully coexist without one country's threatening the other by occupying a part of the other's territory.[49]

In the 1960s the Taiwan issue faded out of China's U.S. policy. China did not take military action against the perceived joint threat from the United States and Taiwan during the period after the Great Leap Forward. This unusual omission was consistent with official emphasis on peaceful coexistence under Liu Shaoqi's leadership. Equally significant was the lack of interest in the Taiwan issue during the Cultural Revolution. This was primarily because U.S. encirclement from Vietnam drew the most attention and appeared much more ominous, but even that threat was scorned by Mao as the last stand of imperialism.[50] Taiwan, in comparison, was a rather minor issue. A realist could argue that the Taiwan issue is missing whenever China is incapable of doing anything about it. Nonetheless, neglect of the Taiwan issue is significant only in the symbolic sense because, in the real sense, even when it is stressed during periods of anti-imperialism, China has never really challenged the United States directly. Failure to use the issue is a reflection of the prevailing drama, not a reflection of China's relative power status.

The Shanghai communiqué repeated word for word China's five cherished principles of peaceful coexistence. In the meantime, Zhou Enlai confirmed that the Taiwan issue was not as urgent as that of Indochina.[51] With the communiqué signed and the withdrawal of U.S. forces under way, China predicted a dismal future for the Nationalists and offered to open talks for a peaceful solution.[52] The Chinese rejoiced: "We use the peace talks as a means of forcing U.S. imperialism, now beset with difficulties at home and abroad, to withdraw its forces from Indochina, Taiwan, and the Taiwan Straits, of promoting a peaceful settlement of the questions of Taiwan, Indochina, and Vietnam, and of alleviating tension in Asia and other parts of the world."[53]

China also agreed to exchange liaison offices with the United States because of the communiqué's "recognition" (the U.S. text reads "acknowledgement") of China's position on Taiwan. Nonetheless, the creation of the liaison offices should be interpreted as a compromise on the Taiwan issue. The Chinese justification is that the offices were established to facilitate a future settlement on the issue.[54]

Chinese reaction to the joint communiqué on normalization in 1979 was more entertaining. Consistent with Zhou Enlai's remark that peace depended on U.S. noninterference, China, immediately after diplomatic normalization with the United States, ceased the two-decade-long practice of symbolically firing on the offshore islands. A new peace offensive was launched toward Taiwan. During his visit to the United States, Vice-Premier Deng Xiaoping promised to try to secure a peaceful solution.[55]

Peace is not guaranteed even if the United States has signed a peace communiqué; the Chinese understand that it is possible for the United States to renege. The pact might have been regarded as a test of U.S. intentions, as Huang Hua argued a year and a half before the joint communiqué was signed: "At least, the one who tears up an agreement will find it difficult to defend its action, and will therefore lose support among third parties."[56] Nonetheless, the Chinese were satisfied in the 1980s. Although it was mentioned occasionally, the Taiwan issue was not the popular topic of bilateral relations that it was before the joint communiqué of August 17, 1982.

In 1982 China finalized its independent foreign policy line. This must have provided the Chinese a good measure of psychological and political relief, China having developed full-fledged relations with the United States and rapprochement with the Soviet Union at the same time. The most important sign of independence was achieving a balance between the two superpowers. In this context, the Taiwan issue once more diminished in importance. Only when the Soviet Union relinquished domination over Eastern European did it again arise as a different sign of independence. In the 1990s, however, it is anticapitalist values, not the Taiwan issue, that symbolize China's anti-imperialism.

Taiwan and Antihegemonism

China managed not to lose face over the Shanghai communiqué of 1972 by allowing some ambiguity on the Taiwan issue. The spirit of the communiqué fully embodies Zhou Enlai's oft-repeated call to seek common ground and put aside differences. Although the two sides agreed to disagree on many issues, the U.S. statement in the communiqué is not inconsistent with Chinese principles on the Taiwan issue. U.S. compliance allowed China to highlight one of the most important messages of the communiqué: antihegemonism. As the communiqué stated, neither side should seek hegemony in the Asia-Pacific region and each is opposed to efforts by any other country or group of countries to establish such hegemony.[57]

As the tension decreased, with the United States affirming "the ultimate objective of the withdrawal of all U.S. forces and military installations from Taiwan" and promising to "progressively reduce its forces and military installations on Taiwan," the Chinese were able to claim that "U.S. imperialism is kicked out of the area. From Asia and Vietnam, U.S. imperialism has moved its forces over to Europe and the Middle East. This has greatly aggravated the contradictions between the United States and the Soviet Union, putting the two dogs at loggerheads. This struggle of theirs is advantageous to the revolution of our people and the people of the world."[58]

The perceived tendency for Taiwan to take advantage of superpower confrontation was growing in the 1970s, especially after two Soviet fleets sailed past Taiwan and a noted Russian reporter paid a visit to the island. According to one Taiwanese source, Foreign Minister Qiao Guanhua reportedly said on May 20, 1975, that "the Soviet Union is watching this area and attempts to avail itself of an opportunity to set its foot on it."[59] It was apparent that the Chinese knew it was unlikely that China could liberate Taiwan immediately even if the United States completely withdrew from the island. As a result, antihegemonism to prevent Soviet influence in Taiwan became an urgent task.

In this atmosphere of anti-imperialism, the Taiwan issue appeared to be a token. Thanks to the Taiwan intelligence service, the world now knows of a 1975 speech by Geng Biao, director of the CCP International Liaison Department, in which he said that Taiwan was regarded as a secondary issue and it was important to shelve differences so that both sides (the United States and China) could cope with a far more serious threat.[60] Huang Hua's speech two years later directly pointed out the necessity of winning over the United States "in order to focus our strength to cope with No. 1 enemy—Soviet revisionist social imperialism"; the same position was revealed in an *Asian Wall Street Journal* interview with China's vice–foreign minister in 1977.[61]

As a result, the Chinese were willing to let the Taiwan issue drag on for the sake of antihegemonism. The Chinese strategy was to make sure that their options would be kept open in the future rather than to push for an immediate solution. Deng Xiaoping was quoted as saying, "We cannot commit ourselves to use nothing other than peaceful means to achieve reunification of the motherland. . . . We cannot tie our hands in this matter."[62] Having said this publicly, China nonetheless went ahead to "emphasize" its beloved antihegemonism once again in the 1979 joint communiqué.

It is ironic that once the theme of antihegemonism was officially acknowledged in the communiqué, there was no need to deemphasize the importance of the Taiwan issue. The issue dominated the Sino-U.S. agenda for the next three years. In short, the Taiwan issue is sacrificed when China is recruiting members for its antihegemonic front but is revitalized afterwards to restore consistency. Since the announcement of the independent foreign policy line at the end of 1982, antihegemonism gradually lost its momentum. With *glasnost* and *perestroika* in the Soviet Union, antihegemonism was even less meaningful. On the one hand, there is no need to set aside the Taiwan issue for the sake of antihegemonism; on the other hand, the dominant open-door image forbids pushing the issue.[63]

Taiwan and the Open Door

Because the open door is official policy, the United States has been expected to assist China in its development. On the Taiwan issue, the United States is expected to assume a double role. As it is perceived that there is a new trend toward U.S. protectionism, the United States is expected to force export-oriented Taiwan to depend less on the U.S. market and shift trade to the increasingly open Chinese market. In 1985 one Chinese document suggests, "Under the circumstance of shrinking world markets and rising protectionism in the United States and Western Europe, Taiwanese products will be increasingly dependent on the mainland market as long as we make a good effort. The continuation of this task can effectively manipulate the operation of the Taiwanese economy and speed up unification of the fatherland."[64]

A more active role for the United States is encouraging Taiwan to take advantage of China's open-door policy. In 1984 Deng Xiaoping asked Prime Minister Margaret Thatcher of Britain to tell President Reagan that the United States had much to contribute on the Taiwan issue.[65] General Secretary Hu Yaobang urged the United States to be more assertive in bringing a peaceful solution to the Taiwan issue in 1986,[66] and Zhao Ziyang said in 1988 that the United States should do less to damage bilateral relations (referring to arms sales to Taiwan) and more to help.[67] Although the open-door policy is an important element of China's theme of peaceful coexistence, the policy invites positive role-playing by the United States; the theme discourages such interference. This is why the open-door policy has ushered in a new era for the China–United States–Taiwan triangle.

The Taiwan Drama

China's use of Taiwan may seem confusing, the numerous intentions behind policy on the issue nebulous and even inconsistent. It is therefore interesting to examine the timing of Chinese contention on the Taiwan issue. As Ross has pointed out, the Chinese are conscious of the possibility of achieving a balance of power between the United States and the Soviet Union. During the 1960s the Chinese were relatively silent on the Taiwan issue. A realist could contend that this might have something to do with the perception of superpower collusion on the Sino-Indian border clashes, the nuclear test ban treaty, and simultaneous superpower intervention by the United States in Vietnam and by the Soviet Union in Czechoslovakia. A realist would also argue that China would avoid dealing with both superpowers at the same time. For example, China started serious normalization talks with the Soviet Union in October 1982 only after China had straightened things out with the United States in their August 17 communiqué.

Did not this omission of the Taiwan issue require some justification? An intriguing question related to this is, Have the Chinese ever thought that they could resolve the Taiwan issue even when they are pressing it? And have the Chinese ever seriously considered an armed invasion of Taiwan since the Korean War era? It is clear that in the offshore islands crises, the Chinese did not target Taiwan.[68] They understood that the issue was not going to be resolved in a hasty manner.[69] If pushing the issue rhetorically or symbolically with military pressure on the offshore islands is not a signal of intention to recover Taiwan, then ignoring the issue cannot be taken as a significant change in policy, as intention never existed in the first place.

The motivations behind the Taiwan policy can be understood differently. The issue was raised in 1954 and 1955 when China launched its peace offensive and when the United States was officially committed to

Taiwan's security through a defense treaty. The Taiwan issue was again highlighted in 1958 to show China's independence (since China challenged one superpower without the backing of the other). In the Shanghai communiqué, the Chinese reminded the United States of its imperialism in Taiwan. In an internally circulated document quoted earlier, anti-imperialism was demonstrated by mentioning the communiqué's potential for kicking the United States out of Taiwan in particular and Asia in general. The use of language has changed since 1979, and "imperialism" has fallen out of favor. Nonetheless, criticism of U.S. interference in Chinese affairs on the Taiwan issue exploded again in the early 1980s.

The timing of the theme of anti-imperialism always helps the Chinese express their sense of independence. They say that they are not afraid to damage relations with the United States if their demands on the Taiwan issue are not satisfied. Of course, "satisfied" must be understood in a symbolic sense. They can be satisfied as long as the issue is put abstractly in the context of peaceful coexistence, something the United States has no intention of disputing. After some sort of agreement or understanding is reached, the Chinese then interpret the peace theme in more concrete terms and struggle to demonstrate that they have never compromised their stand. To avoid disrupting antihegemonism (read anti-Sovietism), this anti-imperialist (read anti-U.S.) rhetoric is sometimes restricted to internally circulated documents.

The two sides agree to disagree on the Taiwan issue but actually put the issue into words that both sides can accept. The effect is twofold: outsiders perceive China to be compromising its position, and the Chinese perceive that peace and antihegemonism are simultaneously actualized. Both principled positions can be preserved because the Chinese would first agree to negotiate at a relatively abstract level and save face for both sides. Anti-imperialism, as reflected in China's concern over the Taiwan issue, is then used to illustrate to both the United States and China their unchanged official position. This creates a problem in bilateral relations and, in turn, compels the Chinese to take their own contention seriously.

In short, the timing of rhetorical anti-imperialist struggle on the Taiwan issue manifests China's consistency regarding its principles. Ignoring the issue or dealing with it in an abstract manner is aimed at dramatizing two other equally important principles of peaceful coexistence and antihegemonism. If the Chinese want the world to buy their anti-imperialist worldview but also want to convince everyone that it is all right to have peace with the imperialist and more important to stop hegemonism, then there must be some mechanism to demonstrate that all three views are correct. The Taiwan issue is a ready and familiar weapon in this sense. The issue is picked up not necessarily because the Chinese really want to threaten Taiwan but because their concern looks real to themselves as well as the outside observer. How can Chinese leaders doubt their own intention to recover Taiwan? As a corollary, then, how can they doubt their sincerity on anti-imperialism, peaceful coexistence, and antihegemonism which is evidenced by emphasizing or deemphasizing the Taiwan issue?

A complicating factor in the issue is the open-door policy. U.S. friendliness can be tested by its willingness to contribute to the peaceful resolution of the Taiwan issue. Especially since sanctions were imposed in the wake of the Tiananmen massacre, the test of friendship cannot be passed simply by transferring technology and opening markets. This is because technology and markets are symbiotic with undesirable Western notions of human rights and democracy. By any account the United States should not directly involve itself in the way China handles its own citizens. The Taiwan issue is different because U.S.-Taiwan relations are close and China expects U.S. influence to be effective. The problem is that Taiwan's recent political and economic achievements have become the source of some degree of U.S. pride. Because China assumes the United States will do something there that it is reluctant to do and will not interfere when China does take drastic action against Taiwan, the Taiwan issue will remain a chronic headache for the United States.

PEACEFUL STRUGGLE

The Civilizer States

Peter Van Ness has argued that China and the United States are the world's two civilizer states, states that project their moral image to the world confident of the attractiveness of their high civilization.[70] China's relations with Southeast Asia and the United States' with Latin America are good examples of this conceptualization. After World War II, China provided the model of communism; the United States, democracy and capitalism. Neither side hesitates to grasp an opportunity to demonstrate its moral influence. The interesting question is what happens when the two civilizer states meet.

The irony in their meeting lies in the way that each struggles to prove the other wrong and to have the other confirm its own moral vision. The difficulty for the United States is that Chinese pride is not debatable because, as Lucian Pye so forcefully argues, it derives from the sense of being Chinese rather than being ideologically pure.[71] In the 1980s, for instance, the Chinese said that they were creating a Chinese version of socialism; anyone who tries to find out what that really means is just asking to be confused: the Chinese themselves are not exactly sure what it means. One thing is certain: their socialism is Chinese. How can the U.S. civilizer state have any impact on China if China's greatness is derived from being

Chinese? Since 1983, and particularly in 1989, China's criticisms of the notion of human rights and democracy as "Western" values have been sufficient for the sake of criticism. These values are inappropriate simply because they are not Chinese.

This attitude toward the outside world protects the Chinese moral regime's pretension of being unique and great—you should learn from me, but you will never learn how to be me. The Chinese image of the United States has changed from one of a barbarian to that of the imperialist, but there is psychological continuity in the sense that the outsiders are denied. The open-door policy that is supposed to extract strength from U.S. society can only succeed, accordingly, if technology can be used to construct *Chinese* socialism.

The Chinese would nonetheless like to have the United States confirm Chinese greatness. While they are unable to do this by force, they manipulate words to discipline the imperialists. On the U.S. side, there is hardly the same notion of being American. The United States derives its pride from its system, institutional strength, and the logic of industrialization. The American style is to look for contacts and demonstrate superiority, whereas the Chinese style is to avoid contact and pretend superiority. The United States then looks awkward, invariably appearing to lose the rhetorical game in order to establish contacts with Chinese society. The Bush administration sent secret missions to China, hoping to reopen the country after the Beijing massacre. Critics charged the United States with engaging in kowtow diplomacy. Interestingly, both governments were satisfied since the United States got the contacts and the Chinese kept the pretension.

A civilizer state's policy is a political statement in its ultimate form. The state tries to prove that the world can be made right by projecting its civilization to the world. It portrays the heroes and the villains and leads the charge against the enemy—militarily if possible, but if not, then rhetorically. For the Chinese, the drama is composed of the pretension that the imperialist is declining, whereas in reality the Chinese are seeking help from it; that technology can be Sinicized, whereas in reality it does not possess true nationality; that the U.S. imperialist can be persuaded to be antihegemonist, whereas in reality the United States has made progress on détente; and that peace works against capitalism, whereas in reality socialism is being transformed at an even faster speed.

United Front

The united front strategy has helped the Chinese pretension survive the vicissitudes of world politics. The united front strategy permits cooperation with a secondary enemy in order to cope with a primary one. Peaceful coexistence with the imperialist United States as a secondary enemy is definitely legitimate in this sense. The strategy nonetheless requires some minor form of struggle with the secondary enemy in order to keep it alert to the possibility that it may become the primary enemy if it does not behave correctly. Anti-imperialism is therefore to be expected. Most importantly, the united front strategy can "pull together all struggles and gaps and contradictions which exist in the enemy camps and use them as a weapon of primary importance against the existing enemy."[72] Antihegemonism can then be victorious.

Although most observers would disagree with the Chinese logic and see the change in its alliance network as a play of politics, the united front strategy has been a consistent thread throughout the PRC's history. This is not to say that security concerns are irrelevant; they are actually extremely important. But how one reacts to a perceived physical threat depends on how the threat is conceptualized; this threat conception suggests what to anticipate, real or imagined. There is no question that antihegemonism role conceptions are partially a product of the Sino-Soviet conflict. The conflict has to be understood as a result of the Soviets' earlier failure to pass the Chinese test of anti-imperialist leadership. Antihegemonism creates the illusion that the Chinese are not standing alone against the Soviet Union and that the Soviet Union is the sole enemy of the world's people.

Peace must be achieved with the United States so that the united front can be activated. Peace cannot be attained at the expense of anti-imperialism lest this send the wrong signals to the world, including the Chinese people, about China's moral integrity. The United States is perceived as in decline so the united front strategy is described as mutually beneficial. Of course, the Chinese are confident that the United States needs China more than China needs the United States. Deng Xiaoping's remark that the Americans would come back after the Beijing massacre may sound arrogant, but that is a typical pretension assumed by the moral regime to create a sense of superiority. This type of self-image will definitely be frustrated in the 1990s as the U.S. civilizer state seems to have made great progress in bringing the former Soviet bloc into the world market. Bilateral relations between the two civilizer states may thus become embittered, as the importance of the strategic China card fades—and so, too, the value of China.[73]

Peaceful struggle has been the main feature of Sino-U.S. relations, and the traditional Chinese habit of shaming has been amply reflected therein. To struggle while lacking the ability to do so requires use of the shaming mechanism to demonstrate a determination to struggle. China's fusses over low-level disputes often risk such disputes' getting out of control. Granting political asylum to China's top woman tennis player in 1983, for example, generated what the United States regarded as an unnecessary disruption. The Chinese called President Reagan the "foreign father" of the young player, a self-contradictory term designed to shame (though the president—and the rest of the world—might not have understood such connotations). Struggle over this type of minor incident is psychologically necessary to show the existence of the struggle, which justifies the use of the united front.

Defining the role of the United States in the world is not an easy task. Which role conceptions to apply at a particular moment depends on the larger worldview of Chinese leaders at that time. The way the relationship with the United States is managed also signals to the rest of the world what the Chinese hold to be the correct world order and how justice can be achieved. The significance of Sino-U.S. relations to the symbolic role of the Chinese state in world affairs helps guarantee that the ambivalence embodied in the style of peaceful struggle will continue in the 1990s.

NOTES

1. Quian Quicken, "New China's Diplomacy: 40 Years On," *Beijing Review* (September 25-October 1, 1989): 15.
2. Wang Chunyan and Wu Ximing, "Deng Xiaoping on Peace and War," *Beijing Review* (April 3–9, 1989): 21.
3. Ibid., p. 23.
4. Weiping Zhang, *Two Strategies* (Chongqing: Chongqing Press: 1991), pp. 131–166.
5. Remarks by General Secretary Jiang Zemin quoted by *World Journal* (December 22, 1989): 20.
6. Charles M. Lichenstein, "China in the UN: The Case of Kampuchea," *World Affairs* 149 (Summer 1986).
7. Jiang quoted by *World Journal*, December 22, 1989, p. 20.
8. Remarks by the Chinese foreign minister, Qian Qichen, quoted in *Mainland China Studies* 32, 7 (January 1990): 3.
9. The United States is sometimes referred to as the international opposition force. See, for example, a news report in *World Journal*, January 18, 1990, p. 16.
10. Chunyan Wang and Ximing Wu, "Deng Xiaoping on Peace and War," *Beijing Review* (April 3–9, 1989): 19.
11. Liyu Ni, "On Zhou Enlai's Diplomatic Theory," *Beijing Review* (April 3–9, 1989): 14–15.
12. See the quote in John Gittings, *China and the World* (New York: Harper & Row, 1974), p. 225.
13. Su Zhengxing, "On the Interaction Between Peace and Development," in International Peace Year China Committee (ed.), *Proceedings of International Peace Year Conference* (Beijing: Social Science Literature, 1986), pp. 73–77.
14. See the discussion by Gittings, *China and the World*, pp. 229–230.
15. Chih-yu Shih, *The Spirit of Chinese Foreign Policy: A Psychocultural View* (London: MacMillan, 1990), p. 145.
16. See Samuel Kim, "Whither Post-Mao Chinese Global Policy?" *International Organization* 35, 3 (Summer 1981): 446.
17. See the discussion by Paul H. B. Goodwin, "Soldiers and Statesmen: Chinese Defense and Foreign Policies in the 1990s," in Samuel Kim (ed.), *China and*

the World: New Directions in Chinese Foreign Relations (Boulder: Westview, 1989), pp. 183–188.

18. For bilateral military cooperation, see Steven I. Levine, "Sino-American Relations: Renormalization and Beyond," in Kim, *China and the World,* pp. 96–99.

19. "China's Internal Affairs Brook No Interference," *Beijing Review* (July 31–August 6, 1989): 10–11.

20. Bruce Cummings, "The Political Economy of China's Turn Outward," in Kim, *China and the World,* p. 225.

21. David Richter, "The Foreign Role in Major Projects," *China Business Review,* (May-June 1988): 32.

22. See Wei Ai, "Retrospect and Prospect of Sino-U.S. Economic and Trade Relations," *Mainland China Studies* 32, 6 (December 1989): 26–27.

23. Samuel Kim, "China and the Third World: In Search of a Peace and Development Line," in Kim, *China and the World,* pp. 159–163.

24. Shen-Chi Liu, "Communist China's Policy Toward Studying Abroad," *Mainland China Studies* 33, 3 (September 1980): 57–69.

25. The real reason may be that China expected the United States to postpone the projects as a part of the sanctions imposed on the heels of China's 1989 crackdown on the prodemocracy movement, so it moved first to give the impression that China did not really have to depend on the United States. See Jim Mann, "China Cancels U.S. Deal for Modernizing F-8 Jet," *Los Angeles Times,* May 14, 1990.

26. See the presidential statement on the issuance of the U.S.-PRC communiqué of August 17, 1982, in Lester L. Wolff and David L. Simon (eds.), *Legislative History of the Taiwan Relations Act* (Jamaica, N.Y.: American Association for Chinese Studies, 1982), pp. 314–315.

27. It is reported that the United States indirectly warned the Taiwanese authorities not to supply the *Goddess of Democracy,* an anti-China propaganda ship manned by Chinese prodemocracy dissidents, lest this should agitate China. The United States also allegedly advised France to halt certain military sales to Taiwan, claiming it is easier to maintain regional security in East Asia if the United States is the sole supplier of arms to Taiwan. For the moral implications of the U.S. policy, see the discussion in Jim Hoagland, "China's Protection Racket," *Washington Post,* May 17, 1990, p. A27.

28. See the discussion in Jung-mao Tien (ed.), *Mainland China, Taiwan, and U.S. Policy* (Cambridge, Mass.: Oelgeschlager, Gunn & Hain, 1983); Charles T. Cross, "Taipei's Identity Crisis," *Foreign Policy* 51 (Summer 1983): 47–63; John W. Garver, "Arms Sales, the Taiwan Question, and Sino-U.S. Relations," *Orbis* 26, 4 (Winter 1983): 999–1035; Veng-si Ho, "Chinese Views on U.S. Arms Sales to Taiwan," *Fletcher Forum* 7, 2 (Summer 1983): 373–384; Martin L. Lasater, *Taiwan Facing Mounting Threat* (Washington, D.C.: Heritage Foundation, 1984); Robert A. Scalapino, "Uncertainties in Future Sino-U.S. Relations," *Orbis* 26, 3 (Fall 1982): 681–696; Allen S. Whiting "Sino-American Relations: The Decade Ahead," *Orbis* 26, 3 (Fall 1982): 697–719; Robert G. Sutter, "Taiwan's Future," *Archived Issue Brief of Congressional Research Service* (March 8, 1983); Byron S. J. Weng, "Taiwan's International Status Today,' *China Quarterly* 99 (September 1984): 462–480; A. James Gregor and Maria Hsia Chang, *The Republic of China and U.S. Policy* (Washington, D.C.:Ethics and Public Policy Center, 1985).

29. Melvin Gurtov and Byng-Moo Hwang, *China Under Threat* (Baltimore: Johns Hopkins University Press, 1980), pp. 91–97.

30. Thomas E. Stolper, *China, Taiwan, and the Offshore Islands* (New York: M. E. Sharpe, 1985), pp. 114–139.

31. Gerald Segal, *Defending China* (London: Oxford University Press, 1985), pp. 122–123.

32. Ibid., pp. 118–120.

33. Robert S. Ross, "International Bargaining and Domestic Politics: U.S.-China Relations Since 1972," *World Politics* 38, 2 (January 1986): 255–287.

34. Stolper, *China, Taiwan, and the Offshore Islands*, p. 121.

35. Ibid., p. 35.

36. See Chang Hu, "An Analysis of the Situation in the Taiwan Strait During 1954–5," *Feiching Yuehpao* (Communist bandit information monthly) 27, 12 (June 1985): 13–15.

37. *Literature on Foreign Relations of the People's Republic of China* 5 (Beijing: World Knowledge Press, 1959), pp. 176–177, 181.

38. Stolper, *China, Taiwan, and the Offshore Islands*, pp. 131–132.

39. See the text of the Shanghai communiqué in Hungdah Chiu (ed.), "Normalizing Relations with People's Republic of China: Problems, Analysis and Documents," Occasional Papers/Reprints in *Contemporary Asian Studies* 2, 14 (1978).

40. "The Great Victory of Chairman Mao's Revolutionary Diplomatic Line," in Propaganda Division, Political Department, Kunming Military Region (ed.), *Outline of Education on Situation for Companies* (Kunming: Kunming Military Region, 1973). The text is translated in H. Chiu (ed.), *Normalizing Relations with the People's Republic of China: Problems, Analysis and Documents*, Occasional Papers/Reprints in *Contemporary Asian Studies* 2, 14 (1978), p. 168.

41. "Secret Foreign Policy Speech of Foreign Minister Huang Hua of the People's Republic of China, July 20, 1977," included in H. Chiu, *Normalizing Relations*, pp. 188–189.

42. Western scholars who see power as the essence of politics believe that China made concessions for the sake of countering the Soviet Union. Taiwanese scholars who see Chinese politics as essentially communist believe that China tricked the United States into normalization for the sake of recovering Taiwan. I believe that both views are correct. Chinese policy is by nature ambiguous.

43. "Chairman Hua Gives Press Conference," *Peking Review* (December 22, 1978): 9–11.

44. "Secret Speech of Huang Hua," p. 184.

45. See the text of the Joint Communiqué of August 17, 1982, in Wolff and Simon, *Legislative History*.

46. "Wu Xueqian on Sino-U.S. Relations in Chicago," *Renmin Ribao*, October 16, 1983, p. 6.

47. "Zhao Ziyang Held News Conference in San Francisco," *Renmin Ribao*, January 15, 1984, p. 6.

48. Quoted in *World Journal*, September 26, 1989, p. 8.

49. Richard Moorsteen and Morton Abramowitz, *Remaking China Policy: U.S.-China Relations and Governmental Decisionmaking* (Cambridge: Harvard University Press, 1971), pp. 103–104.

50. Jonathan Pollack, *Security, Strategy, and the Logic of Chinese Foreign Policy* (Berkeley: Institute of East Asian Studies, University of California, 1981), pp. 34–35.

51. Robert L. Worden, "Taiwan: A Crucial Question in United States-China Relations, in Chiu, *Normalizing Relations*, p. 62.

52. Ibid., pp. 63–64.

53. Kunming Military Region, "The Great Victory," p. 167.

54. King C. Chen, "Peking's Attitude Toward Taiwan," in Chiu, *Normalizing Relations*, p. 36.

55. "Interview of Vice-Premier Deng Xiaoping by U.S. TV Commentators," *Peking Review* (February 16, 1979): 19.

56. "Secret Speech of Huang Hua," p. 187.

57. See the text of the Shanghai communiqué in Chiu, "Normalizing Relations."

58. Kunming Military Region, "The Great Victory," p. 167.

59. Hungdah Chiu, "Normalizing Relations with China: Some Practical and Legal Problems," *Asian Affairs, an American View* 5, 2 (November-December 1977): 83.

60. See "Keng Pia's Talks on 'A Turning Point in China-U.S. Diplomatic Relations,'" *Chinese Law and Government* 10, 1 (Spring 1977), pp. 101-105.

61. Warren H. Phillips, "Peking's Posture," *Asian Wall Street Journal*, October 20, 1977, p. 1.

62. Wolff and Simon, *Legislative History*, p. 68.

63. Ross's theory that the importance of the Taiwan issue on the Chinese agenda depends on China's bargaining position is irrelevant here exactly because his analysis ignores the element of policy motivation. The changing power balance in the world since the mid-1980s has witnessed no significant change in China's Taiwan policy partly because the world is not perceived solely in power terms by the Chinese.

64. Chang Jong-feng, "An Analysis of Factors Affecting Trade Between the Two Sides of the Taiwan Straits via Hong Kong," *Mainland China Studies* 31, 8 (February 1989): 42.

65. *Renmin Ribao*, December 12, 1984, pp. 1, 2.

66. *Central Daily News* (overseas edition), November 26, 1986, summarizes Hu's interview with the *Far Eastern Economic Review* on July 20 and with the *Washington Post* on September 23.

67. Ching Nin, "The United States and China's United Front with Taiwan," *Mainland China Studies* 30, 6 (December 1988): 19.

68. Besides the aforementioned works, also see Allen Whiting, "New Light on Mao," *China Quarterly* 62 (June 1975), pp. 263-270.

69. Stolper, *China, Taiwan, and the Offshore Islands*, p. 120.

70. Peter Van Ness, "The Civilizer State," University of Denver, 1985, mimeograph.

71. Lucian Pye, *The Spirit of Chinese Politics* (Cambridge: MIT Press, 1968), pp. 50–66.

72. Kunming Military Region, "The Great Victory," p. 166.

73. For relevant discussion, see Michael Yahuda, "Sino-American Relations," in Gerald Segal (ed.), *Chinese Politics and Foreign Policy Reform* (New York: Kegan Paul International, 1990), pp. 180–194.

6

UNEASY NEIGHBORS: CHINA'S JAPAN SCRIPT

There is no doubt that Sino-Japanese relations underwent a tumultuous transformation as a result of World War II. Early scholarship presumes that relations between the two are completely different from what they were before the war. Consequently, little scholarly attention is paid to the possibility that the mode of bilateral relations has not really experienced a change per se.[1] Sino-Japanese relations are quite unlike those between China and the United States or Russia because of the historical image and the associated role expectations the Chinese have of Japan. Contemporary Chinese images of the United States and the Soviet Union are of slight historical relevance because the two were considered to be culturally alien a mere century ago. The Japanese, in contrast, belong to the same racial group and have a similar culture. China's long relationship with Japan constrains the Chinese perception of Japan's role in current world politics and is therefore not totally subject to ideologically and politically motivated role conceptions. Changes in rhetoric and mode of interaction since World War II have to be understood within this context.

Japan's rise to world-power status after the Russo-Japanese War was received with ambivalence in China, and Japanese economic success since World War II has obviously evoked similar emotions. The emerging likeness between these two periods could indicate that Japan's postwar dependence on the United States may be regarded as an easily forgotten episode over the long run. Should the Chinese regard the Japanese success story as an Oriental achievement? Or would this be too embarrassing for the culturally superior Chinese, as they see themselves, to acknowledge? Could such embarrassment stir anti-Japanese emotions in China? As a result of the Chinese sense of superiority vis-à-vis Japan, Japan's rise has been a disturbing variable in China's quest for justice. The inability to co-opt Japan into China's scheme of justice combined with the psychological need to make sense of Japan's success relative to China's failure brings uncertainty to East Asia. Against this background, China's effort to organize the East Asian order according to its numerous moral principles is destined to appear ambivalent. Ironically, Chinese leaders have consistently found Japan to be one of the most convenient targets for dramatically demonstrating their commitment to exactly those principles.

A BITTER HISTORY

Breakdown of Harmony

Although historical interaction between China and Japan was limited, the two countries coexisted harmoniously in the fundamental sense that Japan did not challenge China's nominal leadership.[2] China's pretension of being the moral symbol of all under heaven could be maintained largely because the two countries rarely encountered the rest of the world. Even after East Asia was forcibly opened up by the West in the mid-nineteenth century, this somewhat outdated self-image continued to prevail in China, notably its notion of rightful East Asian hierarchy. The persistence of this image was understandable. The Koreans were traditionally subject to Chinese suzerainty, and the Japanese were regarded as "dwarf pirates." It became imperative for the Chinese, faced with Western denial of their moral leadership, to protect the East Asian order so as to maintain that leadership at least at face value. A nominal international order seems to mean more and more as its survival becomes less and less plausible.

Japan was able to transform humiliation in its encounter with the West into an all-embracing modernization movement in part because there existed no pretension of innate superiority. This Westernization led to one fundamental question about Japan's true identity: Was Japan unique in any sense? The answer lay in either Westernism or Japanism. A taste of power was nonetheless psychologically necessary for both notions to make sense. As Kenneth Pyle puts it, "military victories, territorial acquisition, and wartime unity helped relieve anxieties over cultural identity."[3] To colonize an East Asian country in the way that the Western colonial powers had done must have been an attractive option for Japan after it so easily defeated China in 1895. The famous Fukuzawa escape from Asia of 1885 was quoted by Pyle to illustrate the original wave of Westernism (all-round Westernization): "It follows that in making our preset plans we have no time to await the development of neighboring countries and join them in reviving Asia. Rather, we should escape from them and join the company of Western civilized nations. Although China and Korea are our neighbors, this fact should make no difference in our relations with them. We should deal with them as Westerners do. If we keep bad company, we cannot avoid a bad name."[4]

Had it not been for the triple intervention that forced Japan to return newly acquired territories to China, Japan would have joined the ranks of the Western colonial powers. Having been shut out by the West, Japan was suddenly but bitterly aware of its inevitable role as leader in the Orient; the rise of Japanese nationalism was needed as an outlet. As argued in Chapter 2, a new worldview can be most effectively demonstrated by altering a long-term neighborly relationship, in this case with China. After the triple intervention, the conception of neighborly relations shifted immensely. Instead of colonizing Asia, Japan had to modernize Asia. Another quote by Pyle is useful here: "Japan had a mission to extend the blessings of political organization throughout the rest of East Asia and the South Pacific, 'just as the Romans had once done for Europe and the Mediterranean.' Among East Asian peoples 'only the Japanese have the ability for political organization; only the Japanese understand the concept of the nation state.'[5]

In contrast, China was in a state of disarray during this period. The defeat of 1895 enabled conservative court officials to purge the forces of modernization. The conservatives could comfort themselves that the defeat had proved Westernization incapable of solving China's problem—the Oriental (i.e., Japanese) solution had proved more effective. This and various other developments culminated in the Boxer Rebellion of 1900. The absurd pretension that Chinese shadowboxing could counter Western firepower was too bewildering to resist yet resulted in a total defeat and the loss of any post-1895 residual national pride. Many Chinese saw Japan as a perfect model and sought to duplicate the apparent success of constitutionalism there. The collapse of the East Asian hierarchy therefore created the opportunity for more cooperative relationships among the various countries of the region.

The East Asian Coprosperity Sphere

Pan-Asianism. Japan's identity problem was essentially solved when world-power status was bestowed upon Tokyo in the wake of Russia's defeat in 1905, but the Chinese role was still unclear. There was no doubt that the fate of Japan was linked to a strong Asia, but there were two possible parts that China could play for Japan. The underlying feeling was nonetheless Pan-Asian: the Japanese military saw itself as a developer of China; Japanese radicals assisted in China's nationalist revolution; Japanese politicians and citizens were generally interested in Chinese affairs. Chinese and Japanese clearly agreed that Japan could and should provide assistance to China. The ultimate question was, Should China be treated as an equal or as a subordinate?

From the Chinese point of view, Japanese brotherhood was welcome. After the 1895 war, the monarchists (Kang Youwei and Liang Qichao), the warlords (Zhang Zuolin and Duan Qirei), and the revolutionaries (Sun Yat-sen) all turned to Japan for support.[6] Sun Yat-sen glorified Pan-Asianism in this way: "We Asiatics must emancipate Asia and the down-trodden states of Europe and America from European and American oppression. Japan and China must join hands and harmoniously lead the Asiatics to fight for a greater Asiaticism, thus expediting world-peace."[7]

This Pan-Asianism continued even after Japan's colonial ambitions became clear to many Chinese. The most famous example is probably that of Tang Shaoyi, who, during the second Sino-Japanese War, still urged Japan to "hold her own on the Asiatic continent against European aggressors" until international interference "ceases to exist in Asia."[8]

Indeed, after its 1895 victory, and more so after the 1905 Russo-Japanese War, Japan became a model for China. In 1905, 8,000 Chinese students went to study in Japan, compared with 1,300 the previous year.[9] Japan's intervention in China had little impact on the movement of students. In 1936, for example, there were still about 5,000 to 6,000 students in Japan.[10] The belief that Japan could aid China and the willingness of many Japanese to provide help certainly contributed to the strength of Pan-Asianism.

On the Japanese side, former foreign minister Mamoru Shigemitsu's conception of China's role, for example, was consistent with the notion of Pan-Asianism. He considered complete Chinese sovereignty to be in the interest of Japan, and if Japan could assist China restore its sovereignty, China would eventually become dependent on Japan.[11] Some in the Japanese military also saw Pan-Asianism as a legitimate rationale for an aggressive policy in China. Whichever way one looked at it, Japan had to save China. For General Iwane Matsui, the Sino-Japanese dispute "was always a fight between brothers within the 'Asian Family.'" His statement portrays (perhaps in somewhat overstated terms) the nature of Sino-Japanese relations within what was called the Great East Asian Co-prosperity Sphere, a sort of economic bloc in East Asia led by Japan: "we love them too much. It is just the same as in a family when an elder brother has taken all that he can stand from his ill-behaved younger brother and has to chastise him in order to make him behave properly.[12]

Who led whom. It was exactly this elder-younger notion that led to the bitter showdown between brothers. And this trivial contention about who was the elder highlights the delicate nature of social role play and how irksome a particular role expectation can become in the international organizational process. From the realist point of view, the second Sino-Japanese War may not make sense judging from the degree of interdependence the two countries had built up since the beginning of the twentieth century. Japanese investment in China increased from $1 million in 1902 to almost $1.4 billion in 1936, and the Japanese share of total foreign investment in China went from less than 1 percent to 40 percent over the same period (see Table 6.1). In concrete terms, in 1919 about 4 percent of the textile looms in China were Japanese; by 1936 that number had increased to 88 percent. Coal from Japanese-owned mines represented 20 percent of total production in China in 1918, 40 percent in 1937 (see Table 6.2). The number of Japanese firms and Japanese nationals in China witnessed similar expansion, as shown in Table 6.3.

Table 6.1   Japanese Investment in China

	1902	1914	1931	1936
Investment in $ millions	1.0	219.6	1,136.9	1,394.0
Percentage of total foreign investment	(0.1)	(13.6)	(35.1)	(40.0)

Source: Developed from Chi-ming Hou, *Foreign Investment and Economic Development in China, 1840–1937*, Harvard Eastern Asian Series 21 (Cambridge: Harvard University Press, 1965), p. 17.

Table 6.2   Japanese Capital in Cotton Textile, Shipping, and Coal Production in China (as percentage of total foreign capital in China)

	Looms	Yarn Spindles	Coal	Shipping
1897	0	0	—	2.5
1918	—	—	20	—
1919	39	58	—	—
1922	52	71	25	—
1924	58	79	28	32
1928	85	90	35	34
1935	85	90	35	—
1936	88	91	40	—
1937	—	—	40	—

Source: Developed from Chi-ming Hou, *Foreign Investment and Economic Development in China, 1840–1937*, Harvard Eastern Asian Series 21 (Cambridge: Harvard University Press, 1965), pp. 61, 88, 231.

Table 6.3   Estimated Number of Japanese Firms and Residents in China
(percentage in parentheses)

	Firms		Residents
1903	361	(28)	5,287
1906	739	(40)	15,548
1909	1,492	(53)	55,401
1911	1,283	(45)	78,306
1913	1,269	(33)	80,219
1916	1,858	(39)	104,275
1918	4,483	(65)	159,950
1921	6,141	(65)	144,434
1936	—	(—)	435,381

Sources: Albert Feurwerker, *The Foreign Establishment in China in the Early Twentieth Century*, Michigan Papers in Chinese Studies 29 (Ann Arbor: Center for Chinese Studies, University of Michigan, 1976), p. 17; E. B. Schumpeter, "Industrial Development and Government Policy, 1930–1940," in E. B. Schumpeter (ed.), *The Industrialization of Japan and Manchukuo, 1930–1940* (New York: Macmillan, 1940), p. 78.

It was clear who the theoretical leader was. The Chinese contention for leadership, or simply equal status, cannot be understood rationally, since their material interests were so dependent on Japanese support. But Japanese efforts were hardly appreciated in China because the style of Japanese involvement seemed to deny China's self-perceived role in East Asia. Of course, there was no absolute consensus either in China or in Japan as to the correct East Asian order. As the situation developed in Japan, it became increasingly obvious that Shigemitsu's and Kanji Ishiwara's dovish approach was thoroughly absent from the military-dominated decisionmaking process. Not only had the time passed "when other powers or the League of Nations can exercise their policies for the exploitation of China," but Japan had to "act and decide *alone* what is good for China."[13]

It was precisely this Japanese sense of mission that disillusioned Chinese nationalists and pan-Asianists alike. But it is not clear what Chiang Kai-shek's view of the East Asian order was at that time. During the 1930s, his chief preoccupation was consolidating his still shaky regime within the context of warlordism. His strategy seemed to be to placate the Japanese in order to gain time to cement domestic unity, ironically increasing Japanese suspicion and aggression. From the Chinese perspective, it was without a doubt that the Japanese failed the Chinese test of brotherhood. From the twenty-one demands of 1916 to the 1931 Mukden incident, each Japanese intervention in China provoked massive demonstrations, boycotts, and strikes and fostered anti-Japanese sentiments. In order to gain time, Chiang's regime took the Mukden incident to the League of Nations—the first time in Chinese history that China sought international mediation on its own initiative. In a statement issued on November 8, 1931, the Chinese government urged other powers to send "representatives to observe [the] real situation on [the] spot and to secure evidence of flagrant violations of [the] Council's resolution by Japan."[14]

Both the conciliatory approach of the government and the anti-Japanese sentiments of the people alarmed the Japanese. How could the elder brother make sense of the younger brother's seeking help from outside the family or his sons' and daughters' rebelling against their uncle? The implication could be no clearer: either there was no East Asian hierarchy or Japan was not a worthy leader. The vicious circle had started: Japan resorted to harsher discipline in order to curb deviant behavior in the East Asian order, which led the Chinese to realize the utter bankruptcy of Japan's Asianism, which in turn provoked stronger emotive reactions, begetting increased Japanese sanctions. While Pan-Asianism promoted mutual dependence, incongruent mutual role expectations made such dependence senseless. Interdependence had to be sacrificed in the short run to dramatize determination to maintain the integrity of each partner's notions of correct order.

These processes of seeing the emergence, evolution, and exacerbation of incongruent role conceptions; of experiencing anxiety and frustration; and of continuously dramatizing one's own role conception through drastic means shed light on the marginal relevance of power calculus in the outbreak of war. High mutual expectations were followed by frustration. Chinese nationalism, which sought to assert China's equal status, overwhelmed Chiang's realist anxiety of Communist insurgence. Asianism in Japan, which sought to rectify the East Asian hierarchy and China's and Japan's roles therein, inevitably responded vehemently with military invasion.

Collapse of neighborly relations. Throughout China, Sino-Japanese conflict led to a groundswell of patriotism. And yet Chiang remained more concerned about communist insurgency and led a passive, not assertive, war effort that he labeled "resistance." He continued negotiation, through German mediation, with the Japanese military and at one point nearly reached an agreement that would have acknowledged Japanese occupation of north China; later Japanese victory on the battlefield mooted the agreement. Nevertheless, Chiang's efforts to secure a peaceful solution through a Japanese navy connection continued until 1941.[15] Lack of a clear worldview and role conceptions obscured any meaning behind the war, if indeed there had ever been one. Chiang's calculus was still realist in that he deliberately preserved his strength for the final showdown with the Communists. He was forced to lead the war against Japan because his realist yet soft attitude made no sense to his compatriots. It was not until the United States joined the Pacific War that Chiang officially cast his lot with the Allies, from that moment on aware of China's emerging leadership status in the war. While military strategy became relatively active, more important was the development of a worldview: Chiang now saw his China as the leader of an East Asian hierarchy whose final victory he could foresee as early as 1942. In the end, as a traditional Oriental leader would normally do, Chiang agreed to forgive Japan after the war as long as the latter acknowledged its mistake. Chiang would use his virtue (*de*) to make up for Japan's bitterness (*yuan*).

Before either side could formulate a grand notion of a new East Asian order, the area's political scene witnessed drastic changes. Japan was occupied by U.S. troops after the 1945 surrender. With the total bankruptcy of its East Asian Coprosperity Sphere, Japan was ready to receive instruction from whichever nation was willing to assume leadership, and that was the United States. The U.S. view therefore would determine the Japanese view; Japan would be the faithful junior partner of the United States in East Asia. In the meantime, after the Communists look over China following a four-year civil war, Mao decided in 1949 that China would lean to the side of the Soviet Union. The role of the new China would be defined by socialism instead of Asianism. The East Asian order collapsed not because the war had continued or because bitter prewar feelings had resulted in mutual distrust, but because neither side had developed new role expectations for the other. Henceforth, there was no need to examine in detail what the other was doing in order to confirm one's own value. The two ceased to interact with one another. In fact, this lack of mutual role assignment or interaction dramatized to some extent their newly acquired meaning of nationhood under socialism and capitalism respectively. The Cold War image replaced neighborly relations.

NEIGHBORING STRANGERS

The chances for improving international organizational processes in East Asia looked meager in the 1950s. The Cold War had built an invisible wall between the two East Asian neighbors. From the realist point of view, this was because the two superpowers dominated the international stage and disallowed the development of substantial bilateral interaction between China and Japan. In addition, there were no longer Japanese investment activities in China to provide incentive for renewing neighborly relations. Nevertheless, if one examines the bilateral relationship closely, one finds the implicit yet constantly extant assumption in the two societies that Sino-Japanese neighborly relations should be cherished; Pan-Asianism apparently lingered. Later, this chapter illustrates that the Chinese were particularly fond of manipulating this presumed desire for better relations to dramatize higher-level role expectations and worldviews. The Cold War was undermined by those Chinese who were interested in resuming a neighborly relationship rather than straightforwardly opposing Japan as the Cold War required. Policy statements from China revealed that the Chinese intended to cooperate with their East Asian neighbor. The subsequent decision to sacrifice their bilateral relationship could therefore be utilized to shame the Japanese government for not being a good neighbor and express China's sincerity in pursuing morality in world politics. What has blocked development of relations since the end of the war is this pursuit of a moral role that enlivens the realist notion of the Cold War in East Asia.

For the Japanese, even though they lost the war, coordination among East Asian countries still seemed all too natural. It is clear now that the leading Yoshida group, going against the predilection of Secretary of State John Foster Dulles toward containment, had always pushed for accommodating China in postwar East Asian international relations. Since the Japanese had officially and willingly (just look at the peaceful welcome accorded U.S. troops by the Japanese people) accepted the U.S. worldview as theirs, Yoshida's preoccupation with economic revival and its China implications (i.e., market and resources) were never formalized into a contending worldview. The policy of isolating China was therefore adopted against Japan's own interests. One could say that Japanese interests were sacrificed for the sake of the Cold War. It was a sacrifice exactly because Japan cherished its relationship with China but had to shelve it because it was a value incompatible with Cold War realism. Cold War realism was undermined in the long run because it was preserved by reluctantly abandoning the values that came into conflict with it.

When opportunities for better Sino-Japanese relations emerged later in the 1970s, excitement overwhelmed caution about likely incongruence in mutual role expectations. A simple quest for better cooperation is too hazy a concept to provide effective guidance. Later, this general vagueness in role expectations proved to be insufficient to enhance coordination in East Asia, and it was costly. Efforts to reestablish an East Asian order were doomed to be frustrated because of the inevitable yet unpredicted incongruence of role expectations. This leads back to the earlier point that vagueness does not promote organization in the long run whereas clarity often hurts it in the short run.

Anti-imperialism

Tokyo's U.S. policy made it unlikely that the Chinese could get anything of substance out of Japan. Despite the cultural and ethnic kinship between the two peoples, Japan fell into the imperialist camp. Ironically, Japan would thus become a symbolically useful foreign policy element for China. Since China was unable to strike out against the imperialist directly, it might target the imperialist agent in Asia. It would be politically possible and psychologically impressive to win the hearts of the Japanese people and convert the Japanese government. The East Asian order had to be reestablished, but this goal could be sacrificed in the short run to demonstrate China's determination to adhere to correct principles if the Japanese government refused to comply with Chinese anti-imperialism. (In the East Asian context, anti-imperialism would mean two things: U.S. troop withdrawal from Japan and recognition of China rather than Taiwan.) The main thrust of China's Japan policy in the 1950s was to wait for the Japanese government's "reactionary policy" to be abandoned and the Japanese people's anti-imperialist sentiments to be stirred. This stress on the people explains the cautious, moderate nature of China's Japan policy during that decade. It also reflects the lack of role expectation from the Chinese side: Japan was not an essential part of China's quest for justice in this period. East Asia had ceased to be a meaningful locus for international organizational processes.

Power politics cannot completely explain China's lukewarm attitude toward Japan. As argued earlier, the values of a nation determine the meaning of power politics rather than the other way around. China's insensitivity toward a new East Asian order was not only a result of the Cold War, but also a result of the lack of a meaningful role expectation. The case of Taiwan illustrates this point: the Cold War drew the line of containment between China and Taiwan just as it did between China and Japan. If the Cold War had been all-important, China's Japan and Taiwan policies should have been similar. But China had a clear role conception of Taiwan yet none for Japan. China's constant harassment of Nationalist troops occupying the offshore islands suggests that the psychological need to prove one's ability to actualize the correct order cannot be negated by rational calculations of power. Why, then, was there no role expectation for Japan? The reason was a combination of disappointment with Japanese militarism during the war, the outbreak of the Chinese civil war, the U.S. occupation of Japan, and the lack of interaction between the two neighbors. This lack of mutual expectations made the separation of the two neighbors understandable during the Cold War. It would be interesting to examine how Chinese anti-imperialism gradually specified Japan's role in China's emerging notion of East Asian order and how the Chinese expressed their expectations through policies and statements.

Based upon anti-imperialist resolution, the Japanese Communists waged a determined struggle against the U.S. imperialist with the ultimate goal of expulsion of all U.S. troops from Japan. To demonstrate its friendship, China initiated Japanese repatriation even though the two sides had yet to sign a formal peace treaty.[16] In 1952 China and Japan signed an unofficial trade agreement, renewed the following year, and in 1954 a Chinese Red Cross delegation visited Japan. The number of Japanese visitors to China increased rapidly. This people-to-people diplomacy was juxtaposed against Chinese complaints about the Japanese government. It was clearly understood in China that Japanese foreign policy was dominated by the United States and concern over the Cold War. The Chinese government rarely took the Japanese government as its direct counterpart. China's task was to enlighten the Japanese people as to their historical responsibility and hope their government would respond to such pressure. According to Zhou Enlai, fifteen trade and fishing agreements were signed with Japan between 1952 and 1956, so, "inevitably, the impact on the Japanese government was increasingly impressive."[17]

The Japanese government had to pass two tests before it could win the hearts of the Chinese (and, presumably, the Japanese) people. First, it had to forgo diplomatic recognition of Nationalist Taiwan. U.S. support of Nationalist Taiwan was regarded as hard evidence of imperialism, and in recognizing the Nationalists, the Japanese government had only half-heartedly followed the U.S. lead. This pro-imperialist posture had to change before normalization could proceed. In fact, Zhou Enlai once proposed a collective peace pact for the Pacific region and indicated that the San Francisco peace treaty (signed by Japan and Nationalist Taiwan but not China) was not necessarily an obstacle to normalization. In 1957 a joint statement issued by the Japanese Socialist Party and Chinese People's Institute of Foreign Affairs proposed that "certain existing agreements between the people's organizations of the two countries, together with matters on which agreement might be reached, should be developed into agreements between the two governments at an earliest possible date."[18] But despite making proposals and concrete efforts to improve bilateral relations, China was ready to sacrifice everything if Japan refused to cut diplomatic ties with Nationalist Taiwan.

In 1957 Japanese premier Shinsuke Kishi visited both the United States and Taiwan. The following year, China broke off trade with Japan on the pretext (a perfectly justifiable one from the Chinese standpoint) that Japan denied the Chinese trade office the right to fly its national flag. Trade was resumed immediately after Kishi left office in 1959 and the Japanese Export-Import Bank agreed to finance Chinese purchases of Japanese goods. These incidents and China's criticism of Kishi sent the message that China was ready to normalize bilateral relations, had strived for that goal, yet was compelled to forgo it because the Japanese government was still pro-imperialist. China's pursuit of new a relationship with its neighbor was therefore a kind of dramatization: all China's efforts could be sacrificed to express its requirement that the new East Asian order be anti-imperialist. Shame on the Japanese government for wasting all those friendly endeavors!

China's insistence that politics and economics could not be separated stood in direct opposition to Yoshida's concept that Japan's political overtures to the United States should not hinder its economic role. Politicization can be a meaningful gesture, however, only if economic relations are allowed to develop, regardless of politics, so that there will be something of value to sacrifice later. Politicization has little meaning without such economic sacrifice. That China's Japan policy looked ambivalent had much to do with the dominance of the Yoshida group in Japanese politics. Yoshida's disciples contended that Japan, regardless of its actions, was too weak to damage U.S. containment policy; hence, the inclination to advance economically while paying only lip service to the cause of containment was reflected in the Japanese business sector's active exploration of opportunities in China. The Yoshida doctrine therefore paved the way for the Chinese to make an assertive sacrifice. So whenever the Chinese government appeared to be friendly toward the Japanese, businesspeople advanced with official acquiescence. When business relations reached a certain plateau, the Chinese sacrificed them in order to put pressure on the Japanese government.

Politics and economics can be separated only if rhetorical respect for political principles is properly and publicly addressed; at least there should be no open violation of China's principled positions. For the Chinese, developing people-to-people relations is a good way of influencing the opponent. However, relations must be discontinued as soon as the Japanese government violates the moral code, as China detests being seen as driven by material interests at the expense of moral integrity. It is ironic that the Japanese tend to ignore Chinese feelings whenever there is improvement in relations—exactly at that most sensitive point when China would like to determine if the other side has abused newly developed relations. Once the Japanese recognize economic value they are willing to ignore any political stand; in contrast, once the Chinese recognize political position, they are willing to pursue any economic venture despite its political implications. The different premises of the two approaches explain the difference in their policies regarding anti-imperialism.

The second test the Japanese government had to pass concerned the renouncement of militarism. When the security treaty between the United States and Japan was renewed in 1960, mass protest rallies were staged in Beijing. During the Cultural Revolution, accusations of militarism against the Japanese government reached fever pitch. Premier Eisaku Sato's 1969 indication of a Japanese interest in Taiwan's security immediately unleashed a new wave of accusations from China. Even when the two sides finally normalized diplomatic relations in 1972, Zhou Enlai still wanted to remind the Japanese of their historical militarism: "in the half century after 1894, owing to the Japanese militarists' aggression against China, the Chinese people were made to endure tremendous disasters. . . . The past not forgotten is a guide for the future; we should firmly bear the experience and the lesson in mind. . . ."[19] In contrast, in his toast at the same reception, Kakuei Tanaka stated that "we should not forever linger in the dim blind alley of the past."[20] In the 1980s China was alarmed at the possible revival of Japanese militarism. The bilateral relationship was reevaluated in both countries because of this issue.

Instead of detailing the correct East Asian order, China viewed Japan in the 1950s and the 1960s in the larger context of Chinese anti-imperialist rhetoric. Japan's role performance, however, had only marginal relevance to China's own role performance precisely because the Chinese did not really expect the Japanese people to achieve very much under U.S. protection. In the meantime, although the two sides were supposedly in opposite camps, the level of animosity was far from intense. Pan-Asianism no doubt played an important role in alleviating ideological confrontation. In truth, China's leaning to the side of the Soviet Union was not totally voluntary, nor was Japan's reliance on the United States. Interestingly, the division of East Asia by a line of containment did not result in the direct confrontation that a realist would probably assume. Without a clear vision of East Asian order, confrontation served no purpose and made no sense. On the contrary, it provided time for each side to forget the bitter past and reflect upon historical miscommunications surrounding Pan-Asianism. Anti-imperialism as a general principle was thus vague enough to allow low-intensity, low-level interaction and was acceptable to the Japanese, who decided to ignore political rhetoric for the sake of economic interests.

Peaceful Coexistence

In the aftermath of the Great Leap Forward, the moderates Liu Shaoqi and Deng Xiaoping took over the reins of national political and administrative affairs from Mao Zedong, and a distinctive national role conception emerged in China. Liu allegedly advocated reconciliation with imperialism and reactionary regimes and played down the role of the Third World in Chinese diplomacy, though anti-imperialism continued to be useful in interpreting regional conflicts.[21] For example, the Sino-Indian conflict of 1962 was presented as the result of manipulation by the U.S. imperialist. On the whole, in this post–Great Leap Forward period of adjustment and consolidation, China was ready to deal with any country or any social system. Partly to demonstrate unreasonableness on the part of India in the border clashes, China managed to resolve disputes with all its other small neighbors in the region, including Burma and Nepal.

In 1962 Sino-Japanese trade once again reached the level of the early 1950s in terms of the proportion of overall Chinese trade. In 1964 the figure was almost 10 percent, and by 1966 it approached 15 percent. During the Cultural Revolution, though absolute volume decreased, that proportion remained steady. In 1963 the two sides established a China-Japan Friendship Association, which became a model for later people-to-people contacts with other countries. One task of the association was to facilitate an atmosphere conducive to normalization. With respect to commerce, the unofficial Japan-China overall trade agreement was concluded in 1962 and remained in effect for five years, replaced by the annual memorandum trade talks. In the following year, a fisheries agreement was signed, and in 1964 China opened a trade office in Tokyo, even though Japan-based U.S. troops were fighting in Indochina.

Peaceful coexistence as a policy guideline was not inconsistent with anti-imperialist role conceptions, both stressed the importance of people's diplomacy. Both served to exert pressure on the Japanese government. Asia-watchers tend to overemphasize the importance of such growth, though the increase did not compromise the Chinese anti-imperialist stance for several reasons:

> The improvement was probably attributed to the spill over effect of the expansion of the Japanese foreign trade section rather than to China's own efforts. China made no attempt to curtail Japan's share in its market for many possible reasons. First, the bilateral trade could be useful in effecting an estrangement between Japan and the United States. Second, foreign trade was not an important element in China's economy. Third, Japan's economic activity did not carry a colonial implication as it did in Manchukuo in the first half of this century. Japan was seen as a neighbor with no evil intention. Last but not least, Japan's increasing share was by no means an obstacle in China's search for an identity.[22]

Most importantly, however, the Chinese government still had the option of sacrificing people's diplomacy in order to show how much it cherished the correct political order. By exerting pressure on the Japanese government, Beijing deliberately ignored trends in Japanese politics that called for normalization. In 1964, for example, impressed by French diplomatic recognition of China, the Japanese diet turned down Zhou Enlai's proposal for ambassadorial talks by only a narrow margin. This was a clear indicator of a change of mood in Japan, but China refused to capitalize on it. In contrast, China quickly noted Japanese conservatives' occasional symbolic overtures to Taiwan. However, China showed no sign of acknowledging efforts by Yoshimi Furui and Seiichi Tagawa, men who risked their political careers by accepting what were, from the Japanese perspective, humiliating agreements written by the Chinese.[23]

The Japanese, for their part, tried to highlight the value of peace, with an eye on U.S. failure in Vietnam. Peace would promote business, and business would help avoid politics. Regarding Japan's mission in East Asia, a political scientist at Tokyo University concluded in 1976 that Japan's tasks should be "to improve relations with the communist countries of Asia . . . , to revoke the anti-communist overtones from bilateral and regional arrangement . . . , and to maintain strict neutrality *vis-à-vis* the Sino-Soviet conflict."[24]

It is clear that both sides were strategically ready for normalization. What hampered such a move was China's insistence that Japan satisfy certain Chinese role expectations that were incompatible with Japan's self-image. For the Chinese, toleration of U.S. imperialism in Taiwan was unthinkable. The Chinese peaceful coexistence approach could not offset the minimum anti-imperialist request that Japan dump Taiwan and prove its sincerity by recognizing China's full sovereignty over the island. The Japanese, however, strove to extract economics from politics and hoped that they could pay lip service to Cold War rhetoric while edging toward the process of normalization. The self-defined Japanese role as U.S. junior partner did not permit Japan carte blanche to redefine the existing East Asian order. Unfortunately, rhetorical redefinition was a high priority for the Chinese. Contrary to popular impressions, the conservative Sato government in Japan not only laid the groundwork for normalization but actually made such an offer to China in 1972. Zhou Enlai rejected the proposal solely on the grounds that the offer was from the conservative Sato cabinet. China would rather wait for (and in effect made an implicit request for) a less conservative, pro-China premier.[25] The gesture was clearly theatrical, as China agreed to receive Nixon a year later despite his pro-Taiwan record.

Official normalization eventually took place in 1972, after Nixon had publicly opened the door for the Japanese. His junior partner could now confidently and openly proceed with normalization without fear about role implications for the United States. Sato was replaced by Tanaka, who visited Beijing to complete the normalization process. At the reception Zhou highlighted the idea of peaceful coexistence. His toast of "seeking common ground on major points while reserving difference on minor points" sounded less resolute than Tanaka's call to overcome "divergence of view" and reach "agreement in the spirit of seeking common ground on major questions and of mutual understanding and mutual accommodation."[26]

In the joint normalization communiqué, the Japanese reproached themselves for what they had done to the Chinese people during World War II. The Chinese then forgave the Japanese by renouncing war indemnity demands. This exchange allowed the Chinese to pretend that the peace agreement between Japan and Nationalist Taiwan never enjoyed legal status, even though China was not prepared to seek reparations in the first place. Since Japanese militarism was implicitly regretted, there was no need for the Chinese to be fussy about the U.S.-Japan security treaty. A sense of returning to normalcy was confirmed by asserting that "the abnormal state of affairs" was terminated.[27] The Japanese government now respected the Chinese claim to Taiwan, hence Chinese acquiescence to de facto relations between Japan and Taiwan.[28]

The two neighbors struggled to establish normal relations. Consistent with China's peaceful coexistence slogans, the two sides agreed to "establish durable relations of peace and friendship" on the principles of "mutual respect for sovereignty and territorial integrity, mutual non-aggression, non-interference in each other's internal affairs, equality and mutual benefit and peaceful coexistence. . . . In keeping with the foregoing principles . . . all disputes shall be settled by peaceful means without resorting to the use or threat of force.[29] Nonetheless, as the toasts at the reception party suggested, both sides knew there had been differences and both expected disputes. A more clear-cut principle had to be spelled out to clarify proper order in East Asia. This is where the Chinese notion of antihegemonism came into play.

Antihegemonism

Perhaps at the insistence of the Chinese, one clause of the normalization joint communiqué reads: "neither of the two countries should seek hegemony in the Asia-Pacific region." To make it more assertive, they should be "opposed to efforts by any other country . . . to establish such hegemony." Because the Chinese must have implied Soviet hegemony, the Japanese, who were not ready to take on the Soviet Union, must have insisted on the proviso that normalization was "not directed against third countries." The proviso may look fine to the Chinese since, as explained in Chapter 3, Chinese antihegemonism was really targeted at a type of behavior rather than a particular country. Despite the proviso, there was a surge of literature in the following years in China urging the Japanese people to take a resolute stand against Soviet hegemonism.[30]

For the Chinese, the age of anti-imperialism was replaced by the united front against the hegemons, the Soviet Union topping that list. To be a good neighbor, symbolic compliance with China's position on Taiwan was insufficient in the 1970s, a decade affected by the legacy of the Cultural Revolution. Chinese diplomatic rhetoric was still filled with revolutionary spirit, and the emerging Japanese notion of omnidirectional diplomacy lacked revolutionary principle in Chinese eyes. Global détente in the 1970s therefore changed the tempo of international relations in East Asia in a rather limited way by paving the way for normalization, generating new role conceptions, and producing new role expectations. These role conceptions, however, were incongruent. The Chinese revolutionaries generally turned a deaf ear to the Japanese call for mutual understanding and adjustment.

Contrary to observers' claims that exchanges increased in the wake of normalization, there were actually only moderate, incremental changes. The number of Japanese visitors to China rose by about 2,500 per year on average between 1972 and 1977. The number jumped only after the signing of the 1978 long-term trade agreement and the peace and friendship treaty.[31] Trade with Japan as a component of China's overall trade hovered at around 20 percent and steadily increased only in the early 1980s. On the Japanese side, trade with China fluctuated between 2 and 3 percent of overall trade during the 1970s.[32] This incremental development of relations reflected modest improvement in the international organizational process in East Asia. Japan was not ready to comply with China's role expectations, and the Japanese failed to specify what was expected of China aside from the sense of returning to normalcy.

China, this enormous market and supplier of raw materials, was certainly never far from the minds of Japanese businesspeople. In order to exploit that market the Japanese government was asked to join forces against hegemonism in East Asia. In the words of a longtime student of Sino-Japanese relations, the prolonged negotiation for the treaty of peace and friendship "dramatized" the constantly extant "connection between China's bilateral relations with Japan and its global strategy" of antihegemonism.[33] In the aftermath of the 1972 joint communiqué, it became absolutely clear that the Chinese notion of antihegemonism included the obligation to oppose the Soviet Union. Although the Chinese most likely expected rhetorical support, few nations could take on that kind of symbolic obligation without consideration of their own interests. Even if a nation could appreciate the Chinese style, it had no reason to cloak itself in the flag of revolution and permit misunderstanding of its intentions. The Japanese therefore painstakingly maneuvered to avoid letting the wording of the 1972 communiqué reappear in the 1978 treaty. Its omnidirectional diplomacy made little sense of the principle of antihegemonism.

The treaty nonetheless included an antihegemonic clause. The Japanese found this acceptable for two reasons. First, they were comforted by a third-country clause that reads: "The present treaty shall not affect the position of either contracting party regarding its relations with third countries." Second, trade negotiations with China produced an agreement in early 1978 that committed China to $20 billion worth of transactions with Japan over the next eight years, raised to $60 billion in early 1979.

It looked as if East Asia had entered a new era. But the treaty meant different things to different people. Chalmers Johnson quoted the Japan External Trade Organization in saying, "the world is witnessing [in China] the transition of a closed society governed by whimsical political principles into an open system based on sound economics."[34] The Chinese characteristically celebrated the treaty as embodying "the abject bankruptcy of Soviet Socialist imperialist diplomacy."[35] In ignorance—or perhaps sincere hope—the Japanese public saluted the triumph of their omnidirectional foreign policy, making room for China once again in the East Asian order while avoiding Soviet alienation.[36] The fact, of course, was that the Soviets never appreciated the significance of the third-country clause. Furthermore, a peace treaty accommodating antihegemonism was regarded as an innovation by one Chinese observer;[37] in sharp contrast, a Japanese critic denounced the treaty as a second-class agreement precisely because it lacked anything new.[38]

For one brief moment it appeared that both neighbors had got what they were looking for: China, a friend in its united front; Japan, an immense market. It soon proved true that neither the peace treaty nor the trade agreement had created new norms in East Asia. Chinese antihegemonism was never popular in Japan, especially among those who should have benefited most from business opportunities supposedly promoted by the peace treaty and the trade agreement. Being a neighbor of similar Asian origin, cultural background, and sense of historical intimacy makes Japan too attractive a source of potential moral support for China to ignore. The bitterness of the 1950s seemed to dissipate in the 1970s not just because détente had lured them together, or because bilateral relations were too intense to be left unregulated, but also because the emergence of mutual role expectations gave meaning to their neighborly relations. Yet the new relationship was, as usual, based upon each country's own assessment and resulting misconceptions. They were reluctant to make genuine mutual adjustments in addition to the semantic manipulation of treaties and agreements. Misunderstanding and frustration thus generated would inevitably bring back bitter memories of the prewar period.

CONTEMPORARY BITTERNESS

An examination of the conceptions Japan and China have of their own self-roles may enable us to appreciate how they expect each other to behave, which may in turn explain why there has been a rise in mutual misunderstanding. Since the 1970s both countries have been searching in earnest for a national identity. This may have something to do with the way that, as many observers of Japan and China have repeatedly pointed out, both these Oriental societies are extremely concerned with how they are viewed by others and are under constant pressure to conform. For individuals in these circumstances, it becomes imperative to find out exactly which relationship network they are involved in before they take meaningful action. To the extent that everyone is taught to comply with social expectations, the validity and value of social norms must be dramatized and confirmed. The same style of thinking may apply to international relations. Political actors in both societies may have to clarify correct international norms so that they can make sense of the existence of the state in the world and formulate foreign policy accordingly. For the two Oriental societies to interact smoothly, they must follow mutually congruent codes of behavior.

In the 1970s the process of détente eroded the underpinnings of the Cold War. Foreign policy premises based upon superpower confrontation and the superiority of ideology were no longer valid. Neither the United States nor the Soviet Union was able or willing to discipline defecting or uncooperative allies. The USSR and the United States both failed the leadership test in East Asia because neither was ready to take care of its respective junior partner, China and Japan. This leadership failure passed on the responsibility for securing international morality to the East Asian partners, sparking an identity crisis in both societies. The Japanese, under the Sato cabinet, tried unsuccessfully to hide behind the United States, and the Chinese, in contrast, indulged in antihegemonism and their dogged obsession with revolutionary rhetoric. But as events evolved in the 1970s, it was clear that neither unconditional subjection to one superpower nor the mania of revolution against the other provided sufficient guidelines. The two East Asian neighbors had to regulate their relations on their own. The question, "Who am I?" had to be answered first.

Japanese National Identity

The scenario in the late 1970s bore a striking resemblance to that of the early twentieth century. The editor of the *Japanese Interpreter* watched history's repetition with sorrow. He believes that the extreme Westernization of the Meiji period was replayed in the 1950s and 1960s. National self-confidence, achieved after defeating China in 1895 and Russia in 1905, was paralleled by big-power mentality associated with extraordinary economic recovery during the 1960s.[39] The implications of this parallel were alarming since the ultranationalism of the 1930s could have easily resurfaced in the 1980s. Though this anxiety may not be justified, a similar brand of national self-confidence and quest for meaningful national identity certainly connoted an emerging vision of Japan's role in the 1980s.

The Sato cabinet did seriously consider the impact of superpower decline and Japan's role in Asia. In his famous Matsue speech delivered on

September 25, 1969, Sato said, "It is apparent that in the future Japan will gradually assume the leading role in bringing about stability in Asia, with the U.S. cooperating in a limited capacity. . . . It is clear that it is Japan's responsibility to play a major role in aiding these [Asian developing] countries to gain their independence."[40] Eighty years earlier the concept of developing Korea, which later evolved into one of colonizing Korea and China, had first hit Japan. Self-confidence and a sense of leadership arose when the Japanese realized that other East Asian societies were indeed unable to develop themselves effectively. The situation was different in the 1970s, however. The Yoshida group had incorporated the peace doctrine into Japan's foreign policy. There was no emergent sense of rebuilding military capabilities in order to enforce the Japanese development plan throughout Asia. Japanese contribution has taken the form of aid rather than direct intervention, and in the 1980s Japan surpassed the United States to become the world's largest source of economic aid.

A more direct challenge to the Yoshida legacy nonetheless arose in the 1980s. Yasuhiro Nakasone talked about Japan's military policy in a truly nontraditional way and was perhaps the first Japanese prime minister to bind himself to such a controversial position. According to the premier, "True independence is impossible as long as a nation chooses to depend in large measure on the military power of another country for its own territorial security."[41] It was therefore impossible for Japan to rise again if it could not ascertain its role in the world. So Nakasone wanted to promote "independent diplomacy," "transcend the San Francisco System," and carry out transformation by making the Japanese "know Japan itself."[42] In the mid-1980s the Japanese military budget inched above 1 percent of gross national product (GNP), a benchmark set decades earlier. The increase was not really significant quantitatively, but the breakthrough had a symbolic impact not only on the rest of Asia but on Japan itself. Nakasone proudly announced that a "Japanese nation" was being built and unity achieved. He declared that Japan had "reached a turning point" and the Japanese people could walk "in the world with . . . heads held high."[43]

Rising Japanese nationalism might have a tremendous impact on East Asia. If a nascent sense of confidence means a perception of superiority, it would be necessary for the Japanese to look for subordinates to confirm that image. If it means intensive coordination and assistance, then the Asian neighbors must demonstrate their capability and willingness to utilize the opportunities provided by the Japanese. If it means being the richest, the Japanese state must promote a thirst for wealth so that the income gap between Japan and the rest of Asia can be maintained, if not enlarged. If it means all-round independence, the idea of a new military buildup will be entertained. In short, as Pyle's discovery of four contending image conceptions in Japan today suggests, the Japanese can be progressive-idealistic, liberal-realist, mercantile, or neonationalist.[44]

East Asia may play a more and more important role in Japan's search for identity for another reason. Despite its demonstrated ability to render aid to the Third World, Japan is still isolated. The main criticism focuses on Japan's closed market and its apparent eagerness to invest in and therefore heavily influence other economies. Such isolation would make the Japanese look to their East Asian neighbors, as other countries normally and habitually look to their neighbors, for confirmation of their value. The role China can play in Japan's quest for a new identity actually depends on two things: what the Japanese believe they truly want to be and to what extent the Chinese appreciate that conception and cooperate with Japan. The Japanese reaction to China's role performance according to Japan's new image will determine the tempo and the direction of East Asian coordination.

Chinese National Identity

Mao's death and the arrest of the Gang of Four in 1976 brought a new political force to power in China. The Cultural Revolution was officially over and revolutionary rhetoric became less and less relevant as a motivation for both domestic and foreign policy. In contrast to postwar Japan, the aftermath of the Cultural Revolution in China witnessed not confidence but confusion. The atmosphere was fresh but uncertain, people were hopeful yet directionless. While the term "revolutionary diplomacy" (*geming waijiao*) disappeared from the pages of the *Renmin Ribao* toward the end of 1978, "antihegemonism" was still a popular slogan. While the Cultural Revolution was denounced, Mao was still widely quoted by some high-level party leaders. The confusion could be clearly seen in the party's economic policy: forbidding the contract or responsibility system but at the same time ignoring its use at the local level. Deng Xiaoping, who became a vice-chairman of the party in 1978, openly advocated experimentalism—seeking truth from practice.

Discovering truth through practice implied that nearly any measure could be attempted, including seemingly capitalist ones. In foreign policy peaceful coexistence was highlighted and the Chinese were encouraged to familiarize themselves with the realities of capitalist society. In an ironic turn of circumstances, peaceful coexistence became an excuse for war: China sacrificed peace in the short run and launched a punitive attack on Vietnam for allegedly violating and challenging Chinese determination to maintain the status quo. In the meantime, China's peaceful intent could be demonstrated by its efforts to establish or improve diplomatic ties with leading capitalist countries such as the United States and Japan.

The combination of coexistence and antihegemonism inevitably created the impression that China was playing the U.S. card against the Soviet Union. To counter that perception, the Chinese deliberately strove to prove their independence by prodding the United States on a number of minor issues such as arms sales to Taiwan, the defection of a Chinese tennis player, historical debt, and textile quotas. As mentioned before, it was the announcement of an "independent foreign policy" by General Secretary Hu Yaobang in 1982 that set the tone for the coming decade. Still, independence as a general principle could only remotely help daily decision-making. At that time it was not clear how, for example, the principle would work for regional issues in which neither of the superpowers was directly involved. It was Deng in 1989 who finally explained that independence meant adherence to socialist principles (see Chapter 3).

This confusion about China's role in the world at large could by no means guarantee a steady policy current in East Asia. Based upon their factional loyalty, personal interests, and psychopolitical need to be consistent in their outlook, Chinese leaders had to choose one of three versions of the independent foreign policy: antihegemonist (i.e., independent from foreign threat and nonaligned), economic reformist (i.e., free from underdevelopment and dependency), and socialist (i.e., independent from bourgeois influence). As a neighbor, Japan is inevitably a stage on which the various themes on independence can be acted out. On that stage, socialist principles would imply a regulated market and centrally directed investment opportunities. In that case, Japanese businesspeople as well as government aid agencies would have to work and comply with Chinese national planners. Economic reform, once stressed, would probably encourage Japanese business interests to flourish in China. Antihegemonism has many different connotations. It could mean China's opposition to military buildup in Japan, to any Japanese intervention in Taiwanese politics, or even to Japanese acquiescence in superpower intervention in Chinese politics.

Mutual Role Conceptions

The primary Japanese interest in China is commercial. Japanese business cannot but conceive of the colossal Chinese market in certain precise terms. An increase of 100 kilograms per capita in steel consumption in a nation of 1.1 billion, for instance, entails an overall increase of 110 million tons. In this truly "mammoth market," the Japanese have certain advantages over their Western competitors.[45] Japan is closer to China, and the Japanese know the style of the Chinese socialist market better. This is hardly surprising. Indeed, loan agreements between the two countries topped $10 billion in 1980. A modernized China presents a good business prospect for the Japanese, and Japan is eager to assist in China's modernization. But Japan as developer of Asia stirs up unhappy memories among the Chinese people. The Japanese are therefore highly sensitive when making offers. To demonstrate their sincerity, they often start with noncommercial projects, for example, building a hospital.

For a time, the Japanese were especially excited about political trends in China. Students of Sino-Japanese relations have generally noted Japan's sense of guilt for war crimes in China and for rapid postwar development that seemingly came at China's expense (by Japan's ignoring China). Yet the Japanese believed they could soon compensate the Chinese. According to Foreign Minister Tadashi Sonoda, "China has finished the consolidation of its footing, centering on Chairman Hua Guofeng. It has now formulated a realistic plan for modernization, and is taking first steps in that direction. . . . With the team of Premier Hua and Deputy Premier Deng, it appears they are both helping each other. . . . The two must help each other and must walk in unity and solidarity."[46] Hasayoshi Ohira observed during his trip to China in 1980 that "resolute Chinese leaders" had changed his anxiety toward China into confidence.[47]

The Chinese style of politics may have been misleading and caused the Japanese to be overoptimistic. As mentioned earlier, Chinese leaders are extremely concerned about the appearance of harmony. One simple way to achieve harmony is to disguise any sign of disagreement by using dramatic statements to highlight the intended goal without indicating whether one is capable of moving toward that goal in the short run. After repeated Chinese promises and statements of intent, the Japanese were later shocked when none of their expectations materialized. It is quite possible that the Japanese sensed to some extent the fragility of the Hua-Deng coalition. The *Japan Quarterly*, the leading journal on Japanese affairs, suggested that the Japanese utilize technology and capital indispensable for China's modernization to "help strengthen the foundation of the Hua-Deng regime."[48]

In short, the Japanese were ready to advance their business interests in China. They felt that the Chinese were going to take monumental steps toward developing their domestic market, that Chinese politics had stabilized, and that the Chinese people would think, calculate, and act in much the same way an ordinary Japanese businessperson would. With Japanese assistance, the Chinese should, could, and would carry out their modernization projects, appreciate Japanese friendship, and reward the Japanese with more business opportunities.

The Chinese seemed to share the same optimism (although for the Chinese, optimism is often a way of dramatizing their intention). Nonetheless, Hua Guofeng, reflecting the age-old notion of an East Asian Coprosperity Sphere, suggested that China, with its resources, and Japan, with its technology and capital, would "complement each other."[49] The Chinese mass media also carried the message that the two neighbors should "share what each has and supply what each has not."[50] For the Chinese, once the political disputes over Japan's militarism and collusion with Taiwan were resolved, new neighborly relations could be allowed to develop along economic lines. There was no hint of Japanese colonialism.

Disillusion

The political struggle between Hua Guofeng and Deng Xiaoping became more acute toward the end of the 1970s. Hua and his supporters were known as "whateverists" because of their insistence that whatever Mao had said was right. Fortunately for the Japanese, Deng's pragmatic approach of testing theory through practice finally gathered sufficient support and Hua was forced to resign. Though the perception of post-1978 political stability was proved wrong, new hope for stability was nonetheless aroused in 1982 when Deng's steadfast comrade, Hu Yaobang, formally replaced Hua as chairman of the CCP.

In 1983 a campaign to combat spiritual pollution was launched in China. It appeared that Deng's pragmatic alliance was split into reformist and conservative factions, the latter stressing central planning and the former market mechanisms. Hu, the most aggressive member of the reformist group, was finally purged in 1987. Zhao Ziyang shouldered the task of reform for the next two years until he, too, was ousted as general secretary of the party in 1989. The reformist group was left in disarray after the Tiananmen massacre.

In hindsight, Sonoda's analysis appears naive, bordering on absurd. It is exactly this kind of wishful thinking that has made the Japanese subject to the vicissitudes of Chinese politics. Political stability is thought to be an indispensable base for coordinating renewed economic relations; Japanese expectations of an enormous, stable market are left unfulfilled. Underground radical groups in China (e.g., Xieguang, literally, Bloody Lightning) warned Japanese businesspeople that they would become the targets of assassination attempts if they decided to stay in China after the 1989 massacre. China clearly fails the Japanese test for correct role-playing.

More important, of course, are the economic repercussions of all these political maneuvers. Ohira's "resolute" leaders in China never measured up to Japanese role expectations. Chalmers Johnson details the case of Baoshan Iron and Steel.[51] The project was at the heart of Hua Guofeng's ten-year plan, which, according to his political opponents, caused the economy to overheat. Under the leadership of the conservative economist Chen Yun, an economic retrenchment (literally, a dismounting, or *xiama)* movement was launched and the Baoshan project was half cancelled and half postponed. Chinese critics argued that the project was ill contrived, an accusation that embarrassed the primary designer, Nippon. The retrenchment movement also saw the cancellation of other contracts between the two countries. "Resolute" leaders were simply not ready to assist eager Japanese businesspeople.

China's performance in everyday economic activities adds to Japan's disappointment with its western neighbor. The low quality of managers and workers and widespread corruption have led to the following complaints: "The trade imbalance between the two countries cannot now be corrected without a change in China's industrial structure; without improving the quality and lowering the price of manufactured goods China cannot hope to boost sales to Japan. Nor will there be much increase in Japanese direct investment in China or in Sino-Japanese joint business ventures unless the Chinese way of doing things is completely transformed."[52] As one frustrated Japanese observer puts it, better cooperation between the two would require the kind of Japanese involvement in China's economy that "independent" Chinese would never accept.[53] Indeed, the Baoshan failure has led to the emergence in some sectors of "the old attitudes of contempt for China."[54]

The Japanese did worse in Chinese eyes. In the early 1980s, a reported revision of Japanese school textbooks that would have termed Japan's invasion of north China during World War II an "advance" once again raised the specter of Japanese militarism. Prime Minister Nakasone's call to "defend our land by ourselves" had to be justified by some revision in war scholarship, hence the rally to "clear up, one by one, issues that have been left in abeyance all these years since the end of the war."[55] Seisuke Okuno, director general of Japan's National Land Agency, was more provocative when he charged Deng Xiaoping with twisting Japanese intentions during the textbook uproar. He reminded every Asian that Japan "fought to protect itself at a time when the white race had turned Asia into a colony."[56] The implication that Japan had actually intended to liberate China through the war is deeply resented in China. To make matters worse, in 1985 a number of Japanese cabinet ministers visited the Yasukuni Shrine, which commemorates Japanese war dead. The Chinese have never appreciated the simple fact that the Japanese are confused about and looking for their self-image in history, nor have they acknowledged Japanese claims that they, too, are victims of World War II.

A *Renmin Ribao* article explains what disturbs the Chinese: if younger Japanese are "unaware of the history of Japan's invasion of China," "the ghost of militarism" will return.[57] Japanese militarism has no role to play in China's East Asian order. It is not at all surprising that the Chinese were so worked up about what later turned out to be a distorted report about textbook revision. Although the revival of militarism is still but a remote possibility in Japanese politics, the smallest hint of it sets off alarm bells in Beijing. The Chinese have to make their protest loud and clear to counter any suspicion that they would ever tolerate being a colony again. Real militarism is therefore not the issue; the issue is talk of militarism, which can be equally threatening to rhetorically oriented Chinese diplomacy. Militarism in Japan is incompatible with peace, friendship, independence, and patriotism—all of which are essential elements in China's just world.

In this respect, the future does not look promising for China now that the Chinese have discovered that a "new nationalism" based upon chauvinism is being advocated by some members of the Japanese government. The Chinese cannot understand why Japan would want to increase its military budget in the age of détente and superpower negotiation.[58] One Chinese expert on Japan also discovered that "the guiding ideology of a passive defence has been transformed into one of active pre-war preparations to defeat the enemy at first blow."[59] The Chinese are still hopeful, however, even if they are not optimistic. *Beijing Review* concludes that "Japan's political disease cannot be cured overnight," and China has to "wait and see."[60]

Even though the Chinese feel that the problem is rooted in a small faction of right wing agitators, these agitators are seen as creating a tendency which could sabotage Sino-Japanese friendship.[61] Throughout the 1980s, almost all Chinese literature on Japan condemned Japan's tilt toward militarism. By repeatedly specifying what should and should not be, the Chinese might be able comfortably to conduct business with the Japanese while reserving the legitimate right to terminate it later. Given Chinese suspicions, it is thus genuinely important for the survival of neighborly relations in East Asia that Japan succeed in assisting China's modernization. Japan has obviously failed the economic test during the first decade after the peace and friendship treaty. The Chinese complain that the Japanese, like the Hong Kong Chinese and the Taiwanese, only sell China obsolete technology and defective products, although this may have to do more with an insufficiently trained work force or managers trying to make a quick profit in an age of uncertainty. Regardless, the practice by no means signals Japanese friendship. The Chinese leaders certainly feel the Japanese could do much better.

Trade imbalance has also prompted Chinese leaders to reevaluate relations with Japan. China's trade deficit with Japan has skyrocketed since 1985 (see Table 6.4). Relaxation of financial controls in China has meant increased importation of industrial goods and inflation (which is partially alleviated by importing more consumer goods). Only in 1989, after a drop in imports from Japan in the wake of the Beijing massacre, did China finally enjoy a trade surplus. The implication is that China has become increasingly dependent on the world market and, above all, on the Japanese market. The open-door policy appears to be incompatible with independent foreign policy, at least in East Asia. Despite initial predictions in both China and Japan, Chinese oil fields have never produced enough to cover the imbalance. The concern, then, is probably less about who is to blame or how to improve the situation than about the destruction of the myth of *mutual* assistance and *equal* status in East Asia. The right order does not evolve automatically from expectations of its arrival.

Table 6.4   China's Trade Balance with Japan (in $millions)

	Total Balance	Trade Balance with Japan
1978	-297	-1,126
1979	-753	-880
1980	-35	-970
1981	-3,751	-44
1982	6,214	1,583
1983	5,225	-72
1984	2,156	-1,538
1985	-8,155	-6,368

Source: Developed from Harry Harding, *China's Second Revolution: Reform After Mao* (Washington, D.C.: Brookings Institution, 1987), p. 148.

    Signs of unequal capability and Japanese dominance of East Asia (which appeared under Deng's leadership when China gave overwhelming emphasis to economic development) have led to a certain degree of anxiety. As one Chinese observer comments, in Japan "there are still . . . people who regard assistance as pity, intending to use a little money to seal other people's mouths. Some people thought that the developing countries needed them, so their tails rose up in the sky. . . . The consequence would be the creation of strong opposition from other countries, and tragedy for Japan."[62] The attitude boils down to a defiant "Don't think I have to depend on you." Chinese sensitivity was shown most clearly in their criticism of Japanese aid to Southeast Asian countries. As the Chinese see it, Japan's notions of freedom and democracy, open market and world prosperity, and international order are used to strengthen U.S. global strategy. Japan's economic aid is no more than interference in others' domestic affairs and a move toward big-nation diplomacy.[63] This frustration causes the Chinese to take up issues they might rationally have chosen to ignore. The case of the Koka dormitory is a typical example. China's claim to the Koka student dormitory in Kyoto made headlines in China when a Japanese court ordered that it be handed over to Taiwan. Even though the Japanese government had no power to overturn the court's decision, China nevertheless found the ruling unacceptable. If China had exclusive sovereignty over Taiwan, how could the court have behaved as if Taiwan itself had been a sovereign entity? In reality, maybe only the Chinese can appreciate their own anger. The value of the dormitory is disproportionate to the benefits of overall Sino-Japanese economic coordination. The irony is that if the Chinese had ignored the issue, there would have been no violation of sovereignty since the Japanese had no intention of exploiting the implication of sovereignty that worried the Chinese.

One may argue that this is Chinese nationalism. And to some extent it is, but appearances are equally important. China has allowed the Taiwanese airline to fly planes carrying the nationalist flag to Japan. Why is this arrangement not seen as de facto recognition of Taiwan by Japan? Because Taiwanese flights land at a different airport and there is thus no direct violation of China's sovereignty. Nationalism became a conspicuous topic at the end of 1982 when the "independent foreign policy" was launched. Accordingly, the Koka dormitory had a psychological value: is China truly independent if it cannot resist even a minor, marginal, and nominal violation of its sovereignty claim over Taiwan by a friendly country? Can China afford the implication that economic relations are more important than diplomatic rectitude? Is it too much to ask a well-intentioned neighbor to keep out of China's "domestic" affairs? In every case, Japan has respected China's claim to sovereignty over Taiwan, at least rhetorically. In the 1980s, however, the Chinese must have worried (probably more than necessary) that the equal status of the two neighbors would be undermined if the Chinese sent the wrong message that China might be vulnerable to economic pressure from Japan (even though it is).

Mutual Adjustment

Over time, the Chinese and the Japanese may gradually develop more realistic views of each other. To cope with those problems in bilateral relations caused by unfulfilled role expectations by both sides, the two countries established the Twenty-First Century Committee in 1984 to discuss long-term relations. The Chinese brought their peaceful coexistence cliché to the meeting; they hoped that developments in East Asia could demonstrate how countries with dissimilar social systems could maintain good relations. The Japanese reiterated Nakasone's point that the two needed to establish "mutual trust." The key message was nonetheless economic:

> The new possibility of developing Japan-China relations occurred after China had specified its emphasis on the route of economic development. . . . The evolution of a long-term, stable Japan-China relationship cer-

tainly depends on the economic element. The government will be engaged in realistic economic/technological cooperation with China. . . . Later on, various problems will inevitably occur between Japan and China. . . . Through bilateral efforts and self-consciousness, the problems can be resolved before they aggravate to an unsolvable stage.[64]

Again, the understanding that the two should adjust to each other, just like the understanding years before that the two should cooperate closely, gave no real promise that such adaption would become a reality. China's primary interest in independence since 1982 and socialist principles since 1989, and the Japanese preoccupation with market and investment may require a kind of mutual adjustment that would call for changes in priorities. Such a shift presupposes changes either in China's dedication to independence or in Japan's style of business. Otherwise, the adjustment may take a less welcome tone, with China denouncing Japan's betrayal of equal partnership (since Japan exploits rather than assists China's backward market) and Japan resuming its role as the sole developer of Asia (since China cannot make it on its own).

HISTORY REPEATED?

The process of disillusion is incomplete at best. To leaders in both countries, peace and friendship between the two peoples are perhaps too natural to think otherwise. Outside observers, too, predict the emergence of a China-Japan axis in the long run. True, the countries expected problems twenty years ago when their bilateral relationship was normalized, but they basically believed that minor disputes would not undermine a general convergence of views. Unfortunately, this general convergence has never materialized. While peace and friendship remain high guiding principles, exact role expectations associated with such principles have yet to be defined. So the willingness on both sides to share leadership in East Asia does not mean a great deal in actual policy behavior. The Chinese have to demonstrate to the Japanese their capacity to share the position of leadership. The Japanese must prove to the Chinese that they have no intention of assuming some sort of absolute leadership (most importantly, economic and military).

Ironically, leaders in the two countries tend to exaggerate the convergence. Both are constrained by higher-level national roles in the world at large. For the Chinese, they cannot afford to lose Japan as a symbolic good neighbor and still contend, mainly to themselves, that they truly intend to achieve a modernization that requires peace and friendly assistance. This dramatic requirement of good neighborly relations in East Asia became extremely significant after China's punitive war against another major neighbor—Vietnam—in 1979. Who, especially the Chinese themselves, could doubt China's sincerity in being a good neighbor when the Chinese have continued rhetorically to highlight neighborship in spite of Japan's disappointing behavior on the textbook and Taiwan issues? The serious implication of this mentality may not be clear to the Japanese, but it is real: Japan must bear all responsibility if neighborly relationship were to fall apart.

For the Japanese, good neighborly relations with China become more important and symbolic during instances when Japan is the brunt of global criticism for its economic aggressiveness. It is no secret among Japan experts that the Japanese are obsessed with their image in the world. Despite domestic pressure for a more assertive foreign policy, Japan keeps a rather low profile in world politics. Proposals to send Japanese forces to the Middle East battlefield during the 1990 Gulf War were finally squashed despite support of the ruling party. Now Japan has become the largest source of aid in the world and finds itself in the thankless position of trying to make everyone happy. After the 1989 Beijing massacre, Japan led the criticism of China's violation of human rights during a summit of the seven leading industrial nations, but at the same time Japan urged caution and avoided imposition of harsher sanctions. Mediating between China and the West, a whole series of Japanese delegations to China attempted to persuade Beijing to lift martial law, which China did in January 1990. Japan responded by lifting economic sanctions. After all this maneuvering, how could the Chinese ever doubt Japan's goodwill?

Empty talk may generate both good feelings and inflated expectations. High government officials especially like to preserve the feeling of good neighborly relations. Prime Minister Nokoru Takeshita visited China in August 1988, and Premier Li Peng returned the visit in April 1989. They repeated what they had been saying for a decade. In addition to friendship, peace, mutual trust, economic coordination, and promise of the one-China principle, the two leaders alluded to long-term stability in this round of exchanges. There is no reason, then, why good neighborly relations cannot be maintained. In 1992, however, General Secretary Jiang Zemin visited Tokyo, trying in vain to persuade Japan's emperor to come to China and apologize for what Japan had done in China during the war. Japan rebutted by mentioning China's arms sales to the Third World and its troublesome human rights performance. For the first time since 1945, Japan brought the international context into the Sino-Japanese bilateral relations on Japan's own initiative. This kind of practice is destined to generate frustration later.[65]

The fundamental problem lies in Japan's continuous efforts to separate politics from economics and China's insistence that they must be linked. Japan's expectation that the Chinese will forget about political rhetoric and get down to the real business of modernization is not congruent with the Chinese expectation that business can be conducted only after all assume their correct political roles. The Chinese are always ready for retreat primarily because they have so many principles available to fall back on. Socialism, nonalignment, independence, and antihegemonism can all justify a turn in diplomacy. Japanese attempts to strengthen their defense forces and the judgment in the Koka dormitory case came close to initiating a trend toward overthrowing the status quo in East Asian politics. The concept of peaceful coexistence is exactly to preserve that status quo. The Chinese are worried about the intentions of some Japanese politicians rather than the immediate breakdown of the status quo. And they may be forced to use other role conceptions to justify their criticism.

The more rhetorically committed the Chinese are to a certain relationship, the more likely the relationship will be sacrificed for the sake of dramatizing principles that seemed to have been forgotten for the time being. Yet only when the relationship has been damaged will the Chinese ignore the violation of principles, because, once sacrificed, the relationship can no longer be employed to dramatize China's adherence to its principles. For example, during the 1990 dispute between Japan and Taiwan over Diaoyutai Island, China kept an unusually low profile on a supposedly hot, sovereignty-related issue. A realist would point out that China could benefit from better Sino-Japanese relations in the economic field so its people would rather keep silent on this symbolic issue. The realist perspective is partial at best because China's historical tendency to sacrifice existing (or improving) relationships would appear inconsistent with this explanation. On the Diaoyutai issue, one would also have to consider why the Chinese were able to show their goodwill by keeping silent. The answer seems to be that they are sacrificing their firm stand on a sovereignty issue. And this could continue only as long as political factions would agree not to cash in on the issue. There was no guarantee of this, though, as in 1992, a People's Congress resolution included Diaoyutai in China's territory.

This type of alternating sacrifice will always occur because of the multitude of principles in Chinese diplomacy. There is no way the Chinese can cooperate fully with any other country and at the same time maintain integrity on all these self-role conceptions. So once an all-round relationship is expected, the Chinese will consistently feel frustrated because no country can satisfy all five role conceptions simultaneously. The normal response is to dramatize China's sincerity toward a good relationship by mentioning violations but forgiving them temporarily—forgiving them until the day arrives when it is politically and psychologically necessary for the relationship to blow apart so that the Chinese may avoid losing face for being inconsistent. It seems as though the Sino-Japanese relationship will fall into this trap. The Chinese make much of the neighborly relationship and attempt to suppress their frustration. The time will eventually come, however, when the Chinese finally decide that they are fed up with their uncooperative neighbor.

NOTES

1. See the conclusion of Tang Tsou, Tetsuo Najita, and Hideo Take, "Sino-Japanese Relations in the 1970s," in A.D. Cox and A. Conroy (eds.), *China and Japan: Search for Balance Since World War I* (Santa Barbara: ABC-Clio, 1978), p. 431.

2. Jujimura Michio, "Japan's Changing View of Asia," *Japan Quarterly* 24, 4 (1977): 423–424.

3. Kenneth B. Pyle, *The New Generation in Meiji Japan: Problems of Cultural Identity, 1885–1895* (Stanford: Stanford University Press, 1969), pp. 197–198.

4. Ibid., p. 149.

5. Ibid., p. 181.

6. Marius B. Jansen, *Japan and China from War to Peace, 1894–1972* (Chicago: Rand McNally College Publishing, 1975), pp. 131–175.

7. Lyon Sharman, *Sun Yat-sen: His Life and Its Meaning* (Stanford: Stanford University Press, 1968), p. 304.

8. John Hunter Boyle, *China and Japan at War, 1937–1945* (Stanford: Stanford University Press, 1972), p. 164.

9. The increase in number is reflected of both the decline of the Confucian examination system in China and admiration of Japan. The statistics are from Robert S. Schwantes, "Japan's Cultural Foreign Policies," in J. W. Morley (ed.), *Japan's Foreign Policy, 1868–1941* (New York: Columbia University Press, 1974), p. 99.

10. Jansen, *Japan and China from War to Peace*, pp. 75–76.

11. Boyle, *China and Japan at War*, p. 34.

12. Ibid., p. 341.

13. Westel W. Willoughby, *The Sino-Japanese Controversy and the League of Nations* (New York: Greenwood Press, 1968), p. 630.

14. Ibid., p. 146.

15. Yang Tianshi, "Secret Negotiation Between the Japanese 'Civilian Politicans' and the Chiang Kai-shek Group During the Early Period of the War of Resistance," *Lishi Yanjiu*, 1 (1990): 160–175.

16. Zhou Enlai, speech at the third meeting of the First People's Congress, (History studies) in Center of the Chinese Issue Research (ed.), *Special Edition on Zhou Enlai* (Hong Kong: Zilian Press, 1971). p. 272.

17. Ibid., p. 273.

18. Harold C. Hinton, *Communist China in World Politics* (Boston: Houghton Mifflin, 1966), p. 376.

19. "Zambian Vice-President Chona Visits China," *Peking Reviw* (September 22, 1972): 7.

20. Ibid., p. 3.

21. Lowell Dittmer, *Liu Shao-ch'i and the Chinese Cultural Revolution: The Politics of Mass Criticism* (Berkeley: University of California Press, 1974), p. 225.

22. Chih-yu Shih, "The Bitter Neighborship Divided: The Psycho-historical Origin of the Post-war Sino-Japanese Relations," *American Asian Review* 6, 4 (December 1988).

23. Chalmers Johnson, "Japanese-Chinese Relations, 1952–1982," in H. J. Ellison (ed.), *Japan and the Pacific Quadrille* (Boulder: Westview, 1987), p. 111.

24. Sato Seizaburo, "Japan-U.S. Relations—Yesterday and Tomorrow," in Japan Center for International Exchange (ed.), *The Silent Power: Japan's Identity and the World Role* (Tokyo: Simul Press, 1976), p. 211.

25. See the discussion by Seizaburo, pp. 115–117.

26. "Zambian Vice-President," *Peking Review:* 3, 7.

27. Tacao Ishikawa, "The Normalization of Sino-Japanese Relations," in P. Clapp and M. H. Halperin (eds.), *United States–Japanese Relations: The 1970's* (Cambridge: Harvard University Press, 1974), p. 153.

28. Ibid., pp. 158–159.

29. Ibid., pp. 157–158.

30. See, for example, *Peking Review* 18, nos. 19, 20, 35 (1975).

31. Chae-Jin Lin, *China and Japan: New Economic Policy* (Stanford: Hoover Institution Press, 1984), p. 19.

32. *Direction of Trade Statistics Yearbook* (Washington, D.C.: International Monetary Fund, 1984); *Japan Statistical Handbook* (Tokyo: Bureau of Statistics, Office of the Prime Minister, 1971 to 1983); John L. Scherer (ed.), *China Facts and Figures* 4, 7 (Gulf Breeze, Fla.: Academic International Press, 1981, 1984).

33. Herbert S. Yee, "China and Japan: A New Era of Cooperation," in C. Hsueh (ed.), *China's Foreign Relations: New Perspectives* (New York: Praeger, 1982).

34. Johnson, "Japanese-Chinese Relations," p. 21.

35. "Sino-Japanese Relations Will Be Good for Generations Ahead," *Renmin Ribao,* August 14, 1978: 1.

36. See Chihiro Hosoya, "Japan's 'Omnidirectional' Course," *Japan Echo* 5, 4 (1978).

37. Chang Hsiangshan, "Far-reaching Significance of China-Japan Treaty of Peace and Friendship," *Peking Review* 21, 42 (1978): 20.

38. Michimasa Irie, "The Politics of Peace and Friendly Treaty," *Japan Echo* 5, 4 (1978).

39. Kano Tsutomu, "Why the Search for Identity?" in Japan Center of International Exchange, *The Silent Power,* p. 7.

40. Nomura Koichi, "The 'Japan-China Problem' in Modern Political Thought," *Japan Interpreter* 7, 3–4 (1972): 276–277.

41. *Asian Bulletin* (December 1982): 16–17.

42. Kenneth B. Pyle, "In Pursuit of a Grand Design: Nakasone Betwixt the Past and the Future," *Journal of Japanese Studies* 13, 2 (1987): 251, 261.

43. Yamazaki Masato, "History Textbooks That Provide an Asian Outcry," *Japan Quarterly* 34, 1 (1987): 54.

44. Kenneth B. Pyle, "Changing Conceptions of Japan's International Role," in Ellison, *Japan and the Pacific Quadrille,* pp. 203–218.

45. Hosoya, "Japan's 'Omnidirectional' Course," p. 91.

46. Quoted in Robert E. Bedeshi, *The Fragile Entente* (Boulder: Westview, 1983). p. 56.

47. "Japan-China Summit Meeting and China's Foreign Policy," *Japan Quarterly,* 27, 2 (1980): 164.

48. Ibid., pp. 164–165.

49. Ibid., p. 164.

50. Ping Xin, "10 Years of China-Japan Relations," October 4, 1982.

51. Johnson, Japanese-Chinese Relations," p. 122.

52. Nakajima Mineo, "The Precarious Balance of Chinese Socialism" *Japan Quarterly* 35 (1988): 36–37.

53. Shigeru Ishikawsa, "Sino-Japanese Economic Cooperation," *China Quarterly* 109 (1987): 21.

54. Johnson, "Japanese-Chinese Relations," p. 123.

55. Masato, "History Textbooks," p. 54; *Asian Bulletin* (December 1982): 13.

56. Yu Wen, "Okuno Seeks to Reverse Verdict on War," *Beijing Review* (May 9-May 15, 1988).

57. New China News Agency, "Wu Xueqian Met the Japanese Ambassador," p. 1.

58. Ge Genfu, "Japan Tones Up Defence Policy," *Beijing Review* 32, 10 (March 1989): 16–19.

59. Ibid., pp. 17–19.

60. (No Author), "Japan Gets 'War-Responsibility-Phobia'," March 6-March 12, 1989, p. 7.

61. Yu Wen, op. cit.; Guangying Wang, "Documentation: Sino-Japanese Friendship Monument Destroyed for Five Times," Liaowang Zhoukan 51 (1987): 8.

62. Fang Ding, "Why Does the Spoon Surface as the Calabash Is Pressed Down?"

63. Chao Chian, "Northeast Asia Aft Li Peng's Visit to the Soviet Union," *Mainland China Studies* 33, 1 (1990): 10.

64. Wang Zhaoguo Speaks on the First Meeting of the 20th Century Commission on Sino-Japanese Friendship. (No Author)

65. As Allen Whiting has pointed out, the positive image of Japan is found among economists and the older generation; the negative image is popular among the younger generation. See Allen Whiting, *China Eyes Japan* (Berkeley: University of California Press, 1989); for a similar view, see Laura Newby, "Sino-Japanese Relations," in Gerald Segal, ed., *Chinese Politics and Foreign Policy Reform* (New York: Kegan Paul International, 1990), pp. 195–213.

7
MODELING IN THE UN:
CHINA'S THIRD WORLD SCRIPT

Studies of China's Third World policy in recent years have been preoccupied with its inconsistency and changes. The inconsistency can be intuitively explained by Chinese opportunism; changes, by the fluid international environment. Of course, both opportunism and international environment point to the notion of national interests—China will do anything to protect its national interests. Implicit in this perspective is stress on the Chinese *reaction* to the outside world. Politicians as well as scholars seldom attend to China's attempt to moralize world politics and arrange its proper order. The pretension of the moral regime that nations in the international system are constrained by high principles has to be protected, especially when the popular perception is that China is unable to restructure that system. Dramatization is a confusing phenomenon in that China has a number of moral goals that may be consistent logically but are normally incompatible in the daily formation of concrete policy. The psychological need to prove the regime's determination to pursue *all* these goals requires a resort to drastic diplomatic rhetoric and symbolic moves. At different times, different moral goals have to be dramatized. It is often imperative that one principle be sacrificed in the short run for the sake of highlighting another. Changes and inconsistency may well be understood in this psychological perspective.

Instead of examining China's Third World policy in detail, this chapter concentrates on policy motivation. It studies China's attitude toward neighboring Third World countries as well as the Third World as a whole. It discusses the conceptual significance of the United Nations in China's Third World policy and evaluates China's symbolic use of it. The thrust of the chapter concerns China's efforts to organize the Third World by serving as a model for emulation and to convince the world and itself that it is indeed a popular model.

PERSPECTIVES ON CHINA'S THIRD WORLD POLICY

Duality

Most observers note China's call for revolution in the Third World but at the same time are intrigued by its policy of establishing formal relations with as many Third World governments as possible. Journalists take delight in citing Premier Zhou Enlai's 1964 trip to Africa and stressing how his remark, "Africa is ripe for revolution," annoyed his hosts.[1] As a result, only Mali issued a joint communiqué during his trip "fully in accordance with Chinese wishes."[2] This duality in strategy reflects what Alan Hutchison finds to be the unique Chinese characteristic of combining the united front from above and the united front from below.[3] The most clear sign of China's ambivalence was probably in its Southeast Asia policy in 1970s. The Chinese did not attempt to deny their relations with guerrillas active in the member states of the Association of Southeast Asian Nations (ASEAN) but maintained diplomatic relations with many of those states nonetheless. In Angola, for another example, China refused to halt support for rebels of the National Union for the Total Independence of Angola (UNITA) while recognizing the regime of their chief adversary, the Popular Movement for the Liberation of Angola (MPLA).[4]

This duality may be aimed at diverting the United States and the Soviet Union from their aim of containing China. China must sponsor rebel activities to compete with the Soviet Union and recognize reactionary Third World regimes to compete with the United States and Taiwan. The apparent irony in this duality can only be justified by simultaneously promoting antihegemonism against the Soviets and socialism against the U.S. imperialist. The ultimate motivation, as Hutchison puts it, is to "give a welcome boost to internal morale, and show the Chinese that their country has a role to play in world affairs," hence the dramatic statement that "Congo-Brazzaville was a 'vast and important' country, whose leader was a 'world statesman.'"[5] In fact, China's support for rebels is genuine only when it deals with unfriendly governments; it is purely moral or spiritual when China deals with friendly regimes.

Opportunism

A closer look at the duality may suggest that China utilizes rebel movements simply to topple unfriendly regimes. When dealing with a friendly regime, China would rather maintain good relations even at the expense of the revolutionary movement. One observer calls Chinese tactics guerrilla diplomacy in that its "mix of confrontation, stealth, showmanship and obliqueness transcends any theoretical framework."[6] China steadily cut back its support for guerrillas in the ASEAN nations for the sake of promoting good neighborly relations and trade with those countries. China's relationship with Mobutu's Zaire made a 180-degree turn after the two countries established diplomatic ties in 1973, and Mao was quoted as acknowledging his error in attempting to overthrow Mobutu prior to that point.[7]

The charge of opportunism ignores the point that an opportunist looks for genuine gain, not symbolic image. There is no doubt that China made the shift in its Zaire policy to counter Soviet influence in Africa. But how could the Soviets threaten China from Zaire? The issue had to be a symbolic one: who represented the true socialist force. However, one has to ask what China could really gain by having Zaire on its side. As a result of the policy change, the Chinese became embroiled in central African affairs against their will; they had to come to the rescue when Mobutu was threatened by Soviet-armed Angolan dissidents who intruded into Zaire in 1977 and 1978. In the meantime, China denies that it has retreated from the revolutionary front. In fact, the Chinese have thus far refused to sever connections with Southeast Asian revolutionary movements or any other dissident groups they have aided—a policy that makes friendly governments suspicious. What does the opportunist China gain by publicizing unsubstantiated ties with world revolution? Nothing concrete. Supporting an insignificant, right-wing ally shows how sincere China is in enacting its antihegemonic role, as antihegemonism gains reputation if China can win friendship from small states. The united front permits the expedient strategy of cooperating with reactionary nationalist regimes. This may have the appearance of opportunism, but the true motivation is to achieve popularity with the Soviets.

Revolutionary Pragmatism

The duality can also be understood as some kind of revolutionary pragmatism.[8] Chinese long-term national interests, according to this view, are defined by revolutionism. Pragmatic diplomats then further China's defined interests by all available means, even by establishing relations with conservative regimes in the short term. To justify this, China has declared that it is wrong to export revolution. Case in point is Sudan in the 1980s—protracted rebellion against a government friendly to China did not receive Chinese aid.

The Chinese nonetheless support armed struggle and, in the case of Algeria, impressed many African anticolonialist rebels with their quick and active support of the provisional government in the late 1950s. Yet the purpose of Chinese aid to friendly regimes, though occasionally right-wing, is always to assist in developing self-reliance. The Chinese thus continuously write off their Third World debt, as they did in 1983 with Zaire,

Zambia, and Tanzania, or extend it when the debtor appears to be experiencing certain difficulties, as with the Congo.[9] They have signed trade agreements to help Third World countries diversify their markets: agreements with Chile and Peru in the early 1970s purported to make the Latin Americans feel freer and "more Latin American."[10] The Chinese policy is revolutionary because it encourages armed struggle and supports anticolonialism. It is pragmatic because China disregards the nature of the Third World regime it aids.

One cannot make sense of this pragmatism unless one understands antihegemonic morality. Pragmatism that compromised local revolution served the highest level of antihegemonism. On many occasions, Chinese assistance to the Third World seemed to be aimed at shaming the Russians, as they invariably highlighted the point that there were no political strings attached to their aid. The Chinese were pragmatic enough to realize that their battle with the Soviet Union could not be won under constraint of limited resources. As one observer put it, "the Chinese intended to prove that they could look after ordinary Africans as no Europeans of any political complexion had ever been able to do."[11] It is hard to see how China can promote its national interests simply by showing its friendship. The notion of interests has to be symbolic, psychological, and realistically irrelevant. Pragmatism, in its ultimate form, is dramatization of antihegemonic role conceptions.

Functionalism

The recent change in China's diplomatic rhetoric with new emphasis on peace and development has given China's Third World policy a new look—what Samuel Kim terms functionalism[12] rather than a united front approach. China maneuvers to be included in the world economy dominated by the United States and its Second World allies and struggles to maintain a steady flow of aid to the Third World countries at the same time. China has started participating actively in international organizational processes and has offered to contribute to consolidating current international regimes. Functionalism thus takes what was previously termed pragmatism to a multilateral level. Instead of China's being a model and endeavoring to organize the world, its leaders try to adjust to existing reality.[13] The countries of the world are seen to be interdependent, and their Third World components are no longer nebulously dealt with as a homogeneous group.

While this trend toward functionalism does exist, two questions must be asked: What has motivated functionalism? How should one make sense of a counterfunctionalist current in Chinese politics? The rise of functionalism is based upon the belief that with some international assistance

China can catch up economically. This belief exists *before* functionalism has yielded any results. Chinese leaders praise the open-door policy and highlight so-called independent foreign policy just as they originally praised the 1958 Great Leap Forward, which turned out to be a costly failure.[14] The Chinese seem to have decided that the functionalist approach will and should be successful when they announced this new policy to the world. A possibly rational policy position hence turns into a dramatic gesture to convince the world that China can succeed economically. This does not guarantee that all the previous policy currents that disappeared in the process will not reemerge. Peace clearly does not obviate the need to be self-reliant or to struggle continuously for independence in the Third World. The revival of socialist rhetoric since 1989 certainly reminds one of Lucian Pye's observation of the Chinese style of pragmatism: it can be overturned overnight by some kind of make-believe system.[15] Indeed, China's pledge to adhere to the open-door policy appears to be just another make-believe system. In short, an amoral functionalism may do damage to legitimacy whereas a moralized functionalism may reverse functionalism.

China as Challenger

The rise of functionalism has led some observers to conclude that China has proved to be no champion of the Third World. Instead, it is a challenger. China's attempt to maintain the status quo has to do with its new policy of seeking the cheapest possible loans from leading international lending institutions such as the International Monetary Fund (IMF) and the World Bank. Pressure would then be exerted on other potential Third World recipients of international financial aid.[16] China justifies this functionalist approach by grafting the concept of "socialist commodity economy" to the trunk of Maoist Marxism.[17] In turn, China is expected to become active in the world market, putting pressure upon other labor-intensive exporters in the Third World. A more significant problem may be that China currently enjoys a trade surplus with its Third World partners. In the meantime, China's own aid to Third World countries has shrunk in volume and centers on more symbolic projects.[18] All this suggests that China is a competitor with the Third World.

It is not clear to what extent China will tolerate its own competition with the Third World while trying to champion Third World causes. For the Chinese, the charge of being a challenger is groundless since self-reliance is an invariable slogan and no self-reliant country can, theoretically, be seriously hurt in the world market. Nonetheless, prominent Chinese leaders have on several occasions since the early 1980s toured Africa, Asia, and Latin America to assure the Third World's continued confidence in China. Each time, the Chinese brought with them gifts for a few carefully selected hosts. These symbolic moves suggest that the Chinese are still holding tight to their Third World status not to help their modernization program but to confirm their value in the world. Organizing world politics by organizing the Third World will continue to be an alternative approach for the Chinese in their efforts to establish the correct world order.

China as Outsider

A more serious charge against China is that it is not a Third World country at all, reasons for which date back to before the rise of functionalism. One Indian observer finds that the Chinese hypocritically practice the same big-nationism that they themselves are so critical of. In the case of the nonaligned movement, it is argued that the Chinese always had some reservations and waited for others to satisfy their conditions while other Third World countries under Indian leadership were perfectly willing to discuss nonalignment without any preconditions.[19] The Chinese refusal to adopt this open-minded, consensus-seeking approach shows that it is not really a Third World nation. Indeed, many observers point out that China is not a member of the Group of 77, as the Third World countries are known in the United Nations, or the Group of 24, the Third World caucus in the World Bank. This chapter will later return to reasons why China has refused to join Third World groups. All these add up to one thing: that China is obsessed with being an independent nation, not a Third World nation.[20]

But by less subjective measures, too, China is set apart from the rest of the Third World: China ranks "well above other developing nations in per capita GNP, GNP growth rate, physical quality of life, life expectancy, literacy and public education, and military expenditures."[21] Behaving as an outsider while claiming to be a member connotes the psychological need of the moral regime to pretend to popularity. The ultimate test of China's identity may depend on whether China would commit itself to any Third World cause at the expense of its freedom to act independently. There are two ways to bypass this test, however. One way is for China to manipulate the perception of the Third World so that China is seen as a member by most Third World nations no matter how it actually behaves. All the symbolic aid and rhetorical, moral support that China renders might be effective in doing this. The second way is for China to make the Third World follow the Chinese model and hence sinicize the Third World. In this way, the distinction between the Third World cause and China's own cause would be eliminated. China would be truly independent from hegemonism because it would have the popular support of the Third World.

The Chinese Missionary

One interesting perspective on China's Africa policy points to the Chinese as the latest missionaries in Africa and sheds light on China's status as a kind of outsider in the Third World. The Chinese traditionally saw Africans as even more barbaric than Westerners.[22] But the Chinese are obliged to emphasize the ideological parallel between China and Africa, both having suffered from colonialism. As a result, the Chinese incorrectly believe that Africa can follow in China's footsteps, hence the emphasis on people's war, armed struggle, self-reliance, and anti-imperialism.[23] The reality is that Africa is no China—China was never directly under colonial rule; Africa's relationship with its colonial masters was different from China's with the imperialists; many African countries have not had to fight for independence as China did; and peasant-landlord struggle is not necessarily relevant in many tribal states whereas it was critical to the Chinese revolution. Mao's Little Red Book was shipped to Africa by the boatload nevertheless, and a small number of African radicals were converted. The same missionary mentality may apply to Asia, where, as in Africa, observers sometimes find that Maoism has replaced Confucianism as the universal model for emulation.[24]

To spread Maoist lessons in Africa and continue to provide moral support to all those onetime disciples of Mao amount to a de facto attempt to sinicize Africa. Chinese ignorance about Africa is reflected in their tendency to treat it as a homogeneous entity. Even though such ignorance has lately been alleviated to some degree, inability to develop a more sophisticated policy is still obvious. Knowing that African states differ from one another and need to be treated individually is not the same as being able adequately to come to terms with these wide dissimilarities. After advising African leaders to follow China's example in armed struggle during the 1960s, in self-reliance in the 1970s, and in abandoning central planning in the 1980s, China looks set to continue its missionary inclination well into the 1990s. While the Chinese may have an internal logic to justify each of these models, it is hard for their African friends to follow each in turn.[25] Regardless, the missionary's sense of self-worth depends on gathering disciples. Sooner or later, Chinese leaders will once again tour Africa, preaching a new gospel and distributing appropriate gifts to choice adherents, regardless of the constraints this would place on China's own ability to develop its economy.

A POLICY WITH MANY PRINCIPLES

China's doctrine on Third World issues, derived from the aforementioned five sets of norms, includes the notions of intermediate zones, anticolonialism and anti-imperialism, peaceful coexistence, self-reliance, people's war, the three-worlds theory, and the united front strategy. Terms are ceaselessly manufactured and redefined in order to adjust to the changing environment. China has yet, however, to jettison any of these principles rhetorically. Once a term is officially adopted, there is a good chance that it will become a permanent feature of China's normative foreign policy. The nature of the moral regime requires historical continuation of consistent moral pretension. The expanding reservoir of China's Third World jargon not only complicates an analyst's task but also exerts enormous pressure on politicians to comply with all its facets, if not at the same time at least alternately. Understanding the evolution of the logic of these doctrines would be helpful in the analysis of policy motivation regarding the meaning of the Chinese state.

Intermediate Zones

China's socialist worldview depicts the world as divided into the socialist and capitalist camps, with intermediate zones acting as the battlefield between the two. In 1949 China decided to "lean" toward the Soviet side and remained silent on the theory of intermediate zones for almost a decade. The theory reappeared in 1957 perhaps because the Chinese realized that the socialist camp could not fare well under Soviet domination.[26] In 1964 Mao pointed out the existence of a first middle zone, the developing countries, and a second middle zone, the developed world.[27] Herein lie the origins of the three-worlds theory.

The notion of intermediate zones satisfies the perception of a progressive socialist force marching through the ranks of the Third World. More importantly, it provides the Chinese with an imaginary audience who will listen to China's bitter accusations of imperialism and revisionism. China's moral mission would be to convert the intermediate zones, alone or in partnership with the Soviet Union, presumably depending on whether the latter is committed to socialism. Since leaders of the moral regime are psychologically unable to recognize selfish national interests, organizing the intermediate zones is an excellent approach to China's socialist commitment that does not allude to any possible ulterior motive.

Anticolonialism and Anti-imperialism

The socialist worldview also singles out the enemy for developing countries. The doctrine of anticolonialism refers to colonial independence movements before the 1960s. In the 1980s it had more to do with insistence on withdrawing foreign troops from regional conflicts, primarily Soviet troops from Afghanistan and Vietnamese troops from Cambodia. Third World countries are expected to recognize their common enemy, organize themselves, provide mutual assistance, and strike out against the imperialist. The final victory will come when the world's vast countryside "surrounds the world's cities," as in a Chinese peasant revolution. Claiming it shares the same colonial past as the rest of the developing world, the moral regime can comfortably denounce and shame any opponents, as they evidently are on the immoral and unpopular side.

Peaceful Coexistence

The Chinese have advocated peace among nations since 1953.[28] China's peace offensive during the 1955 Bandung conference and later in the 1980s not only reflects China's current stress on domestic economic recovery but also creates a sense of confidence that, ironical as it may sound in view of their economic difficulties, victory belongs to the developing countries. There is no longer a need to export revolution; the will of the developing world shall dominate in the long run, primarily because its numbers are so great.[29] Applied to developing countries, the doctrine calls for a peaceful solution to all Third World interstate disputes. Fighting among developing countries would hurt the Third World cause most of all. This said, the Chinese can then write off any benefit they gain from selling arms to parties in regional conflicts, the most notorious being the Iran-Iraq War in the 1980s. At other times, the moral support for revolution is at best implicit to avoid disrupting normal interstate relations.[30]

The moral regime will not ignore how the apparent dumping of revolution for the sake of peace damages its credit. Zhou Enlai on more than one occasion elaborated the relationship between peace and revolution. He argued that the notion of revolution is composed of anticolonialism, self-reliance, and liberation. Supporting *people's* revolution does not conflict with peace among *states*.[31]

Self-reliance

Isolationist role conceptions suggest that one of China's missions in the Third World is to help these nations achieve self-reliance in order to sever links with imperialism and facilitate its eventual collapse. Although China does not have the resources of a superpower, China can demonstrate its sincere support in every possible fashion and without political strings. In an anticolonial struggle, China will sometimes back all the factions involved. Third World nations are expected to appreciate truly friendly support and gradually phase out the politically motivated assistance given by other powers. This is probably why the Chinese deem South-South cooperation critical to overall development of the Third World.[32] The notion of South-South cooperation extends the scope of self-reliance to include the Third World as a whole. Receiving aid from China is thus more desirable than receiving it from a non–Third World nation. The stress on self-reliance portrays China as a model and the Chinese presence as being morally appealing. The Chinese especially like to pick up projects abandoned by others, despite the drain they present on China's already meager resources. Therefore, granted that the Chinese doctrine of self-reliance reflects China's economic constraint to render aid, China's style of aid serves to evidence its moral commitment.

Armed Struggle

The isolationist view encourages oppressed people to engage in people's war; the doctrine of people's war rejects dependence on one superpower to oppose another; people's war would win true popular support for the new regime. In this regard, the Chinese were interested in supplying light arms to revolutionary forces around the world. They were enthusiastic about training and preaching Mao's guerrilla strategy to Third World resistance groups. Critics may find that Chinese assistance carried a cynical criticism of Soviet style. The Chinese never deny this implication since they felt that Soviet experts and advisers were heavy-handed in their control of guerrilla activities. The difficulty of this doctrine is expressed in the dilemma of choosing between a friendly right-wing regime and a rebellious left-wing opposition. The psychological pressure to resolve this dilemma is never strong, though. If the regime is friendly to China, it accepts or at least recognizes the Chinese model. The normal option is that China continues good relations with the regime but neither actively supplies nor criticizes the activities of the rebels. In any case, the rebels are supposed to demonstrate their popularity by winning a people's war.

Three-Worlds Theory

Revolutionary norms should guide Third World countries in identifying their primary enemy. According to the 1974 version of the three-worlds theory, there are many contradictions in the world, the primary one being that between hegemonism and the developing world. The three-worlds theory provides the basic framework for Chinese foreign policy analysis. The existence of hegemony, practiced by the First World, is certainly the key. This perception of hegemony also satisfies the moral regime's search for a meaningful mission—courageous opposition to hegemonic expansion. It is never ideologically clear why the social imperialist is more dangerous than the capitalist imperialist, although the Chinese justify this view in military terms by arguing that the capitalist imperialist is declining.

The three-worlds theory enables China to shy away from too close a relationship with U.S. capitalism, highlighting China's Third World status and its ultimate conflict with the United States. The theory also allows China to seek cooperation with the Second World, the industrialized countries, without feeling guilty about such cooperation: these countries would become China's primary target if they were to follow in the footsteps of the First World after it is toppled. In this sense the theory satisfies the moral regime's need for a noble pretension and is a timely, self-serving reminder that China will never belong to the imperialist camp—a historically consistent and psychologically comforting self-image.

The United Front Strategy

Statism directs China's attention to security concerns, hence the united front strategy against the United States and, later, the Soviet Union. The anti-Soviet united front strategy forced Third World nations to choose sides even though most of them preferred not to alienate either superpower. United front requirements also kept China out of many Third World organizations that included nations who rejected China's antihegemonic front. The united front strategy helps prioritize moral issues in world politics so that the Chinese have certain criteria for deciding whether socialist imperialism in the Third World is a more serious evil than right-wing reaction. Nonetheless, the united front strategy is flexible enough to have allowed China to shift the primary target of the revolution over the past four decades. And the terminology of the united front also promises China a self-image as a worthy ally.

Because it may appear that the Third World is being manipulated to fit the role China has assigned it, the Chinese often feel obliged to sacrifice some cherished principles to demonstrate their sincerity in consolidating the current united front. The doctrine of people's war therefore received low priority in the 1970s when efforts were being made to woo Third World regimes. Once the united front is morally clothed, any challenge to it, especially from the supposed members of the front, would be extremely threatening and therefore would be dealt with forcefully and not necessarily rationally. The best example might be Vietnam's challenge to China's antihegemonic front. The united front strategy is a way of verifying the Chinese notion of moral world order. Developing nations are practically an inescapable component of the united front because of their numbers and their inability to become a primary threat to China. Vast differences among developing nations, however, make it almost impossible to mold them into a united front. This simple contradiction between wish and reality suggests that the united front strategy, in its ultimate form, is more a psychological drama than the realist strategy it may appear to be at first glance.

Dramatization

Given the changing nature of external challenges, Chinese diplomacy serves to highlight different principles at different times. Why is this not sheer opportunism? Because the doctrine sacrificed this time will probably be reinstalled at the expense of others in due course. It is not in China's national interest to have many seemingly contradictory doctrines. The picture of China busy restoring its credibility on various doctrines best illustrates the Chinese pretension that China is able to organize the Third World to assume its rightful historical role. Since rescuing one doctrine always means sacrificing others in order to achieve a demonstrative effect, any objective notion of national interest would only be obscured over the long course of history.

In the 1950s and 1960s, for example, the need to confirm its value to world communism compelled China, in spite of its peace rhetoric, to supply many Third World guerrillas who were working to topple right-wing and colonial regimes. Anticolonialism was manifested in this period because the use of armed struggle, for example in Rwanda and Vietnam, put peace at risk, and peace was a cherished value for a China facing threats from Taiwan and the United States. In the 1970s antihegemonism and the united front were dramatized by sacrificing the notion of intermediate zones and the notion of capitalism versus socialism. China shamed the hegemons by allying with reactionary Third World regimes like those in Pakistan and Zaire, which, though serious evils in and of themselves, must have been perceived as lesser evils by comparison. As a result of dramatization, China made itself responsible for assisting these two allies in their struggles with India and Angola, respectively, gaining little apart from some vague sense of popularity. In the 1980s peace was promoted through the open-door policy at the expense of self-reliance. Before too long, anti-imperialism and the three-worlds theory reemerged to resolve the national identity crisis caused by the open-door policy in the early 1990s.

Although these examples are sketchy, they do suggest that the classic notion of national interest ignores that the appearance of moral integrity is China's utmost interest. China's enemies always seem to be those who damage its self-perceived moral popularity and prestige. Winning popularity only benefits China in a psychological sense. The coexistence of multiple doctrines may give the Chinese conceptual flexibility in organizing the Third World to deal with different perceived threats, but their efforts result only in outright dramatization, as this flexibility only confuses the Third World and discredits the Chinese argument. Confusion and loss of credit force the Chinese to stick more rigidly to a particular doctrine in the short run to demonstrate their moral purity. This, in turn, will make the next shift look even more dramatic, and so on.

CHINA AND ITS THIRD WORLD NEIGHBORS

For China, the significance of its Third World neighbors is similar to the significance of Japan. The difference is that as Third World countries these neighbors are theoretically more subject to China's influence than is Japan. Historically, China dominated its neighbors, an image the People's Republic has tried to reverse without a great deal of success. Yet the moral regime cannot tolerate *not* being emulated by its neighbors. Reversing China's historical dominance is a role requirement, and China should hence extract itself from the affairs of its Third World neighbors. Superpower intervention in many of these countries, however, could counter China's goodwill and set it back on the track of interference. Superpower intervention means not only direct physical threat but also implies a lack of response to China's friendly overtures. China thus faces an extremely difficult task: drawing a fine line between intervention and assistance. China should help ward off superpower intervention without committing the same sin: a fine line that perhaps only the Chinese themselves can appreciate.

Organizing Neighborly Relations in the Third World

China's Third World neighbors are in one respect different from the Third World as a whole. The policies of these countries have direct implications for China, their model. The temptation to intervene is at times too strong to resist since the moral stakes are high and China usually has some access to these small neighbors' internal politics. In addition, there are many overseas Chinese living in these neighboring countries. What if these Asian societies reject China as a meaningful model? Can the moral regime afford to ignore this kind of cultural defection and still see itself as a moral symbol? Intervention is a psychological imperative. The question is how to encourage people's armed struggle, self-reliance, and anti-imperialism without disturbing peaceful coexistence among states.

The Chinese handle the subtle challenge by presenting their own society as a model worthy of imitation. The Chinese solution to problems in Cambodia, for example, is illustrative. It was based upon the principle of nonintervention. All foreign powers should withdraw, including the Chinese themselves. The connotation is twofold: first, Chinese intervention was justified as a counterforce to other intervening interests; second, implicit in their inflated sense of confidence is Chinese optimism regarding the attractiveness of their model and its eventual triumph if the country could be left in peace. The same line of argument was once applied to Afghanistan.

In the days when Southeast Asian nations served as U.S. allies in regional containment, China encouraged armed struggles in these countries in the belief that local governments dominated by colonialism would be toppled in the end by the forces of history. After some of these countries—Thailand, Malaysia, and Pakistan—developed good working relationships with China, support to native rebel movements gradually declined to the point of being hardly more than a moral gesture. This gesture is noble and theatrical because the Chinese appear to be faithful to their loyal friends despite the suspicion this rhetorical gesture might stir within the local government. The fear of Chinese intervention is therefore quite alive, though the Chinese would probably have difficulty understanding that fear. To use force to gain popularity is simply inconsistent with the style of a moral regime whose attraction is supposed to be self-evident.

In order to convince its neighbors that it has completely jettisoned its imperial past, China has expended considerable efforts to establish relationships with the small countries along its border: Bhutan, Sikkim, and Nepal. These relationships are cherished to a degree that no one can miss their dramatic connotations. The greatest shame to China is the open distrust it attracts despite maneuverings and displays of good intentions. During the Sino-India border disputes, China tried to show the world that even small neighbors had no reason to fear China. China resolved its conflicts with such countries peacefully and without bitterness, so what then did a country like India have to fear? The whole purpose is to create a feeling that China is warmly welcomed by small countries and willingly aids their development. This leaves the impression that there must be something wrong with any country that rejects China's advances.

Though the advent of the open-door policy triggered new fears in the 1980s that China would dump goods on Southeast Asian markets, the Chinese held fast to the belief that everyone would prosper if only they would emulate China's brave decision to join the competitive world market. Chinese scholars came up with a very attractive picture for their anxiety-prone neighbors:

> China's four modernizations . . . will increasingly complement the trade in commodities with ASEAN countries, with each supplying what the other needs. China is an enormous market, and its market capacity will grow with progress in four modernizations and with the rise of the people's purchasing power, thus offering vast fields for its trade with other countries. Economic complimentation will even surpass economic competition. . . . No matter whether China participates or not, international competition is an objective existence. China's participation only adds one more competitive partner.[33]

The Use of Force

Despite its peace offensive, China has engaged in military conflicts with its Third World neighbors. That China has never had a war with a non-neighboring Third World country suggests that wars have more to do with the neighbor element than the Third World element. Nevertheless, because these wars with neighboring countries (specifically, those with South Korea, India, and Vietnam) may have damaged China's claim that it has no intention of meddling in the internal affairs of other countries, the sacrifice of peace must somehow have been seen as conducive to the development of a rightful order in Asia.

Decisions to go to war had more to do with the perception that these countries had abandoned Third World responsibilities and become the puppets of the imperialist or the hegemon. In the case of China's 1979 punitive war against Vietnam, Vietnamese policy was seen as an extension of Soviet hegemonic intervention in Cambodia, and Vietnam itself was labeled a regional hegemon. China launched the war irrespective of its need for resources and a peaceful environment for its recently begun modernization drive. The use of force thus helped China express its seemingly forgotten principle of antihegemonism at the moment when China was actually about to shelve it. Just before the war, China had normalized relations with the United States to signal its intention of returning to international society. By signing an agreement with its historical opponent and sacrificing peace with its neighbor, China count at the same time assert both peaceful intent and antihegemonism.

In each of these conflicts, China has maneuvered to rescue peaceful coexistence principles by unilaterally withdrawing troops after a short limited engagement, illustrating to its neighbors its lack of territorial ambitions. The moral regime still has to organize international politics according to its moral doctrines—if the regime is psychologically unable to enforce them, it demonstrates a *capacity* to enforce them but then gives up any real gains in hopes that the opponents will be moved by this magnanimous gesture of forgiveness. The irony is that China wants a certain moral principle to be followed without enforcing it but at the same time cannot tolerate cultural and moral defection without showing its disapproval. All principles are sacrificed to some extent in an effort to show China's determination to uphold all of them. Though this looks like opportunism on the surface, it can be misleading: China gives up captured territory, wastes resources useful for the domestic economy, creates an opportunity for superpower intervention, and risks its reputation as a peace-loving country all at once and for nothing concrete. The Chinese use force to demonstrate their contempt; they are enamored with the power of disdain because they are convinced of their moral appeal.

The whole process is a drama. The Chinese try to organize regional politics without actually organizing it. They try to demonstrate how refined and legitimate Chinese order and principles are and expect others simply to accept them, at least rhetorically. They adhere to their version of justice single-mindedly and are concerned with their ability to fulfill moral promise in appearance. Consciously as well as subconsciously, they manage to ignore the reality that small Third World neighbors, first and direct targets of their moral influence, are suspicious of their intentions.

Manipulating relationships with small countries and using force together reflect China's frustration and self-deception. This moral drama compels Chinese leaders to disregard give-and-take calculus on the battlefield.

THE THIRD WORLD AS MORAL TARGET

China's Third World policy fundamentally aims at demonstrating that China's principles of organizing world politics have popular support among the Third World countries and that China's willingness to assist these countries is not tainted with big-nationism. Because of the traditional Chinese style of engaging an enemy's mind rather than its muscle, Chinese efforts in the Third World are perhaps less a result of a need for allies than a result of dramatizing. Anyway, it would hardly make sense for China to look for allies to counter the U.S. imperialist and the Soviet hegemon in the Third World since any potential alliance with the Third World would only benefit China symbolically, not strategically.[34] China has little investment in these countries, no military bases, and no historical legacy.

The Third World countries, though, have a conceptually significant impact on China's moral status in the world. The Chinese look for signs of approval in the Third World to confirm their own worldviews. Throughout the 1960s they published maps that showed revolutionary activities around the world. Especially when they face superpower or Second World problems, they are eager to demonstrate how Chinese aid differs from that of the superpower-led blocs in terms of suitability to local conditions and absence of political strings. So the Third World plays a significant role in China's symbolic attempt to organize world politics.

Africa First

China's Third World policy generally targets Africa more than the Middle East and Latin America. According to Chinese conceptualization of world affairs, Middle Eastern politics revolves around anticolonialism and the politics of the Palestinian liberation movement. Since the Chinese are not a religious people, they are simply unable to appreciate the complexity of many Middle Eastern crises and hence largely ignore them. In the 1970s the region became more distinctive in China's views for two reasons. First, it appeared to the Chinese that there was superpower collusion in the Middle East, and this perception fitted nicely into China's antihegemonic worldview. Second, the 1973 oil embargo demonstrated a key weapon available to the resource-abundant Third World in its fight against colonialism. This high-level conceptualization really does not help the formation of concrete policy. On the whole, the Chinese have managed to avoid involvement in Middle Eastern affairs. The only exception is perhaps

South Yemen, which received substantial aid from China. China did not publicize this connection as a model of Sino-Arab relations, however, possibly because it lacked the knowledge (or necessary guiding principle) to deal with this region.

Indeed, when no other set of norms seems to be relevant, statist role conceptions naturally apply. It is exactly because the Middle East is such a conceptually peripheral area that China's policy there appears to be purely opportunistic. The official position is neutrality. Especially since the announcement of its independent foreign policy in 1982, China has endeavored to exploit its Middle Eastern connections as much as possible. During the Iran-Iraq War, Chinese diplomats and the military profited by selling arms to both sides. Meanwhile, the Chinese have developed a relationship of sorts with Israel while at the same time selling ballistic missiles to Saudi Arabia. Independent foreign policy fails to guide China's regional policy because China is never clear about how to be independent when there is no superpower contradiction or when neither of the superpowers is even involved. Most of the time, China's Middle East policy lacks focus because of the vagueness of China's self-image vis-à-vis the countries in the area. There is no moral disorder to be rectified, so there is no consistent policy to be pursued.

Latin America is fairly significant in China's search for justice in world politics. Anticolonialism provides the main theme because of U.S. dominance in the area. Chinese support to guerrilla forces is meager in Latin America, although Maoist rebel factions exist or have existed in most countries across the continent. When antihegemonism prevailed in the 1970s, China's Latin America policy shifted emphasis toward shoring up self-reliance in the region. China signed trade agreements with socialist Chile as well as militarist-nationalist Peru for the sake of diversifying the markets of these two countries, preventing them from falling victim to U.S. business control or politicized Soviet assistance.

China did well in Latin America during the early 1970s as the countries searched for a more independent gesture in world affairs to liberate themselves from U.S. influence and as the influence of East-West détente spread. The Chinese further promoted their popularity by tendering zero-interest loans free of political strings and arranging for delayed repayment schedules. This stands in sharp contrast to Western and Soviet policies. All China got in return, though, was recognition of China's sovereignty over Taiwan, which is actually only of symbolic value.

Africa as the Third World

Africa, in comparison, seems to be the real Third World, where most states are newly born and just throwing off the chains of colonialism; development there is not controlled by any conceptually identifiable historical force. Equally important is the Chinese misperception that Africa is a politically, culturally, and economically retarded and inferior continent. The Chinese contribution should be conspicuous, the Chinese model should be appealing, and the alliance between the superior and the inferior based on equality should be politically striking. China's Africa policy is thus the most dramatic element in its Third World contour.

Development aid. China's Africa policy is concerned with anticolonialism and antihegemonism, where China is able to make a significant moral contribution. China's aid to Africa has always been generous—so much so, in fact, considering China's meager capabilities, that one wonders whether generosity has become the sole purpose of aid. Chinese aid appears in the form of monetary loans, labor support, and material in kind. As mentioned earlier, the Chinese are particularly interested in projects the West has turned down or left unfinished. For example, Chinese hydraulics experts found water in northern Somalia where the British had failed in their previous attempts. Sometimes the Chinese ignore the economic value of the projects to satisfy the local regime's preference for more symbolic construction.[35]

The Tan-Zam Railroad—which neither the West nor the World Bank nor the Soviet Union would touch—has for years been regarded as the showcase of China's Africa policy. For whom is it a showcase? A realist would say Africa as a whole, so that China can win over other African states in its competition with the former colonialists, Taiwan, and the Soviet Union. But would this project not encourage unrealistic expectations among other African states? The Chinese clearly do not have the financial resources to repeat this experience, and it has never occurred to them to do so. In fact, over all these years China has continuously reminded the Africans that aid depends on China's capabilities. The implication is that the Chinese have never really wanted to generate such high expectations from other African states. The showcase, then, if it is one, is not for the Africans but may be for the Chinese, to confirm the correctness of their own method of development.

This psychology can be viewed in several ways. The Chinese technicians working on the railroad were generally interested only in completing the project as soon as possible and were not particularly enthusiastic about training the Africans to take over after it was completed. Problems did indeed arise later when the Chinese team left. When they came back to rescue the railroad, the Tanzanian government had to pay for the travel expenses of the new team.[36] The Chinese were so self-centered that they turned down any and all assistance from outside sources; they tried to construct everything from Chinese materials, and those who died on the job were hailed as martyrs. Precious human resources were poured into this project during post–Cultural Revolution years when essential technicians were only slowly returning from the countryside. All these sacrifices were justified and celebrated in China as winning friends for the Chinese.[37] And this was accepted as legitimate justification. There is no doubt that the project was a heroic effort of self-confirmation and self-actualization on the national level.

Revolutionary aid. The Chinese usually gave only moral support to revolutionary groups. Although no hard evidence has been produced to link China to assassinations or other rebellious activities in Third World countries, China has indeed provided ideological training from time to time. On the one hand, Chinese military aid to established Third World regimes, however, is well documented. On the other hand, Chinese miliary aid to local anticolonial forces is also steady. Whoever comes for help, "progressive" or "backward," the Chinese will render assistance in accordance with their capabilities.[38] Generally speaking, the Chinese try to aid all factions involved in an anticolonial struggle. As a rule, they tend to be closer to minority dissident groups than the major opposition force normally supplied by the Soviet Union, perhaps with the exception of Zimbabwe. China's neutral stand among factions was further extended to include states in the 1980s, so that in Africa, "China would never support one side to oppose the other."[39]

The frequency of remarks about revolution decreased in official Chinese statements during the 1970s and nearly disappeared during the 1980s. This change is not a direct response to the declining Soviet threat. It has more to do with China's self-evaluation of its role in the world than with glasnost in the Soviet Union (which really did not start until China's independent foreign policy was already in full gear). The downplaying of revolution in China makes the style of diplomacy that dramatizes antihegemonism and anticolonialism outdated. As a result, African countries now have to pay the travel expenses of Chinese aid teams. Yet because most states are now independent, relations with states rather than liberation movements have become more important in confirming the moral regime's sense of popularity.

Style. What makes China's aid to Africa truly dramatic is its style. As mentioned several times above, Chinese aid comes with no political strings and does not even require denunciation of the Soviet Union. Chinese aid workers live in conditions similar to local workers—a sharp contrast to teams from other countries, who consume significant local resources in living conditions that could hardly be labeled frugal. Chinese technicians work in the field alongside the locals and avoid generating an air of superiority.

The Chinese style is more like a show, however, if one looks closely at the behavior of the Chinese personnel. The Chinese do not mingle with the local people and seem not to appreciate the African life-style. The Chinese teams do not train their African counterparts well and generally place little trust in them; they would rather do the work themselves. As in the case of Southeast Asia, the Chinese want to establish their popularity in Africa by making their experiences a model for emulation, not by pushing the locals. Chinese technicians' dislike of local culture reveals the theatrical aspect of policy at the national level. The Chinese cause must be noble if they are helping, for free, people whom they neither like nor respect.

The Chinese aid teams also take into consideration the local situation when they implement their projects. Labor-intensive industries that process local materials normally receive priority. The emphasis is invariably on self-reliance and friendship. And self-reliance is at times used to justify China's anti-Soviet advice.

CHINA'S USE OF THE UNITED NATIONS

The Significance of the United Nations

Participation in the United Nations has symbolic function regarding Third World policy since China is not a member of the Group of 77, the Group of 24, or the nonaligned movement. It is widely suspected that China does not want to be constrained by bloc politics, especially as the majority in such a bloc might adopt a position incompatible with that of China. Equally important is China's consistent claim that its antihegemonic policy targets hegemonic behavior rather than hegemonic states. Participation in bloc politics would hinder China's opposition to the hegemonic behavior of other bloc members and constrain it from complimenting nonmembers on their antihegemonism. In particular, China does not see the Third World in economic terms, so economically undeveloped countries willing to serve hegemonic states are unacceptable allies. Many of these perceived Third World defectors are involved in efforts to organize the Third World: good examples include Cuba, India, and Vietnam. China would refuse to deal with them because to do so would hurt the credibility of the united front against hegemonism. (Of course, it is not clear if it is China's dislike of these countries that breeds the perception of their being hegemonic puppets or vice versa.)

Granted the United Nations includes China's friends as well as enemies, the body is better perceived as a battlefield rather than a policymaking unit. Even though the United Nations denounced China as an aggressor during the Korean War, China tends to view the UN positively. A representative from the Chinese Communist Party was in the first Chinese delegation to the United Nations in 1945, and the Chinese consistently quoted the UN Charter in bilateral agreements even before they joined the organization.[40] To make sense of China's UN policy, one has to examine the role-playing nature of the story. First of all, the UN General Assembly provides China with an opportunity to distinguish between Third World defectors and the Third World in general. There is no need to engage in real conflict if China can use polemics to clarify its moral position on Third World issues. Actual punitive action against defectors would hurt China's Third World status because defectors are Third World countries nonetheless. Scolding in the UN forum, in contrast, demonstrates the moral integrity of China's unstressed, but implied, leadership. Peaceful coexistence, antihegemonism, anticolonialism, and the united front can be satisfied at the same time by manipulating the public forum.

Second, as repeatedly mentioned above, it is extremely important for a moral regime to maintain the appearance of popularity in the UN. China's entry was regarded as a victory over U.S. containment policy.[41] It meant that the world recognized China, not that China recognized the status quo. The Chinese were very careful to avoid the appearance of compromise. Just a few years before China's entry, Zhou Enlai was talking about revolutionizing the UN structure.[42] A few years after joining, the Chinese formalized the notion of antihegemonism in the three-worlds theory. Associated with this public recognition of China's status is the opportunity for China to present itself as a model. As discussed in the section on China's policy toward its Third World neighbors, the Chinese are more comfortable with being emulated voluntarily than with imposing their experience forcefully. The UN forum is the perfect setting for such pretended moral popularity. China may criticize the superpowers at will without fear and bask in the applause of Third World nations.

Finally, China's participation has another symbolic effect: China is the only Third World nation with veto power. This simple fact dramatically enhances China's leadership role in the Third World. The element of rich versus poor is added to Security Council meetings traditionally dominated by the theme of East versus West. To a great extent, the Third World countries are seduced by China's position as their representative because of the new political status China took over from Taiwan's Nationalist representative and by China's apparent intention to use this status for Third World causes. It is unlikely that China can resist the temptation to play the role expected of it. In 1985 *Beijing Review* characterized the change in atmosphere that China's presence in the United Nations had brought about: "The increasingly important role of Third World, nonaligned and other peace-loving countries in maintaining the principles of the charter and resisting power politics has made it harder for major powers to manipulate and control the UN. . . . It is of special significance to

strictly . . . oppose in international relations the practice of the big bullying the small, the strong oppressing the weak and the rich exploiting the
poor."[43]

Style of Participation

Nonparticipation. Although China possesses the power of veto, it is reluctant to use what it regards as a tool of hegemony. Instead, China opts
for nonparticipation. According to Kim, this practice allows China more
flexibility. Nonparticipation could mean support or opposition, and the
Chinese could explain their action in different ways to different audiences.[44] Nonparticipation also suggests the self-imposed constraint of the
various principles to which China has pledged allegiance. It is difficult to
satisfy, for example, peace and antihegemonism or antihegemonism and
anti-imperialism at the same time; inaction is perhaps the best action.
China also fears it might end up on the minority side—a sign of a lack of
popularity. This is probably what the moral regime can tolerate least of all.
The practice of nonparticipation explains why the Chinese voting record is
largely consistent with its Third World rhetoric.[45] China simply does not
vote against the Third World if possible. China's first use of its veto was to
delay the entry of Bangladesh on the grounds that the new state was a product of Soviet and Indian interference in Pakistan's affairs and hence not a
peace-loving country. In a later vote, China withdrew its veto and allowed
the country to join after it appeared that China's position was unpopular.

Refusing leadership. Concern for popularity and a positive image constrains China from making a bid for leadership in the United Nations. In
fact, China's participation in the UN helps the Chinese find out what the
Third World really wants, and China analyzes the Third World mood carefully. In an empirical study, Kim finds that the Chinese delegates are patient and sincere listeners.[46] This is again consistent with China's reluctance to impose its own view forcefully, preferring the more delicate and
indirect way. This outright refusal to assume leadership strengthens
China's call for antihegemonism since the Chinese themselves are the perfect example of antihegemonism. China can also avoid being on the unpopular side by shunning any leadership role.

To encourage the Third World to strike against U.S. and Soviet hegemonism in the Chinese way—is this not the best leadership China could
provide? The fear of losing popularity and the psychological desire for
leadership together explain China's relative passivity in organizing the
Third World. Its engagement in the United Nations is invariably rhetorical,
well-calculated, and prepared, and largely consistent with the majority
view of the Third World. This alludes to the unchanged theme of China's
Third World policy: serving as a true model. Indeed, China's polemics

with the Soviet Union and its overall voting record against U.S. positions on world issues substantiated the famous Chinese argument that superpower confrontation was the cause of almost all the problems in the world and shamed the leadership the two provided.[47] In short, refusing leadership is statement of genuine leadership.

Rhetoric. One cannot overlook the polemics between China and the Soviet Union in the United Nations. The Chinese believe that daring to challenge this major power is an important sign of moral purity, although not every Third World country always appreciates China's siding with the United States on some local issues. In reality, the Chinese voting record does not evidence compliance with the United States. The use of rhetoric reflects the traditional Chinese shaming technique. By criticizing the Soviets in public, the Chinese intend to show the world that the superpowers fail morally because they cannot win popular global support. The Chinese hope to encourage others to follow suit in the way Mao did when he carried out peasant revolution and land reform in China. The pretension has to be that if every Third World country dared take on the superpowers in a public forum, it would be possible to reorganize the United Nations. China thus uses the UN primarily to present its worldview and generate popularity.

The use of the UN General Assembly is important in another respect. The Chinese normally do not lobby privately.[48] The moral regime does not encourage lobbying because it implies a lack of moral attractiveness and emphasis on negotiation. Negotiation, in turn, implies the possibility of compromising moral principles for the sake of some less noble material gain. If lobbying is not a legitimate means to get one's message across, the use of a public forum is important. Speaking in front of the General Assembly is more one-way communication than the give-and-take of private lobbying. In addition, one-way communication satisfies some vague sense of superiority in terms of the demonstrated ability to give proper direction and formulate the correct model for the world.[49] In this way, China assures the Third World that dealing with China is a matter of genuine morality, not a carrot-and-stick affair.

Chinese Dramas in the UN

Peace. While both China's constitution and the UN Charter specify peace as a universal goal, the Chinese are ambivalent about the relationship between peace and war. Although China has consistently advocated peaceful coexistence among states, the Chinese also believe that war against a colonialist, a hegemonist, or an imperialist is absolutely justifiable. For example, they supported the Algerian independence struggle against the best interests of the Algerian communist movement.[50] Another matter in which they appear to contradict themselves is the issue of nuclear testing. China and France were the targets of a draft resolution of the UN Conference on Human Environment condemning nuclear testing. China demonstrates its concern for the environment by supporting the Third World on other environmental issues and the opening of a responsible UN office in Nairobi. In short, there are certain reservations in China's peaceful coexistence norms that the other UN members do not appreciate.

One reservation is based upon antihegemonism. China refuses to accept the kind of peace that would strengthen the domination of the superpowers. Until very recently, China refused to recognize the UN peacekeeping role in regional cease-fire agreements (China once fought UN troops in the Korean War). China also accused the United States of using UN troops to invade the Congo in the early 1960s. In the 1960s and the 1970s, when antihegemonism prevailed in Chinese revolutionary diplomacy, this denouncement of UN peacekeeping signaled to the world and the Chinese themselves that joining the UN did not mean that China had foresaken its revolutionary ideology. By uncovering the fraudulent nature of superpower peace overtures, China might ensure a long-term antihegemonic peace.

Another reservation concerns arms control, on which China's position is also a mix of support and opposition. The idea of arms control is honorable, but the manner in which the superpowers propose to go about it is not. As with peacekeeping, the Chinese are constantly worried about a superpower monopoly of nuclear weapons and their use to blackmail the Third World. So the Chinese position on arms control in the UN has been consistent: the nuclear states must agree to the principles of no first use and no use against nonnuclear nations before any meaningful negotiation can begin. From the Chinese perspective, antiproliferation and test ban proposals all appear as attempts at nuclear monopoly. The negative attitude toward arms control again seems to be at odds with the notion of peace, so China has to demonstrate its peaceful intentions in other ways. In the General Assembly China has supported the idea of nuclear-free zones in Latin America, the Middle East, Africa, the South Pacific, South Asia, and the Indian Ocean.[51]

China's efforts to slow down the superpower-sponsored peace process affects neither world politics in general nor arms control between the superpowers in particular. However, dynamic global realities and changing Chinese worldviews worked together to produce China's own peace offensive in the 1980s. Since China launched its reform program in 1978, peace has become more important than antihegemonism. At the same time, superpower détente clearly reached a new stage in the mid-1980s. On the one hand, hegemonism seems to have declined; on the other hand, if China continues to reject arms negotiation or UN peacekeeping, the hegemon could appear to be more peaceful than China! Additionally, to show that China is indeed dedicated to internal reform, there is a new need to demonstrate China's willingness and ability to contribute to external peace processes.

China began to participate in UN disarmament negotiations in 1978.[52] The most dramatic change is probably the rise of China's interest in the UN Truce Supervision Organization in Jerusalem and the UN Transition Assistance Group in Namibia. In 1982 China pledged its full support to peacekeeping and started paying its UN peacekeeping arrears because it realized that peacekeeping was "welcome[d] by the Third World and play[ed] a stabilizing role in keeping conflicts from escalating."[53] In 1988 China became a formal commission member for UN peace maintenance. The Chinese also take a more active approach to arms control. They emphasize the importance of involving every country, not just the nuclear powers, in the disarmament process. After repeating their principle of no first use and arguing that all foreign troops in all nations should be extracted, China made the following proposal in the General Assembly: "the countries possessing the largest arsenals bear a special responsibility for disarmament and should take the lead in drastically reducing their nuclear and conventional armaments. This is the key to progress in disarmament. . . . The United States and the Soviet Union . . . possess the largest nuclear and conventional arsenals, and they also are capable of launching a world war."[54] For this reason, China supports the intermediate-range nuclear forces (INF) treaty between the superpowers, though it remains insufficiently drastic by Chinese standards.[55] To be consistent with previous concern for Third World causes, China also advocates that every country "should have an equal say" in the peace process.[56]

China's peace dramas in the United Nations have really been efforts to actualize China's self-image. Rather than achieving peace, earlier Chinese peace talks aimed at showing the world how the Soviet hegemon had undermined peace. More recent talks present China as part of the world peace process though in fact it is not. Because disarmament is too "complicated," China petitions each country to first demonstrate "good faith" as China has done for decades.[57] Contrary to many journalists' observations, an overall concern for the Third World is constantly present in all China's remarks, although it is not as dramatic as it used to be. The Chinese dilemma is that they despise the superpower-sponsored peace process yet are afraid of being left out in the cold. The aforementioned arms control doctrines help them assert their concern without losing face.

Development. China actively supported the idea of a new international economic order in the 1970s. For the Chinese, the NIEO theme pins the blame for global underdevelopment squarely on the West. They have recommended that all UN organs be reformed according to the NIEO concepts. They are particularly interested in cartels in the style of the Organization of Petroleum Exporting Countries (OPEC), a perfect example of collective self-reliance. Instead of rendering substantive aid to the NIEO, the Chinese have repeatedly demonstrated their familiar style of support in the UN forum by orally encouraging Third World unity and self-reliance, the nationalization of natural resources, and the phasing out of foreign investment. China can indeed be an unambiguous model in this regard.

However, since China's post-Mao modernization campaign began in earnest, North-South interdependence and South-South coordination have received equal stress in the Chinese media. China has started to identify specific responsibilities for the North instead of just demanding a simple shift of wealth to the South. China has presented several propositions to the General Assembly. First, the North should stabilize primary products prices and establish funds to diversify southern commodities. Second, the North should end protectionism. Third, the North must fulfill official development assistance quotas set by the United Nations. Fourth, debtors and creditors should share responsibility for solving the debt crisis. And finally, preferential treatment, like the UN's Programme of Action for African Economic Recovery and Development, should be implemented.[58]

These propositions give the impression of a neutral observer's making suggestions to both the North and South. Indeed, one Chinese commentator proudly claims that the West, the Soviet bloc (before 1990), the Group of 77, and China make up four negotiating parties in most UN economic agencies. China's "unique status" gives it influence.[59] Outside the United Nations, China is competing for capital from the North, and China is probably a good model of how to get northern assistance without sacrificing self-reliance. Economic sanctions imposed on China after the 1989 Tiananmen massacre provided the Chinese with an opportunity to illustrate how they can continue their open-door policy while waiting for the North to resume its economic interaction with China. China needs the North's assistance but can do without if necessary. The true meaning of self-reliance lies more in South-South coordination than in North-South interdependence, since eventually the North will have to come to the rescue of the South in order to save itself.

The same mode of thinking is clearer in the case of the UN Development Programme (UNDP). First of all, China tries to separate itself from the Third World by emphasizing the exchange relationship (as opposed to unilateral UN aid) between the United Nations and China. It is "exchange" because "while donating funds to UN organizations and undertaking their projects, China also receives technical assistance from these organizations," and "mutual cooperation has made rapid progress."[60] The Chinese news media also stresses that the Chinese government shares the financial burden for those cooperative projects aided by the United Nations. A local official is quoted as remarking, "It was not the UN assistance alone that caused these changes; the UN support, however, was a major contributing factor. In the future . . . after residents in [the] county become affluent, they would like to contribute food aid to other developing countries through WFP [the World Food Programme]."[61] In fact, China claims that it has redistributed 5 percent of UNDP funds to support development activities in other countries in order to show that the Chinese will not build their own self-reliance at others' expense. The assistance China has received is described as "supplementary" and "complementary." China has "all along adhered to the principle of independence and self-reliance in its socialist construction" because UN activities are based upon "equality and respect for sovereignty."[62]

Finally, like all other projects China has engaged in, the Chinese experience is presented as a model for the Third World. Chinese-UN *mutual* assistance is praised, and UNDP Administrator Bradford Morse called China's one of the best among the UN's development programs. Despite the widespread impression that China is competing for limited funds with the Third World, China manages to present its UN assistance as a two-way movement, as a model for the other Third World countries, and as a model of how to preserve and even enhance self-reliance with outside assistance. By 1987 the Chinese had received about $6 million from various UN agricultural funds and donated about $6 million and 2 million renminbi. China's contribution to other development organizations reached about U.S.$12 million and 16 million renminbi by 1987, while it received $200 million.

The UN as a Stage

The pattern of UN-Chinese interaction has changed over time. The Chinese use the UN as a stage dramatically to demonstrate China's national self-image and a place to confirm that its popularity has not slipped. China's real contribution to the United Nations, to peace, and to development is debatable. But China's participation in UN activities certainly helps clarify how China would like to be seen. The Chinese make sure their performance—specifically their voting record—is consistent and compatible with Third World interests, at least in appearance.

One philosophical question remaining is, If China actually accepts money from the UN, is not all this moral rhetoric but a smoke screen? Partially. Moral rhetoric and continuous oral commitment to Third World causes would help justify to the Chinese their acceptance of UN aid. This type of moral pretension also reminds the Chinese themselves of the importance of maintaining self-reliance. More significant to international organizational processes is the possibility that China will sacrifice this aid in order to signal the moral decay of the United Nations. China uses the UN to convince itself that its moral principles are popular—or can become popular after the Chinese have staged a few demonstrations of their model and praised a few Third World examples of successful emulation.

THIRD WORLD BETRAYED?

Third World Disillusion

Though the brutality of the 1989 Beijing massacre shocked most in the West, it may not necessarily have alienated the chiefly authoritarian Third World. Third World countries, however, are now able to see that they are dealing with a regime that is not quite popular with its own people. Even for the Chinese, the pretension of the moral regime has been shattered. Some African students in the West have joined their Chinese counterparts in commemorating those killed in the massacre. The incident also reminds the world that the Chinese government is always willing to resort to force despite the rhetoric of peace (though the government may sincerely believe this rhetoric).

The massacre occurred against the background of new revelations of Chinese racism against African students. On Christmas Day 1988, the failure of police to stop an angry Chinese mob escalated a dispute involving African students in Nanjing. In the end, 135 were forcibly detained and allegedly tortured by police.[63] Chinese racism against blacks looks much more threatening now, in view of what happened six months later at Tiananmen.

Perhaps a more serious blow to Chinese morale were the consecutive announcements by nine Third World countries—the Bahamas, Belize, Central Africa, Grenada, Guinea-Bissau, Lesotho, Liberia, Nicaragua, and Niger—that they would establish diplomatic relations with Taiwan. The Chinese on Taiwan were basically doing what the mainlanders had done in the early 1960s: promising economic assistance in return for diplomatic recognition, which would then be used in domestic politics to prove the attractiveness and the popularity of the Chinese (in this case, the Taiwanese) model. These are probably Taiwan's first diplomatic gains at the expense of China. For the Chinese, this is not just a case of losing popularity, it is also a matter of legitimacy, since the Taiwan government still claims partial sovereignty over the Chinese mainland.

There seems to be some disillusion in the Third World with the Chinese model of development, China's capacity to assist the Third World, the popularity of the Chinese regime, the Chinese commitment to Third World causes, and China's usefulness as a Third World ally. China's rhetorical diplomacy in the United Nations is insufficient to consolidate its Third World dramas.

Unfulfilled Dramas

The coexistence of a number of different doctrines in China's Third World policy makes it difficult for the Chinese to indicate their precise role in the Third World and their expectations for Third World conduct. The psychopolitical need for the moral regime to maintain an appearance of consistency is a serious and intriguing constraint. Even though China's self-image has changed over time, outdated doctrines remain valid in theory. Just as China has exploited the Taiwan issue to dramatize China's anti-imperialist concerns and the notion of independence in Sino-U.S. relations, so it has used the Third World to satisfy Chinese notions of popularity. China betrays the Third World in the sense that it determines and alters the needs of the Third World without ever consulting the Third World nations. Consultation in the United Nations only serves to polish official Chinese positions, which can then be presented in a more sophisticated and acceptable manner.

Because of a fear of failure, China does not wish to negotiate with a complex Third World about the root causes of many global issues. If there is no solution to a Third World issue, why should China risk the image of Third World leader by pursuing a solution? The Chinese can do best by assuming their moral doctrines will eventually command popularity. In this way, China's support becomes uncertain. The Third World can expect from China only a degree of rhetorical support whose form they never know in advance. More seriously, they can be almost certain that China will make no substantive effort in the Third World's struggle for equity and autonomy. China's failed leadership is a partial but direct result of the moral regime's reluctance to pursue public leadership.

The same fear of public failure leads to China's unique use of nonparticipation as a form of tacit cooperation or latent regret. The only country that once dared to challenge both superpowers simultaneously may suddenly decide to keep silent at a time when the Third World most needs its moral support. That China has shied away from Third World bloc politics damages the image of the Third World and indicates that the Third World cannot consistently rely on China. Nonparticipation in actual politics may appear especially mysterious because the Third World is unable to appreciate the moral regime's style of publicly saying one thing and actually doing something quite different. The Chinese themselves fail to see the inconsistency between their attitude and their policy toward Israel or toward the Iran-Iraq War. In most other cultures, nonparticipation in high politics would imply lack of interest in low politics. This is not the case for China.

The Third World and, above all, Africa were particularly inattentive to China's call for an antihegemonic united front in the 1970s. The notion of a united front in which imperialist and colonial forces would link with the Third World probably sounded absurd to rational Third World leaders. The Chinese saw Sino-Soviet polemics in the United Nations as a matter of principles and hence more important than the calculation of day-to-day profit for the Third World as a whole. Finally, China's attitude toward the United Nations has at various times been favorable, pessimistic, antagonistic, hopeful, arrogant, negative, and finally accepting.[64]

In the matter of bilateral relations with individual Third World countries, China's call for unity invites cynicism. China has failed to maintain steady and friendly relations with important countries like India, Cuba, and Indonesia. The reckless labeling of these countries as puppets of imperialism or hegemonism only tarnishes the collective Third World image precisely because these countries have assumed some form of leadership in one Third World movement or another. So China's advocacy of a peaceful solution to all Third World disputes has not been applied to China itself (although the Chinese believe they have very good reasons for this inconsistency).

Antihegemonism became irrelevant in the mid-1980s in light of the new reformist leadership in the Soviet Union. The lack of a revolutionary target and the process of détente together make the united front strategy, the theory of intermediate zones, and the three-world theory rather awkward doctrines. This lack of proper role conceptions gives rise to statism, which pays attention to the pursuit of short-run and narrowly defined national interests. Once more, the Third World seems to have been betrayed despite the sporadic gift giving Chinese leaders engage in during Third World visits.

This brings one to the most serious constraint on China's Third World policy: lack of a real ability to assist Third World development. The tendency for the moral regime to search for symbolic signs of its power to fulfill the impossible mission of rectifying world order hampers any serious attempt to break out of the drama of being a model. Even pragmatic leaders like Deng Xiaoping, Zhao Ziyang, and Li Peng hold onto these misconceptions. The tragedy of Tiananmen, followed by reemphasis of socialist ethics, self-reliance, and Third Worldism, only reinforces the pyschocultural significance of these dramas.

Finally, the disaster of the Great Leap Forward, the chaos of the Cultural Revolution, and the indecision and the lack of political support of the reformist leaders should have shown the Third World that there is no such thing as a Chinese model. There is no more serious failure for the moral regime than to be no longer seen as a model for emulation. The Chinese way of organizing the Third World depends solely on the latter's voluntary submission, which can only come about if the moral regime successfully presents itself as a model. The failure of the Chinese development experience directly hinders the establishment of any meaningful causal map depicting the road to modernization.

Remaining Dramas

Chinese dramas nonetheless continue. China has said nothing that damages the Third World as a whole, and China still recognizes the Third World as a powerful force in reorganizing world politics. The Chinese repeat the self-role conceptions that China is a part of the Third World and will continue to be so even after China is modernized. The Chinese may be expected to demonstrate their commitment to Third World causes once in a while to remind themselves of the public perception of China's meaning in the world.

Uncertainty about internal reform is another reason why China must occasionally reiterate its Third World identity. In particular, after the Tiananmen massacre, Chinese leaders turned to their South Asian neighbors, Latin America, the Middle East, and Africa in order to show that international criticism of China's brutality was only a result of manipulation by a minor group of imperialist agents. The moral regime is still popular— or at least is able to pretend to be so when some Third World nations (who the Chinese hope represent the populous Third World as a whole) welcome Chinese visitors.

The cycle will never be perfect, but some sort of cycle does seem to exist. One principle is sacrificed to dramatize another and in due course will itself be dramatized. Neither the world nor Chinese self-identity is static. Exactly because of this dynamism, anti-imperialism will one day make a comeback, and commitment to Third World causes will be highlighted again so that China may pretend to historical consistency. Every drama can and will be repeated till the demise of the moral regime.

NOTES

1. For example, see John Hatch, "China and Africa," *New Statesman*, August 20, 1970: 234.

2. Tareq Y. Ismael, "People's Republic of China and Africa," *Journal of Modern African Studies* 9, 4 (1971): 507.

3. Alan Hutchinson, "China and Africa," *Round Table* 59 (July 1975): 264.

4. Colin Legum, "Gong Dafei: Vice Foreign Minister for African Affairs, the PRC," *Africa Report* (March-April 1983): 22.

5. Hutchinson, "China and Africa," p. 265.

6. Melinda Liu, "Guerilla-style Diplomacy," *Far Eastern Economic Review* (September 8, 1978): 12–13.

7. Philip Snow, *The Star Raft: China's Encounter with Africa* (New York: Weidenfeld & Nicolson, 1988), p. 123.

8. Alaba Ogunsanwo, *China's Policy in Africa* (Cambridge: Cambridge University Press, 1974), pp. 258–267.

9. "Peking Redefines Its Ties," *Africa* 138 (February 1983): 34; Roland Tyrrell, "Zhao's African Odyssey," *Far Eastern Economic Review* 119 (February 3, 1983): 25.

10. Cecil Johnson, "China and Latin America: New Ties and Tactics," *Problems of Communism* 21 (July 1972): 53–66.

11. Snow, *The Star Raft*, p. 158.

12. Samuel Kim, "China and the Third World: In Search of a Peace and Development Line," in S. Kim (ed.), *China and the World: New Directions in Chinese Foreign Relations* (Boulder: Westview, 1989), p. 173.

13. Ibid., p. 169.

14. Chih-yu Shih, "The Demise of China's Moral Regime: The Great Leap Forward in Retrospect," paper presented at the Northeastern Political Science Association annual meeting, November 26, 1989, Philadelphia.

15. Lucian Pye, *The Mandarin and the Cadre* (Ann Arbor: Center of Chinese Studies, University of Michigan, 1988).

16. Robert L. Worden, "International Organizations: China's Third World Policy in Practice," in L. C. Harris and R. L. Worden (eds.), *China and the Third World: Champion or Challenger?* (Dover, Mass.: Auburn House, 1986), pp. 96–97.

17. Carol Lee Hamrin, "Domestic Components and China's Evolving Three Worlds Theory," in Harris and Worden, *China and the Third World*, p. 48.

18. Bruce D. Larkin, "Emerging China's Effects on Third World Economic Choice," in Harris and Worden, *China and the Third World*, pp. 100–119.

19. Gopal Chaudhuri, *China and Nonalignment* (New Delhi: ABC Publishing House, 1986), pp. 167–181.

20. Ibid., p. 169.

21. Lillian C. Harris and Robert L. Worden, "Introduction," in Harris and Worden, *China and the Third World*, p. 1.

22. Snow, *The Star Raft*, pp. 206–212.

23. Ibid., pp. 69–104.

24. Raphael Israeli, "Living in China's Shadow," *Orbis* 31, 3 (Fall 1987): 341.

25. Snow, *The Star Raft*, pp. 136–138.

26. Samuel Kim, "Mao Zedong and China's Changing World View," in J. Hsiung and S. Kim (eds.), *China in the Global Community* (New York: Praeger, 1980), pp. 30–31.

27. Herbert S. Yee, "The Three World Theory and Post-Mao China's Global Strategy," *International Affairs* 59 (Spring 1983): 240–241.

28. See the discussion in Liyu Ni, "On Zhou Enlai's Diplomatic Theory," *Beijing Review* (April 3-9, 1989): 14–15; also see *Selected Work of Zhou Enlai*, Vol. 2 (Beijing: People's Press, 1984), p. 118.

29. "Co-Chairman's Summary of Conclusions," *Beijing Review* (April 18, 1983): v.

30. Peter Van Ness, *Revolution and Chinese Foreign Policy* (Berkeley: University of California Press, 1970), pp. 94–101.

31. Chunyan Wang and Ximing Wu, "Deng Xiaoping on Peace and War," *Beijing Review* (April 3-9, 1989), p. 19.

32. "Co-Chairman's Summary," *Beijing Review*: v.

33. Ji Gouxing, "ASEAN Countries in Political and Economic Perspectives," *Asian Affairs* 18 (June 1987): 166.

34. One good example of this realist perspective is George T. Yu, "China and the Third World," *Asian Survey* 17 (November 1977): 1036–1048.

35. Snow, *The Star Raft*, pp. 156–157.

36. Ibid., p. 182.

37. Ibid., pp. 162–170.

38. Legum, "Gong Dafei," *Africa Report:* 22.

39. "Vice Premier Li on Sino-African Relations," *Beijing Review* (July 9, 1984): 16.

40. Weinberg Chai, "China and the United Nations: Problems of Representation and Alternatives," *Asian Survey* 10 (May 1970): 406–407.

41. Liang Xi, "The United Nations and China," *Wuhandaxue Xuebao* (Wuhan University journal) 4, (1989): 8.

42. *Peking Review* (January 26, 1965): 5–6.

43. "China Marks Signing of UN Charter," *Beijing Review* (July 8, 1985): 6

44. Samuel Kim, "Whither Post-Mao Chinese Global Policy?" *International Organization* 35, 3 (Summer 1981): 442.

45. Trong R. Chai, "China's Policy Toward the Third World and the Superpowers in the UN General Assembly, 1971–1977: A Voting Analysis," *International Organization* 33, 3 (Summer 1979): 391–403.

46. Samuel Kim, *China, the United Nations, and World Order* (Princeton: Princeton University Press, 1978): 129–136.

47. Charles M. Lichenstein, "China in the UN: The Case of Kampuchea," *World Affairs* 149 (Summer 1986): 21–24.

48. Ibid.

49. Chih-yu Shih, *The Spirit of Chinese Foreign Policy: A Psychocultural View* (London: Macmillan, 1990), pp. 138–141.

50. There is no doubt that Chinese support for the struggle also had to do with their wish to hold the second Bandung conference in Algeria, which would have excluded the Soviet Union.

51. William R. Feeney, "Sino-Soviet Competition in the United Nations," *Asian Survey* 17 (Summer 1977): 815–816.

52. For a detailed discussion, see Kim, "Whither Post-Mao Chinese Global Policy?" pp. 442–447.

53. Ted Morello, "Serving the U.N.," *Far Eastern Economic Review* (February 9, 1989): 20.

54. Xueqian Wu, "China's Position on Major World Issues," *Beijing Review* (October 5, 1987): 15.

55. Paul H. B. Godwin, "Soldiers and Statesmen: Chinese Defense and Foreign Policies in the 1990s," in Kim, *China and the World*, p. 194.

56. Wu, "China's Position," *Beijing Review:* 15.

57. Ibid.

58. Fureng Dong, "Socialist Countries' Diversity Ownership," *Beijing Review* (October 5, 1987): 18.

59. Liang, "The United Nations and China," p. 7.

60. *Beijing Review* (February 7, 1983): 19.

61. *Beijing Review* (June 2, 1986): 16.

62. *Beijing Review* (February 7, 1983): 20, 21 and (April 28, 1986): 7.

63. *Far Eastern Economic Review* (January 12, 1989): 12.

64. James Hsiung, *Law and Policy in China's Foreign Relations: A Study of Attitudes and Practice* (New York: Columbia University Press, 1972), p. 174.

8

CONCLUSION:
THE FALLIBLE MORAL REGIME

As argued throughout this book, the Chinese style of organizing world politics is more dramatic than realist. Constrained by cultural imperatives, the moral regime expresses its wishful thinking through extreme diplomatic rhetoric and the occasional use of military force. For the Chinese themselves, the messages primarily serve to indicate their determination and confidence in rectifying the corrupt world order. Instead of forcing others to accept the Chinese view, however, Chinese tactics basically involve shaming, demonstration, self-sacrifice, and modeling. In other words, it is more important to assert that the Chinese vision is impeccable than to achieve that vision. The legitimacy of the Chinese leadership and the Chinese regime is intrinsically dependent on this show of immutable commitment to preserving the right order.

There is an inevitable linkage between external behavior and internal political struggle. China's role in a larger international context has to make sense to its domestic constituency. For this purpose, the view of the external world must comply with the prevailing notion of justice in domestic politics. Yet those who are in power within the moral regime tend to shame those who have lost the battle. In order to maintain external-internal consistency, the external view of those who are purged will have to be frozen, if not denied altogether. Consequently, external policy behavior and its targets of shaming have shifted because domestic politics has never been stable. One quantitative study of China's diplomatic stability actually suggests that the chance any particular dominant worldview will continue as a guideline into the following year is about 28 percent in China, and about 40 percent of the political constituency shifts sides constantly.[1]

Partially for this reason, the Chinese quest for justice is mostly dramatic. China has neither the time and resources for nor interest in actually changing the world. Too much is spent on painstaking struggles to maintain a balance between the need for a consistent outlook and the constantly changing emphasis of domestic politics. For a moral regime to survive in world politics, its leaders cannot afford to shift sides without justifiable reasons. For a moral regime to survive in domestic politics, its leaders cannot afford to allow the moral views of previous leaders to linger too long. The twist is partially resolved dramatically: restating the principles of the previous leadership and sacrificing them immediately afterwards to highlight other principles. Chinese hesitation in the process of Sino-U.S. normalization (see Chapter 5), which resulted from the fluctuating balance between factions during the 1970s, illustrates this point. In this particular case, antihegemonism, peaceful coexistence, and the strategy of the united front were collectively responsible for the confusing outlook. (Scholars looking to explain China's foreign policy in terms of power politics thus miss this critical point: the Chinese mind-set is rarely characterized by clarity. They comfortably live with confusion so long as no one challenges them.)

For China to continue organizing world politics by posing as a model instead of actually doing any organizing, this internal-external linkage must persist, as surely no leader would be interested in dramatizing any national role externally if he or she had nothing to gain in terms of internal legitimacy and moral status. There is one possible reason why a leader might do that, however: if the moral regime still deeply believed in the importance of moral superiority in achieving influence in world politics. This belief in moral power is the definition of the moral regime. One logical caveat exists here. If there is no external-internal linkage, the domestic constituency must have given up the idea of moral politics, thus signaling the end of interest in moral superiority in world politics.

Accordingly, the weakening of the linkage between external behavior and internal political struggle is an indicator of the decline of the moral regime in world politics. This process of weakening appears to have occurred in the 1980s, when, as everyone knows, intense struggle between radical and conservative reformers resulted in several political purges. However, every leader has pledged support for the so-called open-door policy despite allegiance to either antihegemonism or anti-imperialism. The implication is that a certain approach to the external world has gradually developed independently of domestic political struggle; the content of domestic ideology has become less relevant. This process traditionally implies legalist thinking, which emphasizes the wealth and strength of a nation, not its moral standing in the world. Legalist style has been reflected in China's recent willingness to utilize whatever resources it can acquire in the world to promote modernization at home.

The decline of the Chinese moral regime is discussed in the following sections. First, the traditional external-internal linkage is examined in order to show how it is eroding. The next sections show that the internal source of decline was the Great Leap Forward of 1958 and that the decline was reinforced by the open-door policy of the 1980s. Finally, the impact of China's moral decay on its role in international organizational processes is analyzed.

THE WEAKENING LINKAGE

The linkage between domestic and external policy has been well examined elsewhere. Indeed, one can criticize sinologists' obsession with the internal sources of China's external behavior,[2] others may insist that the linkage is clear, if not dominant.[3] As mentioned in Chapter 3, Liberthal, Van Ness, and I all have identified interesting parallels between foreign policy and domestic politics. While the Chinese have never acknowledged factional infighting among the so-called three lines, they do specify three distinct international principles: socialism, peaceful coexistence, and antihegemonism.[4]

In theory, the Chinese could achieve the ideal of socialism by encouraging antihegemonism and anti-imperialism in the Third World while adhering to the principle of peaceful coexistence to deter hegemonic interference in Third World revolution. Of course, the Chinese do not really go out and organize the world like this. The Chinese way of organizing world politics is dramatized by condemning those whose organizational principles stand in opposition to those of China. This is organizing through shaming.

In reality, different political leaders stress different organizing principles, each with a different set of role conceptions; the external-internal linkage exists in leadership. Three different leadership styles in Chinese politics have served as the linkages between domestic political views and external worldviews. According to one recent study, an internal hierarchical leadership that emphasizes socialist principles, employs coercive methods, and builds its strength on organized structures tends to see the world as an asymmetrical relationship between leaders and followers struggling for or against imperialism. An internal leadership style of normalcy that attends to individual needs, utilizes material incentives, and relies on institutional arrangement tends to see the world as a symmetrical relationship among equals regardless of their ideologies. An internal rebellious leadership that despises all authority, favors moral incentives, and adopts the mass line in political struggle tends to see the world as a revolutionary relationship between the victimized Third World and the exploiting hegemony.[5]

Because of the connection between leadership style and external worldview, Chinese diplomatic positions generally change according to a cyclical pattern. As Dorothy Solinger sees it, Chinese leadership style follows the sequence of bureaucratic control, market control, and mass control.[6] Her categories largely match the terminology of hierarchy, normalcy, and rebellion. China's worldview has roughly followed a similar pattern of socialism, peaceful coexistence, and antihegemonism role conceptions. Although Solinger's political economic pattern and this leadership pattern do not fit each other perfectly, both identify cycles. This confirms to an extent the earlier argument that a linkage exists between China's internal and external views.

The linkage, however, has been weakened since the 1980s, and this trend may continue throughout the 1990s. Since the mid-1980s, China's worldview has not changed to an appreciable extent, although the domestic political line has witnessed several upheavals. Leaders who obviously favor the hierarchical style have not yet formulated an argument to reverse the open-door policy. These leaders have been responsible for domestic retrenchment since the early 1980s, through the campaign against spiritual pollution, and bourgeois liberalization to the crackdown on prodemocracy agitation. China's foreign policy positions display surprising continuity. One observer calls this phenomenon in Chinese foreign policy "global learning."[7]

Since 1982 the Chinese have pledged themselves to a so-called independent foreign policy. This policy broke the previously exclusive linkage between the normalcy leadership style and the pro–status quo, pro–U.S., and peaceful coexistence emphasis. The normalcy style of the 1982 leaders was reflected in their predilection for market mechanisms, individual instead of collective responsibility, and a willingness to depoliticize society. However, the independent foreign policy contains all extant principles: socialist role conceptions (by denouncing imperialism and announcing adherence to Marxism-Leninism and Maoism), antihegemonism, and peaceful coexistence. As a result, pro-U.S. gestures were deliberately curbed, at least rhetorically. So the long-established linkage between the normalcy style and the peaceful coexistence worldview is no longer exclusive.

Nevertheless, the rise (or return) of hierarchical leaders (in terms of their preference for centralized control, socialist overtures, and collectivist bias) represented by Chen Yun, Deng Liqun, Peng Zhen, Hu Qiaomu, and later Li Peng and Yao Yilin has never really challenged the line of independent foreign policy. Despite the increasing number of references in 1990 to themes of anti-imperialism and antihegemonism in connection with the United States, the Chinese still welcome U.S. investors, tourists, secret official delegations, and even the Voice of America. And despite the upheavals in the Eastern bloc, where Communist parties were forced to abandon their political monopoly, the Chinese have remained silent on "revisionist" developments there. The hierarchical leadership's traditional obsession with socialist principles has not yet affected China's external view or the open-door policy significantly.

The implication is that the Chinese are not as committed as they once were to applying domestic moral principles to China's role in the world. The weakening of the linkage to some extent reduces the tension between China's relatively low capabilities and the dramatic need to highlight constantly changing positions. As a result, China's role in international organizational processes has become rather passive. Lacking a moral vision, the Chinese no longer have an impact upon others' behavior. Most importantly, the Chinese may dispense with their habitual shaming technique in the long run. Role performance or compliance with China's role expectations by other nations will receive less attention since the role conceptions are generally vague, except that China's independence must be honored.

If domestic moral principles do not guide China's external behavior, the significance of China's external performance in its domestic political struggle will be reduced. In the extreme case, the Chinese would be concerned only when another country is dealing directly with China—how its leaders behave otherwise would be of no interest to China and hence would not require any reaction from China. The possibility of China's involvement in polemics with another country would be much smaller, as would the chance that the other country would feel threatened by China.

In short, the weakening of the external-internal linkage is reflected in two trends: first, the decreasing relevance of domestic moral principles in determining correct world order; second, the decreasing relevance of China's external behavior in judging domestic political legitimacy. The decay is not necessarily irreversible, nor does it mean that the dramatic nature of China's role in international organizational processes will be totally transformed. In order to evaluate the decline of the moral regime in world politics, one must identify the sources of the decline.

THE MORAL DECLINE

Let us recall the characteristics of the moral regime. The fundamental assumption of the moral regime is that persons with higher social status command respect and voluntary submission from subordinates. Those who play the leadership role put themselves forward as models for society. Being a model has historically meant passivity or inaction, and private citizens have been given a free hand in producing wealth for themselves—the regime should *never* compete with citizens for economic resources. This aloofness presents a good example of morally oriented rather than economically oriented leadership. Normally, the stability of the regime depended on rhetorical loyalty and the repeated performance of rituals that confirmed the moral superiority of the national leaders. In times of economic difficulty, however, problems of livelihood were usually taken as signs of moral degeneration. The solution always consisted of a change in leadership, not a change in the Confucian ideology.

The introduction of socialism created confusion in this moral regime. Socialism requires unselfish contributions to the public good by private citizens using their private economic resources. The most striking change after 1949 was that loyalty to the regime had to be proved by economic contributions in addition to submissive rhetoric. In traditional society, submissive rhetoric was enough; under socialism, submissive rhetoric incurs economic obligation. Documents show that socialism developed problems when the cooperative movement started in the mid-1950s.[8] The real drain on moral power was the Great Leap Forward.

The Great Leap Forward

Although the rationale of the Great Leap Forward was well appreciated from the economic point of view, its implementation reflected the nature of moral politics. The campaign was designed to utilize human resources in China in order to make up for the shortage of capital goods. Even before the campaign started, however, the central leadership had already declared it successful and predicted China would overtake Great Britain in fifteen years. Mao was seen as a "great prophet" who foresaw the arrival of "heaven here on earth."[9] What was originally a rational strategy turned into an ultimate test of the Chinese people's will to achieve communism. The moral pressure was so strong that fabricated stories of success flooded Beijing. Whether or not they knew them to be frauds, the leaders were forced to praise these nonexistent achievements in order to preserve the moral integrity of the regime. Waste became the official evidence of moral commitment.

The Great Leap was a total disaster, and its impact on the moral regime was profound. Before, the moral regime could not fail as far as the masses were concerned because they were never involved economically. Now they suffered bitterly from the failure. The moral pretension could not be reinstalled by recruiting a new leader. Economic freedom was no longer guaranteed in a moral regime; instead, supporting the regime became an economic liability. The results were widespread dissatisfaction, vandalism, and even rebellious activities.

Cadres fared far worse under the Great Leap. Since peasants contributed directly to the building of socialism, cadres no longer monopolized the moral rhetoric or the moral status that originally bridged the span between the masses and the central leadership. But they were required to work as hard as (or even harder than) the peasants in order to pose as role models for them. No wonder reports of resignations proliferated. Moreover, the masses hated cadres because they enforced policies of confiscation. Many simply decided to change sides and help the villagers preserve local resources for local use while filing fabricated reports to the center. For the first time in Chinese history, cadres and local leaders took the side of the masses against the regime. While the regime later acknowledged the existence of widespread corruption, the moral implication is shocking: the masses found that their leaders were not morally superior to themselves. (Incidentally, reform in the 1980s has also had a similar effect, putting strong moral pressure on cadres but leaving them behind economically.)[10]

Another repercussion was the development of factionalism at the center. Mao's leadership was directly challenged by Peng Dehuai, who was later purged despite winning the sympathy of many of his comrades.[11] The implication is that no supreme moral being existed. Leaders could no longer assume that their subordinates would submit to them voluntarily. Power had to be pursued, grabbed, and applied ruthlessly. Factionalism at the center created confusion at the lower levels as everyone was uncertain about future policy changes and their political impact. Mutual suspicion was a natural result of this uncertainty as everyone was busy watching which way the political wind was blowing to decide which side to take.

The consequences of this extreme socialist campaign in the Great Leap are multiple: coercion predominated over persuasion; factionalism began to undermine unity; power talk replaced moral talk; power struggle prevailed over concern for harmony. While corruption is not necessarily justified, it has been an open secret. The government has resorted more and more to legalist punishment rather than to moral shaming. People are responding less and less to ideological campaigns[12] but participate in political activities as a form of self-protection and to establish important connections.[13]

After the Great Leap, another devastating movement, the Cultural Revolution, further undermined the integrity of the moral regime. Many see the Great Leap as a prelude to the Cultural Revolution. However, the rationale of each movement is distinctive. The Great Leap aimed at strengthening the political regime; the Cultural Revolution aimed at shaming the political regime (which was responsible for post–Great Leap retrenchment). On the one hand, the Cultural Revolution denounced the *dangquanpai* (current power holders), revealing or even fabricating evidence for the sake of dramatizing their corruption. On the other hand, the Cultural Revolution split society into several Red Guard factions. There were virtually no clear criteria to decide who the true revolutionaries were. Real force determined whose cause was revolutionary and whose was not. Consequently, possession of power was intrinsic to self-protection, and thus power became a value in itself. That Mao was revered as if he were a god could not reverse the trend of factionalism at the center and, more importantly, the masses' knowledge of it. Assailed by open corruption, made-up crimes, Red Guard infighting, purges of leaders, ambiguous interpretations of Mao's remarks, and eventually military intervention, the Chinese moral regime was in serious jeopardy. The Cultural Revolution thus became an immorally carried out search for moral purity. The demise of the Great Leap Forward moral regime made this irony psychoculturally possible.

The rise of legalism in China since the Great Leap has to do with the nature of the moral regime. The erosion of an ethically based authority was not matched by the maturing of social and economic interests that might have provided a new and pluralistic basis for legitimacy. In most societies, moral decay is brought on by modernization that corrodes the traditional political economic structure. In China moral decline came about when the elite tried to use moral authority to pursue modernization—when this failed the moral order lost legitimacy.

The Open-Door Policy

Moral disintegration is certainly a long drawn out process. It began to have a particularly strong impact on China's worldview toward the end of the 1980s. Moral decline is reflected in the rise of legalism, with its emphasis on wealth and strength. Since the 1980s the open-door policy has provided a plethora of opportunities for corruption (i.e., interest in wealth) and reinforced the political power struggle (i.e., interest in strength).

The open-door policy obviously breeds corruption within the party because party members occupy dominant positions at all critical points in society. New opportunities and decentralization of financial power purport to free private enterprises and stimulate the economy, but it has also enabled party officials to utilize their connections to acquire already scarce resources for personal gain. More importantly, people do not hesitate to abuse their social and political connections, especially when the government praises those who are able to enrich themselves.[14] Stories of corruption abound in the popular press on the mainland. One article claims that society is becoming a *baijiazi* (a child who squanders his parents' wealth) as funds earmarked for education, technological upgrading, agricultural development, and scientific research are wasted on banquets, imported cars, and other extravagances.[15]

Political campaigns designed to boost the morale of the masses have clearly failed. Cadres were accused of insufficient faith and self-consciousness in their response to the campaigns against spiritual pollution in 1983 and bourgeois liberalization in 1987.[16] One article concludes that the campaigns failed as a result of peoples' psychological habit of resisting ideological "education."[17] The authorities have now decided to depend on the legalist approach. In its legal campaigns, the party has repeatedly stressed its determination to deal with "serious crime" (*daan* or *yaoan*). Since the June 1989 Tiananmen massacre, which was supposed to consolidate socialist morality, there continue to be numerous reports of corruption.

The open door policy and its social repercussions have had a significant impact on China's view of the world. Relatives and friends of high-ranking party officials benefit from special connections regardless of factional identity. The issue is who has power. One Chinese economist was shocked by this new lust for power: individual demands for power thrive because "using power for oneself becomes a social custom"; it is almost as if "everyone is an official," so no one truly possesses power.[18] As a consequence, all factions have developed a vested interest in the open-door policy to some degree, though no one has complete control over it. Despite their positions on antihegemonism and anti-imperialism, they all have to support the open-door policy to retain the loyalty of their factional supporters.

That the open door has become everyone's policy also has a great deal to do with political realignment in China. The aggressive reformist faction led by Zhao Ziyang formulated the theory of "new authoritarianism," arguing that Zhao needed more centralized power to effectively manage modernization (presumably also to struggle against other factions). The father of the open-door policy, Deng Xiaoping, felt threatened by Zhao, even though he was also worried about potential retrenchment plotted by conservatives. Deng deserted the reformist camp and purged Zhao in 1989. Now that Deng has contracted this marriage of convenience with the conservatives, they cannot clamp down on his policy, at least for the time being, and this further weakens the linkage between factionalism and the open-door policy.

The open-door policy implies that internal moral decline has had an external impact. The lack of genuine moral concern behind the rigid moral drama of the 1970s gave rise to legitimacy crisis after the Gang of Four was purged and the Cultural Revolution was officially denounced. There was no official ideology to make sense of the world situation, internally or externally. The regime has managed to shift responsibility to individuals through decentralization and some degree of economic privatization. Against this background, the open-door policy is supposed to rescue the regime from its legitimacy crisis. Without an official guiding ideology, however, the policy has been taken advantage of (or even abused) in a highly individualized fashion. This has resulted in chaos—inflation, skewed income distribution, an expectation gap, and so on—although the open door has had positive impacts on trade, technology, development, and cultural exchanges. China, however, is now more dependent on the world for imports to curb inflation, for capital to create job opportunities, for exports to gain foreign exchange, and for aid to speed up development projects and infrastructure improvements. As a result, foreign loans have become a component of government revenue in the official budgeting process; foreign trade accounts for over a quarter of the gross national product (GNP).

The continuation of the open-door policy since the early 1980s indicates severance of the linkage between internal political struggle and external views. Both the radicals and the conservatives (whoever they are and however defined) recognize that China's role in the world is to take advantage of the status quo. There is no moral tone associated with it— the Chinese refuse to make moral judgments on world affairs. No attempt is made to reorganize world politics because the status quo is accepted. Ironically, the possibility of bringing China into global organizational processes looks most promising in the 1990s. In 1990 the Chinese reacted moderately to world criticism of their human rights violations, and they are still calling for foreign investment, tourism, and trade. When the moral regime is less offended by foreign moral criticism and less concerned with the moral implications of the retreat from socialism in the rest of the world, the possibility increases that it will accept existing organizational processes.

THE STATIST DRAMA

Chinese Neorealism

In the 1980s Chinese foreign policy reacted to rather than enacted the external situation because the status quo was regarded as legitimate; this does not imply, though, that dramatic style has been discarded. Now that there is less space for antihegemonic and anti-imperialist themes in the mass media, there must be alternative views to help citizens make sense of the world. One of these, the statist view, has come to the forefront. Notions like independence, interdependence, multipolarity, and peace are the most popular terms in a majority of Chinese diplomatic statements. These concepts have components that parallel Western neorealism.

For example, the most exciting vision of interdependence is embodied in Zhao Ziyang's idea of an international circle, according to which China's coastal areas would become integrated into the world market and then serve as "windows." By joining the world market, China would be able to attract foreign investment, earn foreign exchange, and receive foreign technology. China would also enter the world bond market, and toward the end of 1988, China did indeed issue bonds worth over $4 billion on international markets.[19] According to Zhao's idea, the coastal areas would be encouraged to concentrate on light, textile, and other labor-intensive processing industries that "have a great export potential for a long time to come."[20] At the same time, China should create a "mini-climate" favorable to foreign investment, so that joint ventures as well as foreign enterprises are given "all necessary power" to manage their production.[21] The Chinese were looking forward to China's becoming a part of the world market and a "major market for the United States, Japan and Western Europe."[22] Accordingly, China recommends that Third World countries rely on labor-intensive industries in order to benefit from world interdependence.

This loss of autonomy is acceptable because it is reciprocal and voluntary, not forced upon China. The same logic can be applied to international law and organization. China is a member of most UN-affiliated organizations and a party to most international conventions (e.g., on international civil aviation, narcotics, gender discrimination, international telegram, protection of culture and nature, law of the sea, outer space, international postal service, international labor issues, etc.). Recently, China recognized the Convention on the Recognition and Enforcement of Foreign Arbitral Awards and the Convention on Contracts for the International Sale of Goods and accepted their precedence over China's contract law.[23] Since 1984 Chinese experts have served the International Court of Justice. In 1988 China also decided to allow foreign experts to serve as arbitrators in commercial disputes between Chinese and foreign businesses.[24] Since 1989 China has honored the International Trademark Agreement, and it receives aid from the IMF, the World Bank, the Asian Development Bank, and the International Finance Corporation.

All these new developments suggest that neorealism has disciples in China. In an interdependent world, China has realized that "there is no future in confrontation." For a country to establish influence in the world today, the best way "is not to bully its neighbors, but to turn itself into a more affluent and more democratic society by quick, high-quality economic development, sincere cooperation and promoting international economic and cultural exchanges. Its leaders must be broad-minded and willing to absorb what is useful from all other countries, regardless of their political or social orientation. They must improve their people's material and cultural well-being."[25]

As in Western neorealism, current Chinese national interests are not defined in terms of military power but in terms of political, economic, and cultural leverage. Money is no longer a capitalist concept but a "converted form of property created through labor." To enhance labor productivity and create material wealth for the state, goods and services must be measured in terms of money.[26] It is therefore important for the state to promote business opportunities, domestic as well as international, and utilize them to their fullest. In short, Chinese neorealists assign highest priority to economic development. Although they understand the constraints of political power and the significance of economic power, they believe in the peaceful solution of disputes and strive to integrate China into a single world market.

Western Neorealism Compared

Chinese neorealist premises, though, are significantly different from their Western counterparts. According to Western neorealism (or regime literature), new norms emerged in world political economy during and after détente, not just because the United States needed them in order to maintain hegemony but because the phenomena of interdependence and mutual vulnerability associated with international economic structures required them. Literature on regime analysis suggests that international common goods do indeed exist. For instance, the interests international organizations are expected to further are mainly common interests.[27] Moreover, once a legal practice is accepted, changes in a power structure do not necessarily affect its observance. Behavioral changes directly follow regime changes, not changes in power structure.[28] Many factors offset the impact of a change in the balance of power, including the need for convenience in a complex society, inertia, risk of uncertainty involved in changes, expectations of reciprocity, and the concern for reputation.[29] This is especially true for relatively nonpolitical rules and procedures.[30] Détente therefore provides an environment for new international regimes to arise and persist.

Conventional measurement of power resources before détente focused on military power. Regime analysis has become popular among neorealists, however, because military power and, for example, economic power are not fungible nowadays. The use of power has to be contingent upon the issue area. One may wonder whether cooperation is an inevitable compromise of state autonomy or a strategic move to increase, as well as protect, national interests. The former implies leaders' inability to remain invulnerable to environment, the latter their ability to adapt to the environment.[31] Nonetheless, the historical existence of a governing hegemony— Great Britain or, later, the United States—ensures that liberal economic norms prevail in international politics. Since détente, the preservation of that hegemony, however, has depended more and more on nonmilitary resources: technology, rate of market growth, product structure, and so on.[32] Nevertheless, unilateral efforts to maintain a hegemony would almost certainly strain the resources of that hegemony and cause its decline.[33]

Mutual vulnerability consists of common problems shared by industrialized countries. These problems call for collectively agreed-upon solutions that gradually increase these countries' integration. Knowledge of each other's institutions and practices thereby increases enormously and mutual confidence in policymaking arises.[34] Political weight must be attached to all types of nonpolitical arrangements. Some kinds of structural rationality learned through socialization and competitive processes in international politics are believed to constrain all national actors.[35] Such rationality explains why industrialized countries continue to coordinate even though the regulating hegemonic force (the United States) has declined.[36] In fact, scholars have extended the argument into the psychological field and maintain that interdependence is actually community building.[37] Mutual trust is an indispensable element here. The Western industrial societies are so comfortable with one anothers' political (i.e., democratic) styles, legal practices, and ways of thinking and living that it is inconceivable that the use of force or economic sanction would still be within the range of policy options.

The Chinese version of neorealism has different origins. Unlike Western neorealism, which is to a large extent an ex post facto theorization of reality, Chinese neorealism is a policy advocated by politicians. Back in the late 1940s, although the United States worked extremely hard to help its Western allies and Japan recover economically, the evolution of economic interdependence was at best a happy side effect of a military alliance designed to contain communism. The development of mutual vulnerability is a contemporary result. In the United States, it was not until the Nixon administration that politicians like Kissinger recognized and moved to utilize the newly emerged interdependent relationship among the Western industrial societies. In comparison, Chinese neorealism has no real political, economic, or cultural bases that are common to the rest of the world. The Chinese feel that involvement in the interdependent world economy is the best way to go about modernization. This is not because they have already enjoyed the fruits of interdependence but because they want to be a part of it.

As a result of this partial reading of interdependence, the Chinese often fail to appreciate the pattern of interaction among the Western industrial societies. The evolution of interdependent relationships in the West has much to do with a common political style and legal tradition. When disputes arise, negotiation in public as well as private sectors tends to concentrate on professional rather than ideological issues. There is no strong fear of mutual threat; the level of mutual trust is relatively high. Consequently, comments or complaints by politicians of one country about another are not considered as threats or attempts at interference. Take, for example, the problems between Japan and the United States. Although the Japanese do business around the globe, their cultural and political style has yet to be fully understood. Therefore, the political implications of a British interest purchasing a U.S. firm are completely different from those of a

Japanese purchase. Many politicians (a good example is Congressman Richard Gephardt) feel threatened by Japanese economic aggressiveness. Despite this, Japan is still a democratic country and is in part a U.S. post-war creation of the United States. When the notion of interdependence is applied to China, which is neither capitalist nor democratic, the lack of mutual trust can be frustrating on both sides of the Pacific.

First, interdependence for the Chinese is a purely economic concept tied to the notion of independence. The Chinese would like to be accommodated into international interdependent networks without losing independence. This creates confusion, as independence is never on the top of the agenda among Western industrial societies. The coming of 1992 Europe further suggests that concern over a more efficient interdependence prevails against concern over narrowly defined national independence. For the Chinese, since there is no such mutual trust or confidence, a certain degree of national autonomy is always the minimum condition for joining interdependent processes. For Western nations, the processes of interdependence require a sacrifice of independence whose absolute value is in any event questionable among those who interact intensively with one another. (Incidentally, controversy over Japan's role centers exactly on the domestic constraints on Japan's international duties). Seeing countries becoming more and more interdependent, the Chinese inevitably feel frustrated. They simply cannot join without anteing up some degree of independence.

The Chinese notion of independence has changed over time. The so-called independent foreign policy announced in 1982 served as the synoptic slogan (although national autonomy and independence have been constant elements in Chinese diplomatic statements). At that time, independence basically implied China's neutrality between the two superpowers or, at least, not attaching to "any big power or group of powers" or yielding to "pressure from any big power."[38] When tension between the two superpowers eased during the course of the mid-1980s, China's independent foreign policy began to focus on the theme of coexistence. Instead of coexistence with capitalism, as in the 1950s and the 1960s, or with revisionism, as in the 1960s and the 1970s, coexistence now involves relations among *nation-states*. Relaxation in U.S.-Soviet relations "will not change" China's foreign policy and its "strategic position, role and importance in the world."[39] So in politics, China sees a trend toward independence, not interdependence:

> Competition exists not only between the United States and the Soviet Union, and the East and the West, but also among various countries with the same social system, such as the United States and Japan, the United States and Western Europe, and Europe and Japan. On the one hand, the world economy is moving towards integration; on the other hand *countries think about problems mainly in terms of their national and state in-*

terests and not world integration. Therefore . . . the world has [not] entered a period of accommodation. Competition predominates. When everyone will be hurt by competition and lacks the means to compete, accommodation occurs. Not long afterwards, they clash again because of
competition. Then the cycle of competition-clash-accommodation is
repeated.[40]

The mutual consultative processes involved in global interdependence
are threatening to the Chinese notion of independence. For example, the
United States criticized China's sale of arms to Iran and Iraq, which in
turn raised Chinese suspicions of U.S. intentions. Similar criticism by the
United States regarding a German firm's indirect involvement in the possible production of chemical weapons by Libya earned a favorable response from West Germany and no accusation of interference. In the first
place, selling arms to two warring parties is not an ethical act even by
China's standards. Who cares, though, in these days when the tempo of
diplomacy is set by legalism? If there's a profit to be had, China has signaled its willingness to grab for it. Unfortunately, in the interdependent
world, any armed conflict in the Middle East threatens global economic
prosperity, so China's behavior can hardly be tolerated. External criticism
thus collides directly with the Chinese notion of independent foreign
policy.

China's Reappraisal

Since the collapse of communism in Eastern Europe, Western interdependent societies seem to have turned their sights on authoritarianism. China's
crackdown on the prodemocracy movement in 1989 was universally condemned in a West whose people should best understand the value of interdependence and assist China's participation in it. What is striking to the
Chinese is that the West is ready to use economic leverage within the interdependent network against China. Western investment, tourism, and aid
plummeted after June 1989; from the Chinese perspective, the West
abused interdependence and turned it against China's independence.
China's foreign policy analysis and worldview have thus witnessed a subtle shift in emphasis. The notion of multipolarity began to dominate Chinese mass media at the beginning of the 1990s. This multipolar view is
closer to the classic notion of realism than to neorealism and tends to
stress conflict rather than interdependence. Instead of cooperation, the
Chinese predict that the race for technological superiority will be the locus
of battle in the 1990s. In the meantime, the analysis continues, ideological conflicts will persist and become "more acute."[41]

Rising concern about China's independent position in the world and
the continued call to open China wider to the outside world together pose

a dilemma for China. In the late 1980s, China's independent foreign policy was never seriously challenged. There was no clear trade-off between interdependence and independence. When issues like arms sales to Saudi Arabia or population policy came up, China basically resorted to rhetorical protest. The situation is different in the 1990s. China's desire to join the interdependent world is used against China. Maintaining the balance between political independence and economic interdependence has become quite a conceptual task.

The Third World seems to have a more conspicuous role in China's foreign policy in the 1990s. High-level officials toured Africa, the Middle East, and South Asia shortly after the 1989 crackdown, promising a new round of aid. The Chinese are again worried that "sharpening polarization between North and South will surely intensify world contradictions," hence the urge for a "new international economic order."[42] The NIEO has lost momentum among Third World countries and has fallen out of favor with those Chinese who have stressed South-South cooperation in recent years. The Chinese argue that the Third World is playing an increasingly important role in world politics. For China, Third World countries can be a huge political force to be used in dealings with the West.

The tone of confrontation is too obvious to miss in China's new Third World rhetoric. The Chinese admire the unity of the Third World, which allows any small or weak country to expect the whole Third World to be on its side when facing superpower intervention. The condemnation of the U.S. invasion of Panama is seen as one good example of this unity. According to the Chinese, the strength of the Third World was reflected in the UN Assembly in November 1989 when the developing countries defeated a resolution on freedom of speech proposed by the West. The Chinese believed that the resolution was "designed to interfere in the internal affairs of Third World countries." The Third World is now politically mature and capable of "defusing world tension and safeguarding world peace."[43]

This tendency to look at the world in power terms is competing with, if not replacing, talk of interdependence. When the U.S. State Department published its human rights report in 1990, the Chinese were outraged by its criticism of China. For the Chinese, international law does not require that all nations share the same culture, ideology, or socioeconomic system. As far as the Chinese are concerned, using human rights is an international legal pretension, a power play. Why should any country be interested in China's suppression of counterrevolution? Here, the Chinese challenge the whole legitimacy of international law: "Development of international law is largely influenced by Western politics, economics, and culture. Some of the related ideologies and principles . . . smack of colonialism, imperialism and hegemonism."[44] While these charges may be true, interdependence among the Western societies is based on this kind of international law, however biased it might be. As Western criticism of China's human rights violations mounted in the early 1990s, China was forced to publish its own white paper on human rights in 1991, asserting that the right of survival is the highest right, a collective right that dictates China's anti-imperialist policy and has priority above and beyond any bourgeois individual right. For the Chinese, the implication of Western human rights policy has been clear enough for some time already:

> "Human rights" has become a catch phrase these days in the West. The United States . . . has assumed the role of world policemen. . . . Washington also applies sanction[s] at will against anybody it thinks a "bad guy" by its human rights criteria. It seems that in today's world only the U.S. government respects and protects human rights. . . .
> Clearly, the "respect and protection" of human rights are but a pretext under which [the] U.S. government wantonly interferes with other countries' internal affairs and violates their sovereignty.[45]

The political repercussions of power play are serious. On the one hand, China finds itself in a multipolar world. On the other, norms and relationships in this world are not ready to accommodate the Chinese way of thinking. Partially as a result of this perception, the percentage of China's military budget in the 1990 annual budget increased by more than 3 percent over 1989. It's small wonder that despite the urge to open wider, invite more investment, and obtain more low-interest international loans, China has started talking about self-reliance in its ultimate pursuit of development: "Historical experience also tells us that even under conditions of opening to the outside world, we cannot expect others to freely transfer high technologies to us. The development of modern science technology requires, first and above all, reliance on the strength and wisdom of China's own scientists and technicians. Only through our own achievements can we be qualified to participate fully in international exchanges and cooperation."[46]

Li Peng's government work report delivered in March 1990 contains points that contrast with theories of the late 1980s. A significant omission is the term "interdependence." Instead, the world political economy is seen as being in serious disarray. For example, the developed countries are urged to adopt an "active attitude" and accept "responsibility" for alleviating Third World debt, which is caused by "unreasonable international economic relations," asymmetric exchanges, and resultant "ruthless exploitation." This perception collides with the once official view that the U.S. budget deficit would understandably require a very patient, prolonged process of debt relief. More importantly, the report notes with alarm the realignment of various world forces (in Eastern Europe particularly), increasing "tumult and instability." The report expresses confidence that China's friendship with the Third World will be praised for being able to survive the test of chaos. After accusing the United States of engaging in hegemonism, the report looks to a new international *political* order for a solution:

> The drastically changing international situation has further brought the issue of establishing a new international political order in front of the whole world. The Chinese government has consistently proposed that all countries in the world . . . develop mutual cooperation and promote common prosperity. Attempts at imposing one's own ideology, values, and even social institutions on others through political, economic and cultural means are ultimately unfeasible. . . . As long as [we] follow the five principles [of peaceful coexistence] precisely, [all] countries can develop and establish normal and friendly relationships however different their national conditions are, [all] international disputes can be resolved with reasonable measures however complicated the situations are.[47]

MORAL DECLINE

This effort to preserve Chinese independence is matched by an internal campaign to strengthen socialist ideological indoctrination and to discover the uniqueness of Chinese socialism. Deng Xiaoping's analysis of the current world situation, quoted in Chapter 3, is certainly a reminder that the Chinese intend to stay independent of larger forces in the world market. Basically, Deng takes the neo-Marxist approach and argues that China can be independent only if it adheres to socialism. The point here is not really what he means by socialism. The message is that being independent is the new drama that may dominate China's worldview throughout the decade. One wonders if this pretension will jeopardize China's position in the world market in the long run.

In general, China ceased to be a threat to the outside world in the 1980s. Few still believe that China would risk military confrontation for abstract moral principles such as anti-imperialism and antihegemonism. History connotes a different perspective, however. In 1962, for example, China's main concern was internal development (consolidation and adjustment), and diplomatic statements were filled with calls for peace. Nonetheless, China launched an effective attack on Indian troops who had challenged China's willingness and ability to protect its borders. China's punitive war against Vietnam was a virtual replay of the 1962 war in terms of diplomacy and internal development constraints. The weaker China looks, the more the Chinese are concerned about the appearance of independence, and the more dangerous they may become.

There is good psychological reason for this. Especially when nations did not take China's warnings seriously in the late 1980s and early 1990s, it was necessary for the Chinese to employ diplomatic statements to condemn those who, according to the Chinese, interfered in their internal affairs. These statements, like similar ones before, only created misunderstanding and anxiety within the Western industrial societies. Countries like the United States, however, would not feel as threatened as they had in the 1950s and the 1960s for obvious reasons: China's capabilities are clearly weak, communism is fading on a worldwide scale, and there would be no Soviet protection for the Chinese. The implication for the Chinese must be terrible—their moral power witnessed substantial decline in the 1980s. For the moral regime, this represents a total loss of face and even carries dangerous undertones. If their regime is not respected in the world, the Chinese people normally will not respect the regime. This must be particularly worrisome to Chinese leaders at a time when the regime is also suffering from internal moral decay and legitimacy crisis.

A solution does not appear to be on hand. Even though China has reduced the size of its armed forces, makes frequent declarations of its peaceful intent, and occasionally suffers from sluggish economic growth, it is likely that the Chinese will use force on some minor issue to demonstrate their independence. Two political targets are the Nanshas and Taiwan. Indeed, China clashed with Vietnam over the Nanshas in 1988. At the time of the 1990 presidential election in Taiwan, Chinese troops conducted military exercises in the coastal provinces presumably to demonstrate China's concern over the alleged predilection of the president-elect, Lee Teng-hui, for an independent Taiwanese state.

The other element of legalist thinking is equally important here: wealth. The moral decline in China's foreign policy is also reflected in China's willingness to utilize the status quo to carry out modernization. The principal goal is of course to attract international resources in the form of aid, direct investment, and joint ventures. As mentioned in Chapter 7, China is competing with other Third World countries for the limited resources available in such international organizations as the IMF and the World Bank. It does so by accepting the dominant voting rights of the Western countries, notably the United States. It will also join the General Agreement on Tariffs and Trade (GATT) in spite of the latter's strict regulation of its members' domestic development policy. This is inconsistent with China's previous position that international organizations should be operated according to egalitarian principles.

This dependence on world financial organizations for modernization certainly constrains China's ability to ignore Western protests of human rights violations after the 1989 crackdown. Money has become a value and openly so. Moral decline enables Chinese leaders to realize the fruit of interdependence without worrying about the charge of commercial materialism. This new acquisitive attitude has two opposite implications. First, the Chinese will not give up opportunities in international interdependence without justifiable reason since money (i.e., foreign capital) is a legitimate value. Second, however, it would be psychologically dramatic if the regime decided to give up those opportunities for the sake of other seemingly forgotten values. In short, interdependence is a political economic regime as well as a psychocultural regime.

There are therefore two trends working against each other. One stresses independence and has historically led to dramatic policy behavior. The other stresses interdependence and is a new element in China's worldview—but a statist element because of internal moral decline. Independence refers to political concern and China's ability to manage its internal affairs in appearance. Interdependence alludes to economic concerns and China's willingness to sacrifice national autonomy to satisfy conditions for foreign aid. The traditional statist (and legalist) role conceptions make sense of both trends since political strength and economic welfare are all legitimate goals.[48]

The moral regime is by no means infallible in spite of its demonstrated ability to survive. The most appropriate role conceptions available in Chinese psychoculture for coping with moral decline are statist ones. Chinese statism, however, assumes the existence of chaos and the need for self-protection in world politics. The Chinese (and also the Japanese) thus have been unable to appreciate the essence of Western neorealism whereby classic realist concern over narrowly defined national interests is outdated. This inconsistency between China's statism and Western neorealism causes an adjustment problem for the Chinese in their moral decline. China's statism so far refuses to recognize that China cannot resort to coercive, punitive action without eventually hurting China itself in the long run. This realization of mutual vulnerability is a critical element shared by most of the Western industrial societies.[49]

The moral decline thus creates a fatal problem for the Chinese regime. Statist role conceptions that come to justify moral decline and rescue the regime from its legitimacy crisis are outdated according to the Western notion of neorealism. Statism thus turns into a drama that enables China to pretend to independence. The regime would still look bad, having lost face, respect, and dignity because of its inability to attract external resources without negative political repercussions. The use of force to save face (i.e., the appearance of independence), a tendency of the moral regime, is therefore a possible and sensible option for the future. The stylistic legacy of the moral regime (which always relies on rhetoric) is, unfortunately, despised by cynical citizens and politicians witnessing the moral decline. This reinforces the predilection of the regime for appealing to more drastic policy options. Coercive style would speed up moral decline, invite more external criticism, and further political retrenchment.

This vicious circle may continue until China eventually revises or abandons the statist pretension of independence.

NOTES

1. Chih-yu Shih, "A Marhov Model of Diplomatic Change and Continuity in Mainland China," *Issues and Studies* 28, 6 (June 1992): 1–15.

2. For a different view, see David Bachman in S. Kim (ed.), *China and the World: New Directions in Chinese Foreign Relations* (Boulder: Westview, 1989), pp. 31–54.

3. For example, Thomas Gottlieb, *Chinese Foreign Policy Factionalism and the Origins of the Strategic Triangle* (Santa Monica, Calif.: Rand, 1977); Kenneth Liberthal, "The Background in Chinese Politics," in H. J. Ellison (ed.), *The Sino-Soviet Conflict: A Global Perspective* (Seattle: University of Washington Press, 1982), pp. 3–28.

4. For a discussion of the Chinese style of engaging in factional politics through code words not through association of policy lines or factional identity, see Lucian Pye, *The Dynamics of Chinese Politics* (Cambridge, Mass.: Oelgeschlager, Gunn & Hain, 1981).

5. Since 1911, the hierarchical leaders have included Yuan Shikai, Chiang Kai-shek, Mao Zedong (before he launched the Cultural Revolution in 1966), and Deng Xiaoping (after the antidemocracy crackdown in 1986); those who were part of the normalcy style include Liu Shaoqi, Zhou Enlai, and Deng Xiaoping (before 1987); the rebellious leaders are leaders of the May Fourth movement, Mao (after 1966), and Jiang Qing. For more discussion, see Chih-yu Shih, *The Spirit of Chinese Foreign Policy: A Psychocultural View* (London: Macmillan, 1990), pp. 62–94.

6. See the conclusion of Dorothy J. Solinger, *Chinese Business Under Socialism* (Berkeley: University of California Press, 1984).

7. Remarks by Samuel Kim in a speech on Chinese foreign policy at Ramapo College, Mahwah, New Jersey, May 4, 1990.

8. Cheng Chu-yuan, "Basic Problems of the Chinese Communists' Agricultural Collectivization," *Minzhu Pinglun* (Democratic commentary) 7, 11 (June 1956).

9. Richard Wilson, *The People's Emperor* (Garden City, N.Y.: Doubleday, 1980), pp. 361, 369.

10. Victor Nee and Su Sijin, "Institutional Change and Economic Growth in China: The View from the Villages," *Journal of Asian Studies* 49, 1 (February 1990): 3–25.

11. For the impact of the purge of Peng on party unity, see Hu Yinghang and Guan Yushu, "The 1959 Lushan Conference and Its Historical Lessons," *Qiushixuekan* (Pragmatic learning journal), 2 (1985): 71–78.

12. For more information, see *First Ten Points, Later Ten Points,* and *Revised Later Ten Points* collected in Richard Baum and Frederick C. Teiwis, *Ssu-Ch'ing: The Socialist Education Movement, 1962–1966* (Berkeley: University of California Press, 1968).

13. Andrew G. Walder, *Communist Neo-Traditionalism: Work and Authority in Chinese Industry* (Berkeley: University of California Press, 1988).

14. "Becoming Rich Is an Honor," *Liaowang Zhoukan* (Outlook weekly) 5 (1984): 1.

15. Yan Sun, "Warning Messages from National People's Congress," *Banyuetan* (Chats bimonthly) 8 (1988): 52–53.

16. "Raise Confidence and Self-Consciousness in Our Party Rectification," *Liaowang Zhoukan* (Outlook weekly) 2 (1984): 1.

17. *Xuexi Yuekan* (Learning monthly) 8 (1986): 33

18. Wu Jiaxiang, *Control over Corruption*, mimeograph in Columbia University's East Asian Library.

19. New China News Agency quoted in economic information section in *Mainland China Studies* 31, 10 (April 1989): 91.

20. "Coastal Areas Urged to Boost Exports," *Beijing Review* 29, 38 (September 22, 1986): 8.

21. Ibid.

22. Huan Xiang, "World Prospects for the Years Ahead," *Beijing Review* 31, 3 (January 18–24, 1988): 20.

23. See the discussion in Samuel Kim, "China and the Third World," in Kim, *China and the World*, p. 172.

24. Hsu Kuang-tai, "A Study of International Trade Arbitration in Communist China," *Mainland China Studies* 31, 10 (April 1989): 18–19.

25. Huan Xiang, "International Conflicts and Our Choices," *Beijing Review* 27, 48 (November 26, 1984): 18.

26. "Special Economic Zone Typifies Open Policy," *Beijing Review* 27, 48 (November 26, 1984): 21.

27. See Mancur Olson, *The Logic of Collective Action* (Cambridge: Harvard University Press, 1965).

28. Stephen D. Krasner, "Structural Causes and Regime Consequences," *International Organization* 36, 2 (Spring 1982).

29. See Oran Young, "Regime Dynamics," *International Organization* 36, 2 (Spring 1982): 93–114.

30. See the discussion in Louis Henkin, *How Nations Behave* (New York: Columbia University Press, 1979).

31. See the discussion in David Baldwin, "Power Analysis and World Politics," *World Politics* 31 (January 1979): 661–694; Robert Keohane and Joseph Nye, *Power and Interdependence* (Boston: Little, Brown, 1977).

32. Robert Gilpin, *The Political Economy of International Relations* (Princeton: Princeton University Press, 1987).

33. George Modelski, "Long Cycles and the Strategy of U.S. International Economic Policy," in D. Rapkin and W. Avery (eds.), *America in a Changing World Political Economy* (New York: Longman, 1982).

34. Richard Cooper, *The Economics of Interdependence* (New York: Columbia University Press, 1980); Richard Cooper, "Interdependence and Foreign Policy in the Seventies," *World Politics* 24, 2 (1972): 159–181.

35. Kenneth Waltz, *Theory of International Politics* (Menlo Park, Calif.: Addison-Wesley, 1979).

36. Robert Keohane, *After Hegemony* (Princeton: Princeton University Press, 1984).

37. See Karl W. Deutsch et al., *Political Community and the North Atlantic Area* (Princeton: Princeton University Press, 1968).

38. Hu Yaobang's government work report, *Beijing Review* 25, 37 (September 1982): 29.

39. Huan Xiang, "World Prospects."

40. Ibid., emphasis added.

41. Qian Qichen on the world situation, *Beijing Review* 33, 3 (January 15-21, 1990): 14–19.

42. Liu Xin, "North-South Gap Continues to Widen," *Beijing Review* 33, 10 (March 5-11, 1990): 16.

43. Chen Jiabao, "Third World's Role in International Affairs," *Beijing Review* 33, 4 (January 22-28, 1990): 14–16.

44. Yi Ding, "Upholding the Five Principles of Peaceful Coexistence," *Beijing Review* 33, 9 (February 26–March 4, 1990): 15.

45. Xin Li, "Human Rights Concern or Power Politics," *Beijing Review* 33, 10 (March 5-11, 1990): 14.

46. Song Jian, "The Key to Modernization—Science and Technology," *Beijing Review* 33, 4 (January 22-28, 1990): 22.

47. All the remarks are from Li Peng's government work report and are quoted in *World Journal* (March 22, 1990): 19.

48. For a somewhat pessimistic view, see Lillian Craig Harris, "Directions of Change," in Gerald Segal (ed.), *Chinese Politics and Foreign Policy Reform* (New York: Kegan Paul International, 1990).

49. Keohane and Nye, *Power and Interdependence.*

BIBLIOGRAPHY

Adelman, Jonathan, and Chih-yu Shih, "War East and West," *Annual of Chinese Political Science Association* No. 18 (December 1990).

Armstrong, J., *Revolutionary Diplomacy* (Berkeley: University of California Press, 1977).

Backman, Carl W., "Role Theory and International Relations," *International Studies Quarterly* 14, 3 (September 1970): 310–319.

Baldwin, David, "Power Analysis and World Politics," *World Politics* 31 (January 1979).

Bamba, Nobuya, *Japanese Diplomacy in Dilemma* (Kyoto: Minerva Press, 1972).

Baum, Richard, and Frederick C. Teiwis, *Ssu-Ch'ing: The Socialist Education Movement, 1962–1966* (Berkeley: University of California Press, 1968).

Bedeshi, Robert E., *The Fragile Entente* (Boulder: Westview, 1983).

Boulding, Kenneth, "National Images and International Systems," *Journal of Conflict Resolution* 3 (1959).

Boyle, John Hunter, *China and Japan at War, 1937–1945* (Stanford: Stanford University Press, 1972).

Caporaso, James A., *The Structure and Function of European Integration* (Pacific Palisades, Calif.: Goodyear, 1974).

Caudill, William, and C. Schooler, "Child Behavior and Child Rearing in Japan and the United States: An Interim Report," *Journal of Nervous and Mental Disease* 157, 5 (November 1973).

Chai, Ch'u, and Weinberg Chai (eds.), *The Sacred Books of Confucius and Other Confucian Classics* (New Hyde Park, N.Y.: University Books, 1965).

Chai, Trong R., "China's Policy Toward the Third World and the Superpowers in the UN General Assembly, 1971–1977: A Voting Analysis," *International Organization* 33, 3 (Summer 1979).

Chai, Weinberg, "China and the United Nations: Problems of Representation and Alternatives," *Asian Survey* 10 (May 1970).

Chan, Steve, "Chinese Conflict Calculus and Behavior," *World Politics* 30 (April 1978).

Chandler, William, *The Science of History: A Cybernetic Approach* (New York: Gordon and Breach, 1984).

Chang, Hu, "An Analysis of the Situation of the Taiwan Straits During 1954–5," *Feiching Yuepao* (Communist bandit information monthly) 27, 12 (June 1985).

Chang, Jong-feng, "An Analysis of Factors Affecting Trade Between the Two Sides of the Taiwan Straits via Hong Kong," *Mainland China Studies* 31, 8 (February 1989).

Chang, Ya-chun, "Gorbachev's Visit to Beijing and Sino-Soviet Relations," *Mainland China Studies* 32, 2 (July 1989).

Chao, Chian, "Northeast Asia After Li Peng's Visit to the Soviet Union," *Mainland China Studies* 33, 1 (June 1990).

Chaudhuri, Gopal, *China and Nonalignment* (New Delhi: ABC Publishing House, 1986).

Cheng, Chu-yuan, "Basic Problems of Chinese Communists' Agricultural Collectivization," *Mingzhu Pinglun* 7, 11 (June 1956).

Chinese Commission (ed.), *Collections of Scholarly Discussions in International Peace Year* (Beijing: Social Science Literature, 1986).

Chinese Communist Party, *The Tenth National Congress of the Communist Party of China Documents* (Beijing: Foreign Languages Press, 1973).

Ching, Nin, "The United States and China's United Front with Taiwan," *Mainland China Studies* 30, 6 (December 1988).

Chiu, Hungdah (ed.), *Normalizing Relations with the People's Republic of China: Problems, Analysis and Documents*, Occasional Papers/Reprints in Contemporary Asian Studies 2, 14 (1978).

Clapp, P., and M. H. Halperin (eds.), *United States–Japanese Relations: The 1970's* (Cambridge: Harvard University Press, 1974).

Claude, Inis L., Jr., *Swords and Plowshares* (New York: Random House, 1971).

Conrad, Brandt, *Stalin's Failure in China* (Cambridge: Harvard University Press, 1958).

Cooper, Richard, *The Economics of Interdependence* (New York: Columbia University Press, 1980).

———, "Interdependence and Foreign Policy in the Seventies," *World Politics* 24, 2 (1972).

Cottam, Martha, *Foreign Policy Decision Making: The Influence of Cognition* (Boulder: Westview, 1986).

Cox, A. D., and A. Conroy (eds.), *China and Japan: Search for Balance Since World War I* (Santa Barbara: ABC-Clio, 1978).

Cranmer-Byng, John, "The Chinese View of Their Place in the World," *China Quarterly* 53 (1973).

Cross, Charles T., "Taipei's Identity Crisis," *Foreign Policy* 51 (Summer 1983).

Crump, J. I., Jr., *Intrigues, Studies of the Chan-kuo Ts'e* (Ann Arbor: University of Michigan Press, 1964).

Cummings, L., and B. Staw (eds.), *Research in Organizational Behavior* 9 (London: Jai Press, 1987).

———, *Research in Organizational Behavior* 7 (London: Jai Press, 1985).

Dallin, Alexander, and George Breslauer, *Political Terror in Communist Systems* (Stanford: Stanford University Press, 1970).

Deutsch, Karl W., et al., *Political Community and the North Atlantic Area* (Princeton: Princeton University Press, 1968).

Dittmer, Lowell, *Liu Shao-ch'i and the Chinese Cultural Revolution: The Politics of Mass Criticism* (Berkeley: University of California Press, 1974).

Editorial, *Mainland China Studies* 32, 9 (March 1990).

Ellison, Herbert J. (ed.) *Japan and the Pacific Quadrille* (Boulder: Westview, 1987).

———, *The Sino-Soviet Conflict: The Global Perspective* (Seattle: University of Washington Press, 1982).

Fairbank, John K., *The United States and China* (Cambridge: Harvard University Press, 1983).

Falk, Richard, *A Global Approach to National Policy* (Cambridge: Harvard University Press, 1975).

Falkowski, L. (ed.), *Psychological Models in International Politics* (Boulder: Westview, 1979).

Fan, K., *Mao Tse-tung and Lin Piao* (Garden City, N.Y.: Anchor Books, 1972).

Feeney, William R., "Sino-Soviet Competition in the United Nations," *Asian Survey* 17 (Summer 1977).

Feurwerker, Albert, *The Foreign Establishment in China in the Early Twentieth Century*, Michigan Papers in Chinese Studies 29 (Ann Arbor: Center for Chinese Studies, University of Michigan, 1976).

Garver, John, "Arms Sales, the Taiwan Question, and Sino-U.S. Relations," *Orbis* 26, 4 (Winter 1982).

————, *China's Decision for Rapprochement with the United States, 1968–1971* (Boulder: Westview, 1982).

Gecas, Viktor, "The Self-concept," *Annual Review of Sociology* 8 (1982): 1–33.

Gilpin, Robert, *The Political Economy of International Relations* (Princeton: Princeton University Press, 1987).

Gittings, John, *The World and China, 1922–1972* (New York: Harper & Row, 1974).

Godwin, Paul H. B. (ed.), *The Chinese Defense Establishment: Continuity and Change in the 1980s* (Boulder: Westview, 1983).

Gottlieb, Thomas, *Chinese Foreign Policy Factionalism and the Origins of the Strategic Triangle* (Santa Monica, Calif.: Rand, 1977).

Gregor, A. James, and Maria Hsia Chang, *The Republic of China and U.S. Policy* (Washington, D.C.: Ethics and Public Policy Center, 1985).

Griffith, William E. (ed.), *The Sino-Soviet Rift* (Cambridge: MIT Press, 1964).

Gurtov, Melvin, and Byng-Moo Hwang, *China Under Threat* (Baltimore: Johns Hopkins University Press, 1980).

Harding, Harry, *China's Second Revolution: Reform After Mao* (Washington, D.C.: Brookings Institution, 1987).

Hare, A. Paul, *Social Interaction as Drama* (Beverly Hills, Calif.: Sage, 1985).

Harris, L. C., and R. L. Worden (eds.), *China and the Third World: Champion or Challenger?* (Dover, Mass.: Auburn House, 1986).

Hayes, David C., "An Organizational Perspective on a Psychotechnical System Perspective," *Accounting, Organization, and Society* 5, 1 (1980).

Headquarters of the Great Resisting-America-Aiding-Korea Movement (ed.), *The Great Resisting-America-Aiding-Korea Movement* (Beijing: People's Press, 1954).

Henkin, Louis, *How Nations Behave* (New York: Columbia University Press, 1979).

Hermann, Margaret (ed.), *Political Psychology* (San Francisco: Jossey-Bass Publishers, 1986).

Hinton, Harold C., *Communist China in World Politics* (Boston: Houghton Mifflin, 1966).

Hirano, Kenichiro, "International Cultural Conflicts: Causes and Remedies," *Japan Review of International Affairs* 2, 2 (Fall-Winter 1988): 143–164.

Ho, Veng-si, "Chinese Views on U.S. Arms Sales to Taiwan," *Fletcher Forum* 7, 2 (Summer 1983).

Holsti, Karl J., "National Role Conceptions in the Study of Foreign Policy," *International Studies Quarterly* 14, 3 (September 1970): 233–309.

Hosoya, Chihiro, "Japan's 'Omnidirectional' Course," *Japan Echo* 5, 4 (1978).

Hou, Chi-ming, *Foreign Investment and Economic Development in China, 1840–1937*, Harvard Eastern Asian Series 21 (Cambridge: Harvard University Press, 1965).

Hsiung, James, *Law and Policy in China's Foreign Relations: A Study of Attitudes and Practice* (New York: Columbia University Press, 1972).

Hsiung, James, and Samuel Kim (eds.), *China in the Global Community* (New York: Praeger, 1980).

Hsu Kuang-tai, "A Study of International Trade Arbitration in Communist China," *Mainland China Studies* 31, 10 (April 1989).

Hsueh, Chun-tu, *China's Foreign Relations: New Perspectives* (New York: Praeger, 1982).

Hu Yinghang and Guan Yushu, "1959 Lushan Conference and Its Historical Lessons," *Xiushixuekan* 2 (1985): 71–78.

Hutchison, Alan, "China and Africa," *Round Table* 59 (July 1975).

Institute of International Relations (ed.), *Collection of Original Documents Concerning the Disputes Between Russia and Bandits* (Taipei: Institute of International Relations, 1968).

Irie, Michimasa, "The Politics of Peace and Friendly Treaty," *Japan Echo* 5, 4 (1978).

Ishikawa, Shigeru, "Sino-Japanese Economic Cooperation," *China Quarterly* 109 (1987).

Ismael, Tareq Y., "People's Republic of China and Africa," *Journal of Modern African Studies* 9, 4 (1971).

Israeli, Raphael, "Living in China's Shadow," *Orbis* 31, 3 (Fall 1987).

Jansen, Marius B., *Japan and China from War to Peace, 1894–1972* (Chicago: Rand McNally College Publishing, 1975).

Japan Center for International Exchange (ed.), *The Silent Power: Japan's Identity and the World Role* (Tokyo: Simul Press, 1976).

Jervis, Robert, "Security Regime," *International Organization* 36, 2 (Spring 1982).

Ji Gouxing, "ASEAN Countries in Political and Economic Perspectives," *Asian Affairs* 18 (June 1987).

Johnson, Cecil, "China and Latin America: New Ties and Tactics," *Problems of Communism* 21 (July 1972).

Kaplan, Morton, *System and Process in International Politics* (New York: John Wiley and Sons, 1957).

"Keng Piao's Talk on 'A Turning Point in China-U.S. Diplomatic Relations,'" *Chinese Law and Government* 10, 1 (Spring 1977).

Keohane, Robert, *After Hegemony* (Princeton: Princeton University Press, 1984).

Keohane, Robert, and Joseph Nye, *Power and Interdependence* (Boston: Little, Brown, 1977).

Kim, Samuel, "Whither Post-Mao Chinese Global Policy?" *International Organization* 35, 3 (Summer 1981).

———, *China, the United Nations, and World Order* (Princeton: Princeton University Press, 1978).

———, "Behavioral Dimensions of Chinese Multilateral Diplomacy," *China Quarterly* 72 (1977).

———, *China and the World: New Directions in Chinese Foreign Relations* (Boulder: Westview, 1989).

Kissinger, Henry, *Years of Upheaval* (Boston: Little, Brown, 1982).

Koichi, Nomura, "The 'Japan-China' Problem in Modern Political Thought," *Japan Interpreter* 7, 3–4 (1972): 276–277.

Krasner, Stephen D., "Structural Causes and Regime Consequences," *International Organization* 36, 2 (Spring 1982).

————, *Defending National Interest* (Princeton: Princeton University Press, 1978).

Krippendorff, K. (ed.), *Communications and Control in Society* (New York: Gordon and Breach, 1979).

Lasater, Martin L., *Taiwan Facing Mounting Threat* (Washington, D.C.: Heritage Foundation, 1984).

Lebow, Richard N., *Between War and Peace* (Baltimore: Johns Hopkins University Press, 1981).

Liang, Xi, "The United Nations and China," *Wuhandaxue Xuebao* 4 (1985): 3–9.

Lichenstein, Charles M., "China in the UN: The Case of Kampuchea," *World Affairs* 149 (Summer 1986).

Lin, Chae-Jin, *China and Japan: New Economic Policy* (Stanford: Hoover Institution Press, 1984).

Lindblom, Charles, *Politics and Market* (New York: Basic Books, 1978).

Literature on Foreign Relations of the People's Republic of China 1 (Beijing: World Knowledge Press, 1959).

Literature on Foreign Relations of the People's Republic of China 5 (Beijing: World Knowledge Press, 1957).

Liu, Sheng-Chi, "Communist China's Policy Toward Studying Abroad," *Mainland China Studies* 33, 3 (September 1980): 57–69.

Maltz, Maxwell, *Psycho-cybernetics* (New York: Pocket Books, 1966).

Mancall, Mark, *China at Center: 300 Years of Foreign Policy* (New York: Free Press, 1984).

Mao Zedong, *Mao Zedong on the United Front*, Guo Zhiming et al. (eds.), (Beijing: China Literature and History Publisher, 1987).

Masato, Yamazaki, "History Textbooks That Provoke an Asian Outcry," *Japan Quarterly* 34, 1 (1987).

Michio, Jujimura, "Japan's Changing View of Asia," *Japan Quarterly* 24, 4 (1977).

Mineo, Nakajima, "The Precarious Balance of Chinese Socialism," *Japan Quarterly* 35 (1988).

Moorsteen, Richard, and Morton Abramowitz, *Remaking China Policy: U.S.-China Relations and Governmental Decisionmaking* (Cambridge: Harvard University Press, 1971).

Morley, J. W. (ed.), *Japan's Foreign Policy, 1868–1941* (New York: Columbia University Press, 1974).

Mueller, Peter G., and Douglas A. Ross, *China and Japan—Emerging Global Powers* (New York: Praeger, 1975).

Nee, Victor, and Su Sijin, "Institutional Change and Economic Growth in China: The View from the Villages," *Journal of Asian Studies* 49, 1 (February 1990).

Ng-quinn, Michael, "Effects of Bipolarity on Chinese Foreign Policy," *Survey* 26, 2 (1982).

Ogunsanwo, Alaba, *China's Policy in Africa* (Cambridge: Cambridge University Press, 1974).

Olson, Mancur, *The Logic of Collective Action* (Cambridge: Harvard University Press, 1965).

Pinder C., and L. Moore (eds.), *Middle Range Theory and the Study of Organization* (Boston: Martinus Nijhoff, 1980).

Pollack, Jonathan, *Security, Strategy, and the Logic of Chinese Foreign Policy* (Berkeley: Institute of East Asian Studies, University of California, 1981).

Pye, Lucian, *The Mandarin and the Cadre* (Ann Arbor: Center of Chinese Studies, University of Michigan, 1988).

————, *Asian Power and Authority* (Cambridge: Harvard University Press, 1985).

————, *The Dynamics of Chinese Politics* (Cambridge, Mass.: Oelgeschlager, Gunn & Hain, 1981.)

————, The Spirit of Chinese Politics (Cambridge: MIT Press, 1968).

Pyle, Kenneth B., "In Pursuit of a Grand Design: Nakasone Betwixt the Past and the Future," *Journal of Japanese Studies* 13, 2 (1987).

————, *The New Generation in Meiji Japan: Problems of Cultural Identity, 1885–1895* (Stanford: Stanford University Press, 1969).

Rapkin, D., and W. Avery (eds.), *America in a Changing World Political Economy* (New York: Longman, 1982).

Richter, David, "The Foreign Role in Major Projects," *China Business Review* (May-June 1988).

Robinson, Thomas, *The Sino-Soviet Border Dispute: Background, Development and the March 1969 Clashes,* (Santa Monica, Calif.: Rand, 1970).

Rosenberg, William G., and Marilyn B. Young, *Transforming Russia and China* (New York: Oxford University Press, 1982).

Ross, Robert S., "International Bargaining and Domestic Politics: U.S.-China Relations Since 1972," *World Politics* 38, 2 (January 1986).

Ruggie, John G., "International Regimes, Transactions, and Change: Embedded Liberalism in the Postwar Economic Order," *International Organization* 36, 2 (Spring 1982).

Scalapino, Robert A., "Uncertainties in Future Sino-U.S. Relations: The Decade Ahead," Orbis 26, 3 (Fall 1982).

Scherer, John L. (ed.), *China Facts and Figures* 7 (Gulf Breeze, Fla.: Academic International Press, 1984).

————, *China Facts and Figures* 4 (Gulf Breeze, Fla.: Academic International Press, 1981).

Schumpeter, E. B. (ed.), *The Industrialization of Japan and Manchukuo, 1930–1940* (New York: Macmillan, 1940).

Schwartz, Harry, *Tsars, Mandarins and Commissars: A History of Chinese-Russian Relations* (Garden City, N.Y.: Doubleday, 1973).

Segal, Gerald, *Defending China* (London: Oxford University Press, 1985).

———— (ed.), *Chinese Politics and Foreign Policy Reform* (New York: Kegan Paul International, 1990).

Sharman, Lyon, *Sun Yat-sen: His Life and Its Meaning* (Stanford: Stanford University Press, 1968).

Shih, Chih-yu, *The Spirit of Chinese Foreign Policy: A Psychocultural View* (London: Macmillan, 1990).

————, "The Demise of a Moral Regime: The Great Leap Forward in Retrospect," paper presented at the Northeastern Political Science Association annual meeting, Philadelphia, 1989.

————, "The Bitter Neighborship Divided: The Psycho-historical Origin of the Post-war Sino-Japanese Relations," *American Asian Review* 6, 4 (December 1988).

————, "A Markov Model of Diplomatic Change and Continuity in Mainland China," *Issues and Studies* 28, 6 (June 1992): 1–15.

Skocpol, Theda, *State and Social Revolution* (Cambridge: Cambridge University Press, 1979).

Smith, Roger K., "Explaining the Non-proliferation Regime," *International Organization* 41, 2 (Spring 1987).

Snow, Philip, *The Star Raft: China's Encounter with Africa* (New York: Weidenfeld & Nicolson, 1988).

Solinger, Dorothy, *Chinese Business Under Socialism* (Berkeley: University of California Press, 1984).

————, *Three Versions of Chinese Social Socialism* (Boulder: Westview, 1983).

Solomon, Richard, *Mao's Revolution and the Chinese Political Culture* (Berkeley: University of California Press, 1971).

Stein, Susan, "Coordination and Collaboration: Regimes in an Anarchic World," *International Organization* 36, 2 (Spring 1982).

Stoessinger, John G., *Crusaders and Pragmatists* (New York: W. W. Norton, 1979).

————, *Nations in Darkness* (New York: Random House, 1975).

Stolper, Thomas E., *China, Taiwan, and the Offshore Islands* (New York: M. E. Sharpe, 1985).

Sutter, Robert G., "Taiwan's Future," *Archived Issue Brief of Congressional Research Service* (March 8, 1983).

Taylor, Robert, *The Sino-Japanese Axis* (New York: St. Martin's, 1983).

Thompson, James D., *Organization in Action* (New York: McGraw-Hill, 1967).

Tien, Hung-mao (ed.), *Mainland China, Taiwan, and U.S. Policy* (Cambridge, Mass.: Oelgeschlager, Gunn & Hain, 1983).

U.S. Congress, Senate Subcommittee on National Security and International Operations of the Committee on Government Operations, *Peking's Approach to Negotiation* (Washington, D.C.: Government Printing Office, 1969).

Van Ness, Peter, "The Civilizer State," University of Denver, 1985, mimeograph.

————, *Revolution and Chinese Foreign Policy* (Berkeley: University of California Press, 1970).

Walder, Andrew G., *Communist Neo-Traditionalism: Work and Authority in Chinese Industry* (Berkeley: University of California Press, 1986).

Walker, Stephen, and Martin Sampson (eds.), *Role Theory and Foreign Policy Analysis* (Durham, N.C.: Duke University Press, 1987).

Waltz, Kenneth, *Theory of International Politics* (Menlo Park, Calif.: Addison-Wesley, 1979).

Wang, Shaoguang, "Deconstructing the Relationship Between Mao and His Followers: A New Approach to the Cultural Revolution," *Chinese Political Science Review* 1 (January 1988).

Wei, Ai, "Retrospect and Prospect of Sino-U.S. Economic and Trade Relations," *Mainland China Studies* 32, 6 (December 1989).

Weick, Karl E., *The Social Psychology of Organizing* (Menlo Park, Calif.: Addison-Wesley, 1969).

Weng, Byron S. J., "Taiwan's International Status Today," *China Quarterly* 99 (September 1984).

Whiting, Allen, *China Eyes Japan* (Berkeley: University of California Press, 1989).

————, "New Light on Mao," *China Quarterly* 62 (June 1975).

————, *The Chinese Calculus of Deterrence* (Ann Arbor: University of Michigan Press, 1974).

Wich, Richard, *Sino-Soviet Crisis Politics* (Cambridge: Harvard University Press, 1980).

Willoughby, Westel W., *The Sino-Japanese Controversy and the League of Nations* (New York: Greenwood Press, 1968).

Wilson, Dick, *The People's Emperor* (Garden City, N.Y.: Doubleday, 1980).

Wilson, Richard, et al. (eds.), *Value Change in Chinese Society* (New York: Praeger, 1979).

Wolff, Lester L., and David L. Simon (eds.), *Legislative History of the Taiwan Relations Act* (Jamaica, N.Y.: American Association for Chinese Studies, 1982).

Wu, Jiaxiang, *Control over Corruption*, mimeograph in Columbia University's East Asian Library.

Xie Yixian, *Basic Theory of International Struggle and Basic Principles of Chinese Foreign Policy* (Beijing: Institute of Diplomacy, 1983).

Yang, Tianshi, "Secret Negotiation Between the Japanese 'Civilian Politicians' and the Chiang Kaishek Group During the Early Period of the War of Resistance," *Lishi Yenjiu* (History studies) 1 (1990).

Yee, Herbert S., "The Three World Theory and Post-Mao China's Global Strategy," *International Affairs* 59 (Spring 1983).

Yeh, Potang, "Communist China Stricken by Changes in East Europe," *Mainland China Studies* 23, 9 (March 1990).

Young, Oran, "Regime Dynamics," *International Organization* 36, 2 (Spring 1982).

Yu, George T., "China and the Third World," *Asian Survey* 17 (November 1977).

Yu Yingshih, "Between Tao and the Regime," *Chinese Culture Monthly* 60 (October 1984): 102–128.

Zacher, Mark W., "Trade Gaps, Analytical Gaps: Regime Analysis and International Commodity Trade Regulation," *International Organization* 41, 2 (Spring 1987).

Zhang, Weiping, *Two Strategies* (Chongqing: Chongqing Press, 1991).

Zhao Quansheng, "Achieving Maximum Advantage: Rigidity and Flexibility in Chinese Foreign Policy," paper presented at the American Political Science Association annual meeting, San Francisco, September 1, 1990.

Zhou Enlai, *Special Edition on Zhou Enlai*, Center of Chinese Issue Research (ed.) (Hong Kong: Zilian Press, 1971).

INDEX

233

About the Book
and the Author

Looking at China's foreign policy, this book focuses on the Confucian-based need of Chinese leaders to present themselves as the supreme moral rectifiers of the world order.

Shih outlines the diplomatic principles cherished by the Chinese—socialism, antihegemonism, peaceful coexistence, statism, and isolationism—and explores how each has been applied in the past forty years. He argues, for example, that China's policy toward the Soviet Union was aimed primarily at shaming the Soviets for their betrayal of socialism; its United States policy demonstrates China's anti-imperialist integrity; its Japan policy blames the Japanese for a failed Asiatic brotherhood; and its Third World policy is intended to be a model for emulation. The application of these principles has enabled Beijing always to find a moral niche in world affairs; the seeming contradiction among the principles has been ignored, because the need to clarify China's moral role outweighs other national interests.

This unusual perspective on China's foreign affairs also challenges the realist calculation of national interests, one couched purely in terms of military balance or economic development.

CHIH-YU SHIH is associate professor of mainland Chinese affairs in the Graduate Institute of Political Science at National Taiwan University. He has contributed to the *Journal of Social, Political and Economic Studies, Sino-Soviet Affairs, China Quarterly* (Seoul), *Journal of Economics and International Relations, Behavioral Science, Issues and Studies, Political Psychology, American Asian Review,* and *Asian Profile.* The author of *The Spirit of Chinese Foreign Policy: A Psychocultural View* (1990), he is also coeditor of *Contending Dramas: A Cognitive Approach to International Organization,* and coauthor of *Symbolic War: The Chinese Use of Force,*

1840–1980 (forthcoming). He has published three books in Chinese: *The Principles of Chinese Political Economy, The Deep Structures of Taiwan Straits Exchange Relations*, and *Managing Taiwan Straits Exchanges*. His current interest is Chinese economic culture and legal culture.